T. J. Smith
Sept '95'

English II: . . . N—KB3 Systems

CONTEMPORARY CHESS OPENINGS
GENERAL EDITOR : R. G. WADE

English II: ... N-KB3 Systems

JOHN WATSON

B. T. Batsford Ltd. *London*

To my mother

First published 1979
© John Watson 1979
ISBN 0 7134 2087 1
Set by Hope Services, Abingdon, Oxon.
Printed in Great Britain by
Billing & Son Ltd
London, Guildford & Worcester
for the publishers
B. T. Batsford Limited
4 Fitzhardinge Street, London W1H 0AH

CONTENTS

ACKNOWLEDGEMENTS

I should like to express my gratitude to everyone who assisted me with the writing of *The English Opening*. In particular, Ken Rogoff, Evan Michaelides, and Bill Martz provided much analysis and encouragement, while Jon Frankle and Chris Chase offered their books and madcap hospitality on numerous occasions. I am also indebted to Eric Helmreich of the Boston Chess Studio for his generous provision of books and magazines, to Burt Hochberg for his counsel, to Kevin O'Connell for the use of his game files and to Bob Wade for checking game sources.

My deepest thanks go to Kenneth J. Case, who laboriously proofed and criticized the entire manuscript, and, most importantly, to Cindy Royce for several years of dedication to every phase of its preparation. Without her help and friendship, the book would never have seen the light of publication in its present form.

INTRODUCTION

The English Opening is devided into four books: —

English I: ... P—K4 deals with 1 P—QB4 P—K4;

English II: ... N—KB3 deals with 1 P—QB4 N—KB3 and for the sake of convenience excludes variations in which Black plays early either ... P—K4 or ... P—QB4. Thus a game which begins 1 P—QB4 N—KB3 2 N—QB3 P—Q4 3 Px P Nx P 4 P—KN3 P—QB4 may be found in *English III:* ... *P—QB4* under the order 1 P—QB4 P—QB4 2 N—QB3 N—KB3 3 P—KN3 P—Q4 4 Px P Nx P;

English III: ... P—QB4 deals with 1 P—QB4 P—QB4;

English IV is made up with other important variations like 1 ... P—K3, 1 ... P—KN3, 1 ... P—KB4, 1 ... P—QB3 and 1 ... P—QN3.

WHO PLAYS THE ENGLISH?

The best players in the world! Korchnoi, Larsen, Polugaevsky, and Uhlmann have used 1 P—QB4 (or 1 N—KB3 and 2 P—QB4) as their main weapon over many years; and Smyslov, Petrosian, Tal, Portisch, Hübner, and Hort have shown a marked liking for it. Also, no discussion of English Opening greats can exclude Mikhail Botvinnik; while of the other world champions, even Spassky, Fischer, and Karpov (normally 1 P—K4 adherents) have had recourse to the English in key situations. Newer devotees are many, Andersson and Miles being prominent examples.

The cause for such enthusiasm may be found in the intriguing balance of tactical and strategical challenges offered by the English. Hardly any other opening is so assured of increasing popularity in the years to come.

In my opinion there are three other outstanding players whose creative contributions to the theory of 1 P—QB4 deserve special notice: Pal Benko, Ludek Pachman, and Mark Taimanov. Each of these has had his influence on innumerable variations through the years and has brought respectability to many higherto disreputable lines.

TRANSPOSITIONS

While almost every chess opening can be confusing with regard to move order and the crisscrossing of variations, the English is likely the most convoluted of all. Even 1 P—QB4 regulars are often manouvered into lines they wished to avoid, and the whole subject is rendered even more complicated by the existence of multitudinous 'reversed variations', in which White adopts a normal Black set-up, or vice-versa (see below).

Books on the English Opening have generally tended to ignore transpositions and left the reader to his own devices. In this book, transpositional possibilities are mentioned throughout the text for immediate reference; but the important tool in this regard is the Index of Variations and Transpositions (page 106). By use of the index, the reader should be able to locate the pages of the book which analyze any logical sequence of early moves, without having to thumb through five or six chapters in hopes of finding the author's move order.

The Index also explains much that is not apparent in the Table of Contents. After 1 P—QB4 N—KB3, for example, there are countless games every year with 2 N—KB3 (or with 1 N—KB3 N—KB3 2 P—QB4). Where does one find analysis on this sequence? Of course that depends on what happens next, and one can find a specific answer in the section on alternatives to 2 N—QB3.

Finally, one may find the Index useful in forming a comprehensive personal repertoire for either colour.

BIBLIOGRAPHY

I have tapped many sources over the last several years, including older theoretical works (e.g. Pachman, Euwe), games collections, and particularly many magazines and tournament books. The references I relied most heavily on were:

Books:

Keene, R. *Flank Openings* (2nd Edition, Sussex 1970)

Schwarz, R. *Englisch/Bremer Partie* (Hamburg 1963)

Shatskes, B.A. *The English Opening*, translated from Russian by Ralph Lawrence (Chicago 1973)

Taimanov, M. *Slawisch bis Reti-Eröffnung* (1st Edition, Berlin 1971; 3rd Edition, Berlin 1976)

Cafferty B. *English Opening* (1st Edition, Nottingham 1973; 2nd Edition, Nottingham 1977)

Comment on the last three books is unavoidable, for even the casual browser may be confused by the fact that the text and diagrams of all three bear a striking resemblance. In fact, Shatskes' is an original work, and the title page of the first edition of Cafferty states that it is a translation of '*English Opening* by B. Shatskes.' I used it as such, since Cafferty's few revisions and additions were easily distinguishable from the original.

In the case of Taimanov's book, one observes the collaboration of Shatskes, whose work on the 1 P–QB4 section (slightly over a third of the book) doubtless accounts for the similarity of exemplary games, analysis, and conclusions.

Periodicals and Pamphlets

Chess Archives	*Sahovski Informator* (1–25)
Chess Life and Review	*Shakmatny Bulletin*
Modern Chess Theory	*Shakmatny v SSSR*
The Reti (Weinstein; Dallas 1976)	*The Chess player* (1–15)

All analysis in the book is the author's unless otherwise indicated. Very elementary notes (or variations pointed out by all annotators) I have sometimes left unaccredited.

SYMBOLS

ch	Check
$\triangle$	With the idea of
$\pm$ ($\mp$)	Some advantage for White(Black) (sometimes convertible to a win)
$\pm$ ($\mp$)	Clear advantage for White(Black) (usually convertible to a win)
$\pm\pm$ ($\mp\mp$)	White(Black) has a clearly won position
$=$	The position is balanced or equal
∞	The position is complicated and unclear
!	Strong move
!!	Excellent move
!?	Interesting move
?!	Not the best move, although with some value (e.g. trickiness)
?	Weak move
??	Blunder
(!)	Probably a good move (e.g. could use more tests)
(?)	Probably a bad move (e.g. could use more tests)
½–½	Draw agreed
1–0	Black resigns
0–1	White resigns
(1–0,75)	White went on to win in 75 moves
Ch	Championship
Tu	Trade Union
corres	Correspondence game
Top L	Top League
W or B	beside each diagram indicates which player is to move

1 GRÜNFELD-RELATED I:4 P–KN3 P–KN3

Black may play . . . N–KB3 and . . . P–KN3 with the idea of . . . P–Q3 (see Chapters 5 to 7), or with . . . P–Q4. That this latter move is quite compatible with a kingside fianchetto has been shown in the Grünfeld Defence to 1 P–Q4, and also holds true for the related positions of this (and the next) chapter:

1 P–QB4	N–KB3
2 N–QB3	P–Q4
3 PxP	NxP
4 P–KN3	P–KN3

Systems with an early . . . P–QB4 are analysed in *English I*. Independent is 4 . . . NxN 5 NPxN B–Q2!? 6 B–KN2 B–B3. After 7 N–B3 N–Q2 8 0–0 ±, Black still has to cope with the potential strength of White's centre; yet his position is certainly solid.

5 B–N2

Now Black has to make a decision about his attacked knight. We will examine:

A 5 . . . NxN
B 5 . . . N–N3 (The Czech Variant)

The move 5 . . . NxN has not been popular since Smyslov employed it against Botvinnik in their 1958 World Championship match. Pribyl and Bagirov (veterans of 2 . . . P–Q4) have recently revived this exchange with some new twists, but they themselves prefer the more complicated 5 . . . N–N3.

That retreat, previously considered insignificant (see **B**, introduction), fights for control of d4 and has been played extensively by Czechoslovakian internationals, notably Jansa, Hort, Pribyl, and Smejkal. Hence the name 'Czech Variant', although others, notably Polugaevsky, Vaganian, and Martz, have done much to refine the theory of 5 . . . N–N3. I feel that White obtains a certain pull in most variations; nevertheless, Black's conception is logical and will remain in tournament praxis for some time to come.

A

5 . . .	NxN
6 NPxN	B–N2 (1)

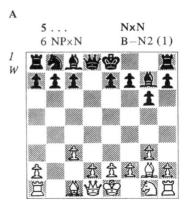

1
W

On 6 ... **P–QB4** 7 R–N1 N–B3 8 Q–R4 Q–B2 9 **B–QR3!? P–K3** 10 Q–N5?! is Larsen–Castro, Biel 1976. After 10 . . . B–Q2!, White could not play 11 QxNP? R–QN1 or 11 BxBP? N–R4 and had to play 11 Q–N2 Q–R4 =. But simply 9 **P–Q4!** △ B–B4 renders this move order suspect. From the diagram:
A1 7 P–KR4
A2 7 N–B3
A3 7 R–N1
And these rarely-seen alternatives:
(a) 7 **P–KB4!?** P–QB4 8 N–R3 0–0 9 0–0 N–B3 10 R–N1 N–R4 (Here 10 . . . Q–B2 △ . . . B–K3 or . . . B–Q2 is simpler.) 11 N–B2 R–N1 12 Q–B2 Q–B2 (or 12 . . . P–N3) 13 P–Q3 P–QN4 (13 . . . P–N3! =) 14 P–K4 ∞ Wright–Schmidt, Dresden 1969 (1–0, 42). Hardly convincing.
(b) 7 **Q–N3** N–B3! (Or 7 ... **N–Q2**; but Black does not mind taking on doubled pawns in return for the powerful king's bishop.) 8 N–B3 0–0 9 0–0 N–R4 10 Q–B2 P–QB4 11 P–Q3 B–B4 (△ . . . P–B5) 12 P–K4 B–Q2 13 B–N5 R–B1 14 Q–Q2 B–N4! = Botvinnik–Smyslov Match (18), 1958.
(c) 7 **B–QR3** N–Q2! (With the idea of cutting down the bishop's scope by . . . P–QB4. An example of poor Black play is 7 . . . **0–0** 8 R–N1 R–K1?! 9 RxNP BxR 10 BxB N–Q2 11 BxR QxB 12 N–B3 N–K4 13 0–0 ± Levenfish-Goldenov, 15th USSR Championship 1947.) 8 N–B3 P–QB4 9 Q–R4 (Else 9 . . . Q–R4) 9 . . . 0–0 10 R–QN1 P–QR3 11 P–B4 Botvinnik–Smyslov Match (10), 1958. Here 11 . . . Q–B2 12 0–0 R–R2! is Bronstein's

wily suggestion, threatening . . . P–QN4. Black stands well.

A1
7 P–KR4
Theory is hard to keep up with. In 1975, Pytel called 7 P–KR4, played against him by Sliwa, a 'novelty'; while in 1963 Schwarz gave it '!' and called it 'best according to theory,' quoting five games (including two by Sliwa!).
7 . . .   P–KR3
7 . . . **P–KR4** 8 N–R3 0–0 9 Q–N3 N–B3 10 N–B4 P–K3 11 0–0 Q–Q2 12 P–Q4 ± Sliwa-Johannessen, Marianske Lazne 1961.
8 N–R3
(a) 8 **N–B3** 0–0 9 R–QN1 P–QB4 (or 9 . . . P–QB3) 10 P–B4 N–B3 11 R–N5?! Q–Q3 12 P–Q3 R–N1 13 B–K3 P–N3 14 Q–B1 K–R2 15 0–0 P–K4 16 B–Q2 B–N5 ½–½ (∓) Keres–Ilivitsky, Göteborg 1955.
(b) 8 **P–R4** 0–0 9 B–QR3 N–Q2 10 N–R3 P–QB4 (10 . . . P–QB3=) 11 N–B4 P–K4 12 N–Q5 ± Petrosian–Ilivitsky, 21st USSR Championship 1954.
(c) 8 **R–N1** N–Q2 9 B–QR3 R–QN1 10 N–R3 N–N3?! (10 . . . 0–0 =) 11 0–0 0–0 12 Q–B1! ± (△ P–Q3, P–QB4) Sliwa–Pytel, Poland 1975.
8 . . .   0–0
9 Q–N3   N–Q2
10 N–B4 P–K3 11 P–Q4 P–QB4 12 P–K3 R–N1 13 **P–R4** ± Schwarz's improvement on 13 0–0? P–QN4 ∓ Langeweg–Johannessen, Zevenaa 1961. White has space and the more active pieces.

A2

    7 N—B3

This is particularly important because of the move order 1 P—QB4 N—KB3 2 N—QB3 P—Q4 3 P×P N×P 4 N—B3 P—KN3, etc.; or 1 N—KB3 N—KB3 2 P—QB4 P—Q4 3 P×P N×P 4 N—B3 P—KN3 etc.

    7 . . .   0—0
    8 0—0   P—QB4

After **8 . . . N—Q2, 9 R—N1** transposes to A3, and **9 P—Q4 N—N3!** 10 B—B4 N—Q4 11 B—Q2 P—QB4 12 Q—N3 P×P ∞ was Romanishin–Gutman, Spartakiade 1975.

    9 Q—R4!

Now **9 R—N1 N—B3 10 P—B4?!** (10 Q—R4, see next note) 10 . . . P—N3! 11 B—N2 B×B 12 R×B B—N2 13 P—Q3 Q—Q2 14 Q—B1 P—B3 (△ . . . P—K4) is equal, D. Byrne–Averbakh, USA–USSR 1954.

    9 . . .   N—Q2

Often seen is 9 . . . N—B3, when **10 Q—R3** can be parried by 10 . . . Q—R4! =; but more subtle is **10 R—N1** (which Byrne could have tried) and now:

(a) 10 . . . **Q—B2** 11 P—Q4 B—Q2? 12 B—KB4! Q—B1 13 Q—R3 with great pressure, Stein–Polugayevsky, Leningrad 1971.

(b) 10 . . . **Q—R4?** (the difference of one tempo . . .!) 11 Q×Q N×Q 12 N—N5! R—N1 13 N—K4 with a much better ending, Bang–Dubinin, corres 1972 (1–0, 42).

(c) 10 . . . **N—R4!?** (the most recent try, and likely best) 11 P—Q3 P—N3 (11 . . . B×P 12 B—R6!) 12 Q—R4 B—N2 13 B—R6 B×N 14 B×B (3) B×B 15 Q×B R—B1 Karpov–Korchnoi (30), 1978, and here 16 P—KR4! △ P—R5 would have

kept Black busy defending (±).

    10 R—N1   P—K4

10 . . . N—N3 11 Q—R5 P—B5 12 B—R3 ±. or **10 . . . P—KR3** 11 Q—R3! Q—B2 12 P—Q4 P×P 13 P×P N—N3 14 B—B4 Q—Q1 15 P—K4 ± Hübner–Savon, Sukhumi 1972. Historically, this game is significant as it first indicated one of White's most dangerous positional threats.

    11 P—Q3   P—QR3
    12 N—N5   R—N1

13 N—K4 Q—B2 14 B—K3!? (Simpler is **14 P—QB4** △ N—B3—Q5, an idea that Petrosian has been using for years.) 14 . . . P—R3 and Tal–Bagirov, USSR Ch 1972 continued **15 P—KB4!?** with complications, whereas **15 P—QB4** was still very strong and at least ±.

A3

    7 R—N1

The most direct move, and that most often played.

    7 . . .   N—Q2

Not 7 . . . 0—0? 8 R×NP!. The White KB can be blocked by:

(a) 7 . . . **P—QB3?!** 8 N—B3 (or 8 P—Q4!–Taimanov/Pribyl) 8 . . . 0—0 (8 . . . Q—R4!?) 9 0—0 N—Q2 10 P—B4 (or 10 Q—B2 Q—B2 11 P—Q4 P—K4 12 R—Q1 ± Tal–Mukhin, Sukhumi 1972) 10 . . . P—K4 11 P—Q3 Q—B2 12 B—QR3! R—Q1 13 N—N5 N—B1 14 P—B5 N—K3 15 N—K4 N—Q5 16 P—K3± Olafsson–Golombek, Hastings 1955-56.

(b) 7 . . . **N—B3!?** 8 N—B3 (8 Q—R4 0—0 9 N—R3—Cafferty) 8 . . . 0—0 9 0—0 P—N3! 10 B—QR3 (10 N—Q4 N×N 11 B×R B—B4!) 10 . . . R—N1

11 Q R4 B—Q2 12 Q B2 R—K1 =
Nikolayevsky–Savon, 34th USSR
Ch 1966-67.

8 N—B3

Obviously **8 B×P?** B×B 9 R×B
N—N3 10 P—K3 Q—B1 11 Q—B3
P—QB3 is undesirable. Alternatively:
(a) **8 P—QB4** 0—0 9 N—B3 R—N1
10 0—0 P—N3   11 P—Q4 P—K4
12 B—QR3 R—K1 13 P×P B—N2 =
Botvinnik–Smyslov (14) 1958. Here
it's worth remarking that Botvinnik
recommended playing P—QB4 only
in response to Black's . . . P—QB4.
(b) **8 Q—B2** R—QN1 9 P—Q3
P—N3 10 N—B3 B—N2 11 0—0
0—0 12 R—Q1 P—QB4 = Korchnoi–
D. Byrne, Palma de Mallorca 1968.
White let Black play all the standard
consolidating moves.

8 . . .   0—0

The immediate **8 . . . N—N3**
diverged from A32 below after
9 Q—N3!? B—K3 10 Q—R3 0—0
11 P—Q3 B—Q4   12 0—0 P—K4
13 N—Q2 B×B   14 K×B with
slightly better minor pieces and
pressure on the queen's wing,
de Roode–van Mil, Netherlands
Junior Ch 1977 (1-0, 46).

9 0—0 (2)

A31 9 . . . P—K4
A32 9 . . . N—N3

A33 9 . . . P—QB4

A31

9 . . .   P—K4

The old move.

10 P—Q4   P—QB3
11 P—K4

11 P—QR4 P×P 12 P×P N—N3
13 P—K4? B—N5 14 B—N2 Q—Q2
15 R—K1 QR—Q1∓ Siems–Koskinen,
1958. An example of the kind of
pressure Black hopes for. By contrast, **11 P—K4** (the text move)
11 . . . P×P 12 P×P N—N3?!
13 P—KR3 would be fruitless.

11 . . .   Q—R4
12 Q—B2 P×P   13 P×P N—N3
14 B—Q2 **Q—R5(?)** 15 Q×Q N×Q
16 KR—B1 ± Botvinnik–Smyslov
(16), 1958. But Smyslov might
have tried **14 . . . Q—R4!** with
possibilities of pressuring the White
centre or even attacking via . . .
B—R6, . . . P—KB4, etc. Better,
according to Botvinnik, was 14
B—K3 △ 14 . . . B—K3 15 P—QR4!.

The strange thing about all this
is that I have found no other master
examples of this line, even though
it seems interesting, consistent, and
no worse than, say, 9 . . . P—QB4.
White's play to hold his centre is
not easy; 9 . . . P—K4 deserves
further tests.

A32

9 . . .   N—N3!?

Also seldom played; Black avoids
weakening pawn advances.

10 N—Q4!?

Shatskes' clever suggestion, intending to bring the knight to a5 or
c5 via b3. Schwarz gives:

(a) **10 P–Q4 B–B4** 'to be tested,' but this looks excellent for Black. Podgayets–Shereshevsky, USSR Armed Forces Ch 1974 saw: (b) **10 Q–B2 B–Q2!** 11 P–Q3 B–R5 12 Q–Q2 B–QB3 13 P–B4 R–K1! = (△ 14 B–N2? Bx N! and 15 ... NxP ∓∓).

(c) **10 N–N5** △ N–K4–B5 is a safe idea, as in Swoboda–Tomaszewsky, Graz 1978.

   10 ...   Bx N

An example of declining might be **10 ... P–QB3** 11 N–N3 Q–B2 12 Q–B2 (If there is any general rule here for White, it might be: Don't move your centre pawns too fast.) 12 ... P–K4 13 P–Q3 N–Q4 14 P–QB4 (or 14 P–K4 △ P–Q4) 14 ... N–K2 15 B–N2 P–N3 16 P–K3 ∞.

In Marović–Kirov, Maribor 1977, Black was less protective of his queenside: **10 ... R–N1** 11 N–N3 R–K1?! 12 Q–B2 P–K4 13 P–Q3 B–B4 14 N–B5 (14 N–R5 P–QB3 15 P–QB4!? ±) 14 ... P–QB3, and now instead of **15 P–K4 B–QB1!**, **15 P–QR4!** would have kept e4 free for the knight and increased White's superiority.

   11 PxB   QxP

Interesting would be the attempt to blockade by **11 ... P–QB3**. Then **12 B–N2 B–K3** 13 P–QR4 Q–Q2 looks double-edged; White might continue his offer with **12 P–Q3** e.g. **12 ... P–B3** 13 B–R6 △ 14 P–K3, or **12 ... QxP** 13 B–N2 Q–Q3 14 Q–Q2 with attacking chances.

After the text (**11 ... QxP**), Soltis gives **12 B–N2 Q–Q3** 13 Q–B2 with 'an attack on both sides of the board.' **12 ... Q–R5**

is probably better (13 Q–B1 P–QB3 14 Q–B3 P–B3); anyway, that attack is hard to demonstrate. **12 P–Q3!**, reserving options as to the disposition of White's QB, looks better and quite unclear.

A33

   9 ...   P–QB4

The move in vogue. Nevertheless, Black's position is rather airy.

   10 P–Q4

White faces a plesant choice:
(a) **10 P–B4 Q–B2** 11 P–Q3 seems to retain a riskless edge, although in Portisch–Polugayevsky, Budapest 1969, Black defended well by 11 ... R–N1 12 B–B4 P–K4 13 B–Q2 P–N3 14 N–N5 B–N2 15 N–K4 Q–B3 16 P–B3 N–B3 17 N–B3 Q–Q2 18 B–K3 N–K1! (△ ... N–B2–K3). White's advantage was minimal and the game concluded peacefully. Also **10 ... R–N1!?** 11 B–N2 P–K4 12 N–K1 R–K1 13 N–B2? P–K5! ∓ worked out well for Black in Taimanov–Savon, Sukhumi, 1972. But a major alternative is (b) **10 Q–R4!**, transposing into the main line of A2, which looked excellent for White.

   10 ...   Q–R4

Pribyl went so far as to give Polugayevsky a '?' for 10 P–Q4 in their 1973 game in Tallinn. But after 10 ... Q–R4, the fault was in Polugayevsky's answer **11 Q–B2?**, after which 11 ... N–N3 12 N–Q2 PxP 13 PxP B–B4 14 P–K4 QR–B1 won a big advantage for Black (½–½, 21, but the position was ∓).

   11 Q–N3!

But this turns the tables, as White's next move is hardly to be avoided.

11 ...   N–B3

11 ... P–K4 12 B–K3!± (Gheorghiu).

12 Q–R3

The point: an ending against White's active bishops and queenside attack is very difficult. We follow Gheorghiu–Stoica, Bucharest 1973: 12 ... Q× Q 13 B× Q N –K5 14 KR–B1 P–N3!? 15 N–N5 N× N 16 B× R B–B4 17 P–K4 R× B 18 P× B N–B6ch 19 K–N2 N–Q7 20 R–N2 N–B5 21 R–N3 N× B! (21 ... N–Q7 22 P× P ±) 22 R× N P× QP 23 P× QP B× P 24 R–Q3 ± and Gheorghiu managed to convert his advantage to a win.

CONCLUSION: In the critical line 7 R –N1 N–Q2 8 N –B3 0–0 9 0–0, both 9 ... P–K4 and 9 ... N–N3 are more careful strategies than 9 ... P–QB4, which will turn in White's favour after either 10 Q–R4 or 10 P–Q4.

B

5 ...   N–N3 (3)

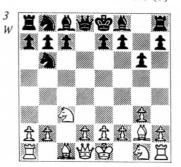

3
W

This retreat loses time, but makes a target of White's centre rather than strengthening it by 5 ... N× N. The modernity of 5 ... N–N3 (the 'Czech Variant') is shown by Schwarz's designation of '?' and Taimanov's 1971 comment: 'disadvantageous is the retreat to b6.' In reply, 6 P–Q4 or 6 N–B3 B–N2 7 0–0 0–0 8 P–Q4 are variations of the Neo-Grünfeld, properly a 1 P–Q4 opening which we do not treat here. Most English players have preferred systems based on P–Q3, either with or without N–KB3. The idea is to avoid committing the centre pawns until they are supported by some pieces. White's KB exerts pressure on the h1–a8 diagonal as usual, and he has attacking possibilities on both wings as well as the strategy of a 'creeping advance' in the centre. Black too can choose from a wide range of plans (e.g. involving ... P–K4 and ... N–Q5 or ... P–KB4), so extremely complex play normally results.

We shall now examine the older treatment with 6 N–B3 (B2), and the recent strategy 6 P–Q3 (B3). Of course 6 P–Q3 often transposes to B2 if White plays an early N–KB3. Aside from these moves, there is only:

B1

6 P–KR4!?

A move that keeps on popping up, but is probably premature.

6 ...   P–KR3!

6 ... B–N2? 7 P–R5 P–QB3 8 P–Q3 justifies White's strategy. 6 ...P–KR4 was also unsatisfactory after 7 N–B3 B–N2 8 0–0 0–0 9 P–Q3 P–QB3 10 N–KN5

QN–Q2 11 P–Q4! N–B3 12
P–K4 ± Dubinin–Zhdanov, 4th
USSR Corr Ch 1960. In general,
Black should prefer not to cede g5
if there is a reasonable alternative.

7 P–B4?!
Probably not best, but at least consistent. **7 P–Q3** N–B3 8 N–B3
(8 **P–R5** P–N4 9 P–B4 Px P
10 PxP R–KN1) 8 . . . B–N2
9 B–Q2 P–K4 was Marsalek–Savon,
Warsaw 1969, and White had only
weakened his kingside.

7 . . . QN–Q2!
8 P–R4
Nor does this help matters, as
White can do nothing on the queenside after Black's reply; but **8 P–R5**
PxP 9 RxP R–KN1 10 K–B2
N–B3 looks ∓.

8 . . . P–QR4
9 P–R5 PxP
10 P–K4?! R–KN1
11 KN–K2 N–B3
12 P–Q4 B–N5 ∓
Suba–Pribyl, Lublin 1974 (0–1,
33).

B2
6 N–B3 B–N2
This line is important in any case
because it can arise from 1 P–QB4
N–KB3 2 N–QB3 P–KN3 3 N–B3
P–Q4 4 PxP etc., or from 1 P–QB4
N–KB3 2 N–QB3 P–KN3 3 P–KN3
B–N2 4 B–N2 0–0 5 N–B3
P–Q4 6 PxP etc.

7 0–0
We analyze from this move order
for the sake of simplicity. Once
White is committed to N–KB3, I
know of no plan in which leaving
the king in the centre or castling
queenside is a serious option.

7 . . . 0–0
8 P–Q3
Taimanov–Vaganian, USSR Ch
1971 went **8 P–N3** N–B3 9 B–N2
P–K4 10 R–B1 '±' (Taimanov).
This is worth a try, though the
assessment seems premature, as
White will have to struggle to
achieve anything tangible.

8 . . . N–B3
(a) 8 . . . **P–QB4?!** 9 Q–N3
(9 P–QR4 is also good.) 9 . . .
N–B3 10 N–K4 P–B5 11 PxP
N–R4 12 Q–B2 N(4)xP 13 R–Q1
Q–K1 14 P–QR4 ± was Mikenas–
Simagin, 22nd USSR Ch 1955. Odd
that Simagin, known for moving his
pieces in openings where others
move pawns, should choose this
position for the move 8 . . . P–QB4?!
(b) 8 . . . **P–QB3** 9 B–K3 **P–QR4**
10 Q–B2 N–R3 11 P–QR3 N–Q2
12 QR–N1 N–B3 13 P–QN4 ±,
the Black side of which looks a bit
random, was Stolyar–Tarasov, 24th
USSR Ch 1957. Simply 9 . . .
QN–Q2 △ . . . N–B3–Q4 was preferable; White could play Q–B1,
B–R6 and/or P–QN4–N5 with
initiative.
Now: **B21** 9 B–K3
B22 9 B–Q2
B23 9 P–QR4
A curious idea was **9 P–QR3** P–
K4 10 B–N5! P–B3 **11 B–Q2**
P–QR4 12 P–QN4 K–R1 13 P–
N5 of Nehmert–Tukmakov, Bath
1973. A draw was agreed at this
point, but 13 . . . **N–Q5** 14 NxN
PxN 15 N–R4 or 13 . . . **N–K2**
14 N–K4 looks better for White.
Moreover, **11 B–K3** (in place of
11 B–Q2) was a promising move,
intending P–Q4. Doubtless Black

should play 9 . . . P–KR3 to avoid
10 B–N5.

B21

9 B–K3

The advantages of 9 B–K3 over
9 B–Q2 are its control over d4 and
its ability to reach c5 (and sometimes a3), adding strength to a
central pawn advance. Also, d2 is
left free for White's queen or king's
knight. The disadvantages are that
the bishop may be attacked at some
point by . . . N–Q4 (forcing exchanges at a loss of tempo); and
that White's knight is prevented
from capturing its counterpart on
d4 after . . . P–K4 and . . . N–Q5,
so that White cannot rid himself of
the interloper without conceding
his valuable QB.

There are two basic plans versus
9 B–K3:

B211 9 . . . P–KR3
B212 9 . . . P–K4
    9 . . . N–Q5?! is rather over-
anxious (not to mention dull):
10 N× N B× N 11 B× B Q× B 12 Q–
B2 P–QB3 13 P–K3 Q–N2 (?)
14 N–K4 ± Stolyar-Klaman, 24th
USSR Ch 1957.

B211

9 . . .   P–KR3 (4)
    10 Q–B1

Preparing R–Q1, P–Q4, etc.
Other tries from the diagram:
(a) **10 P–QR4** P–QR4 11 B× N?!
P× B   12 N–Q2 P–K4, which
Andersson gives as ∓. Black's
bishops more than compensate for
his weakened queenside (as in
Chapter 6).

**4
W**

(b) **10 P–QR3** P–K4 11 R–B1 N–Q5
12 N–K4 P–QB3 13 B–Q2 R–K1
14 N–K1!? B–N5 15 P–B3 B–K3
16 N–B5 B–QB1 = Bilek-Smejkal,
Kapfenburg 1970 (but 1–0, 32).
(c) **10 R–B1 R–K1?!** (**10** . . . P–K4
11 N–Q2 N–Q5 12 N(2)–K4
P–QB3 13 P–QN4 P–R3 14 N–B5
Q–K2 = Geller-Savon, War Anni-
versary, Moscow 1970) 11 N–Q2!
N–Q5 (11 . . . N–N5!?) 12 B× N!
B× B 13 N–N5 P–QB3 14 N× B
Q× N 15 Q–B2 R–N1 16 N–N3
Q–QR5?!   17   Q–Q2!   K–R2
18 N–B5 and White held the reins
in Taimanov-Vaganian, Vilnus 1975.
    10 . . .   K–R2
    11 R–Q1   P–K4
    11 . . . **R–K1** 12 P–Q4 N–B5
13 N–K5! ± Furman-Platonov, 40th
USSR Ch 1972.
    12 B–B5!
    12 P–Q4?! P× P   13 N–QN5
N–Q4 14 N(3)× P N× B 15 Q× N(3)
N× N 16 N× N R–K1! ∓ Smyczak-
Prit ☗, Lublin 1974 (½ –½, 41).
    12 . . .   R–K1
    13 P–K3   P–QR4
    13 . . . **N–Q2** 14 B–QR3 P–QR4
doesn't really help after 15 N–N5
N–B3 16 P–Q4 ± , and **13** . . . **P–B4**
is problematic: 14 P–Q4 P–K5
15 P–Q5!? or 15 N–K5.

14 P–Q4   P–K5
15 N–K5 Nx N   16 Px N Q–N4
17 Nx P± Tal–Jansa, Skopje 1972.
The dark squares are falling.
Thus 9 . . . P–KR3 evidently fails
to equalize.

B212
    9 . . .   **P–K4**
    10 Q–B1
10 Q–Q2 is about the same, but
uses the d2 square and renders
R–Q1, B–B5, P–K3 etc. less playable (see also note (c) to 14 P–QN4).
10 P–QR4 P–QR4 transposes to
B23.
    10 . . .   N–Q5
In view of what follows, Black
should consider the more venturesome **10 . . . R–K1!? Δ 11 B–R6
B–R1.**
    11 B–R6   Nx Nch
    12 Bx N   P–QB3
    12 . . . B–R6?! 13 Bx B Kx B
14 Bx NP Bx R 15 Bx R Bx KP
16 Nx B Nx B 17 Q–B3 P–KB3
18 P–Q4 ± (Gheorghiu).
    13 Bx B   Kx B
    14 P–QN4 (5)

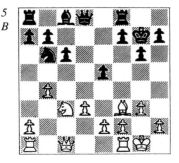

5
B

White has a classic minority
attack on the queenside and some
pressure on the dark squares. If his

advantage seems negligible, just
witness what can happen to Black!:
(a) **14 . . . N–Q4?!** 15 P–N5 N–K2
16 R–Q1 P–B3 17 Q–N2 R–B2
18 P–K3 Q–K1?! 19 N–K4 N–B4
20 Px P Px P   21 N–B5 N–Q3
22 QR–B1 ±   Gheorghiu–Martz,
Lone Pine, 1975.
(b) **14 . . . B–R6?!** 15 R–Q1 Q–K2
16 Q–N2 KR–Q1 17 P–R4 N–Q4
18 P–N5 Nx N 19 Qx N P–QB4
20 P–R5 QR–B1 21 P–N6! ±.
(c) **14 . . . B–K3!** is the right move,
as in Robatsch–Polugayevsky, Sochi
1974, Δ 15 P–N5 Px P or 15 N–K4
B–Q4 or 15 Q–N2 P–B3 (±?). In
that game, Robatsch's queen was
on d2 rather than c1 (due to his
10 Q–Q2) and after 15 KR–B1,
Polugayevsky centralized with 15 . . .
N–B5! and 16 . . . N–Q3. He won
in 35, although the opening position
was not responsible.

B22
    9 B–Q2   P–KR3
A theoretically important alternative is **9 . . . P–K4**, after which
White can play **10 Q–B1** and
B–R6, as in B21, or as in these
exciting encounters:
(a) **10 N–K4 P–QR4!?** 11 N–B5
N–Q2! 12 B–N5?! (12 N–QR4–
Tukmakov) 12 . . . Q–K1 13 Nx N
Qx N 14 Q–Q2 R–K1 15 QR–B1
Q–Q3! 16 B–R6 P–K5! 17 B–B4?
(17 Px P Qx Q   18 Bx Q Bx P
19 R–N1 B–B3 ∓–Tukmakov)
17 . . . Px N! 18 Bx Q Px B(7)
19 Kx P Px B 20 P–K3 B–K3 and
Black, with . . . B–Q4ch coming,
had a decisive attack (0–1, 46,
after many vicissitudes) in Rashkovsky–Tukmakov, USSR Ch 1972.

(b) **10 R–B1** P–QR4! (10 . . .
P–KR3 11 Q–B2 B–N5 12 Q–N! ±
—see also the text) 11 Q–B2
N–Q5?! 12 Nx N Px N 13 N–K4
N–Q4 14 Q–B5 R–K1 15 KR–K1
P–QB3 16 B–N5! Q–Q2 17 Q–
R3!? (17 P–KR3 P–R3 18 B–Q2 △
Q–Q6 ±) 17 . . . P–R3 18 B–Q2
R–Q1 19 N–B5 Q–B2 20 Q–N3
R–R2! 21 P–QR3 P–KN4 22
R–B2 R–Q3? 23 N–K4! R–Q1
24 Nx NP! P–R5 25 Q–R2 Px N
26 Bx N ± (though eventually drawn)
Uhlmann–Tukmakov, Madrid 1973.
(Annotations by Uhlmann).

10 R–B1
(a) **10 R–N1** ('!'—Andersson, whose
notes we follow:) 10 . . . P–QR4
11 N–QR4 Nx N 12 Qx N B–Q2
13 KR–B1 P–K4 14 Q–Q1 R–R2
15 B–K3 N–Q5 16 Q–Q2 K–R2
17 Bx N! Px B 18 Q–B4 B–QB3
19 R–B4 R–R3 20 R(1) QB1
(△ 21 Nx P) 20 . . . Bx N! 21 Qx B
P–QB3 22 P–KR4 Q–K2! Andersson–Olafsson, Nice 1974, and here
by means of 23 R–B5! P–R4
24 P–KN4, White could have kept
some edge.
(b) **10 P–QR3** P–K4 11 P–QN4
P–R3 (11 . . . N–Q5 12 P–QR4! △
P–R5–6 ±—Jansa) 12 N–K4 N–Q5
13 Nx N Px N 14 N–B5 P–QB3
15 Q–N3 N–Q2 16 QR–B1
Johanessen–Jansa, Nice 1974. White
had somewhat the better of it (but
0–1, 33).

From the games in these two
notes, it may be seen that the exchange of Black's knight on d4 can
further White's positional plans
despite the opening of the king file.
10 . . .   K–R2
10 . . . P–K4 11 Q–B2 B–N5

12 Q–N1 ± (Uhlmann).
    11 Q–B2   B–N5
    12 Q–N1! (6)

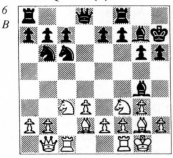

A pretty idea; White supports
P–QN4 and is able to use his rooks
in the centre. Now 12 . . . P–K4
13 P–KR3 B–K3 14 N–K4 B–Q4
15 P–K3! ± was the stem game,
Portisch–Uhlmann, Amsterdam
1971, which White won in 41
moves. See how Uhlmann was
recompensed for this lesson by his
victory in the text:
    12 . . .   Q–Q2
13 KR–K1 P–B4!? (13 . . . P–K4
14 N–K4 △ N–B5±—Uhlmann) 14
P–N4 P–K4 15 P–N5 N–K2
(15 . . . N–Q5 16 Nx N Px N
17 N–Q1 ±—Uhlmann) 16 B–K3
P–B5 17 B–B5 R–B2 (It's not
clear that 16 . . . P–B5, ceding e4
to White, was essential; but otherwise White could mount his queenside attack undisturbed by means
of P–QR4–R5.) 18 N–Q2!
N(3)–Q4 19 Bx N(7)! Nx N
20 Rx N Qx B 21 N–K4! (21 Bx P
P–K5!∓—Uhlmann) 21 . . . P–KR4
22 Q–N3 (△ Qx R!) 22 . . . B–R3
23 Q–Q5! QR–KB1 (23 . . .
R–QN1 24 R–B5! ±—Uhlmann)
24 Qx NP Px P 25 RPx P P–R5
26 Px P Qx P 27 Rx P K–N2
28 P–K3! Q–Q1 29 R(1)–QB1

QxP 30 QxP±± (Δ 30 . . . Qx NP
31 Rx Rch Rx R 32 Qx Rch! etc.)
Uhlmann–Vaganian, Skopje 1976.
A very 'English' exploitation of
Black's formation!

B23

9 P–QR4

This threatens P–R5–R6; after
9 . . . P QR4, White will occupy
b5 to further his ambitions on the
queenside.

    9 . . .   P–QR4
   10 B–K3   P–K4
  10 . . . B–B4 11 R–B1 Q–Q2
12 N–KN5!± Dvoretsky–Chekhov,
USSR 1973.
    11 N QN5
  11 Bx N(?!) Px B   12 N–Q2
B–K3 13 N B4 P–B4 14 Q–N3
('!' Schwarz), and now 14 . . .
R–R3 Δ . . . R–B2, . . . N–Q5
seems fine.
    11 . . .   N Q4?!
Dvoretsky gives **11 . . . N–Q5**
12 N(3)x N Px N 13 B–B4 P–QB3
14 N–Q6 ±. Perhaps '±' if that,
would be more accurate after
14 . . . P–N4! 15 Nx B Px B
16 Nx N Qx N, for instance 17 Px P
B–R3 **18 P–B5** K–R1 19 K–R1
R–KN1 20 B–K4 R–N5 with
attack, or **18 Q–Q2** QR–K1
19 QR K1 R–K2 etc.
    12 B–B5
  12 B–Q2 was the try in Olafsson–Martz, Lanzarote 1974: 12 . . .
P–R3 13 R–B1 B–K3 14 R–B5
N(4)–N5 **15 Bx N?!** Px B 16 N–Q2
Q–K2 17 R–B1 KR–B1! 18
Rx N!∞. Krnić suggests **15 N–R3!?**
Δ Q–B1, N–B4; but there are so
many options on each move that
one must forego assessment!

    12 . . .   R–K1
13 R–B1 B–N5?! (Dvoretsky
mentions 13 . . . P–R3 (!).) 14
P–R3 B–K3 15 P–K4! N–B3?!
(Better 15 . . . N(4)–N5, but
16 P–Q4! is ± –Dvoretsky) 16 N–N5
B–QB1? 17 Q–N3 and White was
winning (17 . . . Q–Q2 18 P–R4),
Dvoretsky–Gulko, USSR Ch 1973.
CONCLUSION: 6 N–B3 seems to
favour White slightly, for he has a
better-defined plan, i.e. attack on
the queenside and in the centre
with the support of his influential
KB and open QB file. If Black plays
. . . P–K4, he restricts his own KB
and grants his opponent Sicilian-
like pressure. Several world-class
players have nevertheless success-
fully championed the Black position, which is at any rate well-
centralized.

B3

  6 P–Q3   B–N2
  7 B–K3 (7)

7
B

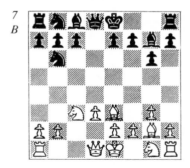

  Leaving the KB unmasked (see
B31). Other ideas are curious
indeed:
(a) **7 B–Q2** N–B3?! 8 Q–B1
N–Q5 9 N–B3 P–QB4? (9 . . .
Nx Nch; 9 . . . P–K4) 10 N–K4

B–B4 11 N×N! P×N 12 B–R6
R–QB1 13 Q–Q2 0–0 14 P–KR4!
B×B (Polugaevsky recommends 14
. . . N–Q2, but I see no good defence to 15 P–R5, e.g. 15 . . .
P×P 16 P–KN4!!) 15 Q×B B×N
16 B×B Q–Q3 17 P–R5 with a
powerful attack, Polugayevsky–Sax,
Hilversum 1973. This is instructive,
but the opening is rather irrational,
since 7 . . . N–B3?! allows 8 B× Nch!,
and White's QB is well-placed on d2
for this position (compare B31,
note to 9 Q–B1). Against 7 B–Q2,
7 . . . P –KR3 and 7 . . . QN–Q2
8 Q–B1 P–KR3 are reasonable for
Black; also 7 . . . 0–0 8 Q–B1
transposes into the text.
(b) Benko–Krnić, Sombor 1976
continued 7 P–KR4!? P–KR3
8 B–Q2 N–B3 (possible is 8 . . .
0–0 9 Q–B1 K–R2. Then 10
P–B4!? △ P –R5 as in Panno–Hort
of B32 is unclear: 10 . . . P–KR4!?)
9 Q–B1 (or 9 B× Nch) 9 . . . N–Q5
10 N–B3 P–QB3 11 N–K4 N–Q4
12 R–QN1! Q–N3 13 N×N B×N
14 P–QN4 B–N5! 15 N–B5 R–Q1
16 Q–B4! N–B3 17 R–QB1±. A
very complex game!

Black has several ways of tackling
the diagrammed position:
B31 7 . . . N–B3
B32 7 . . . 0–0
B33 7 . . . P–KR3
  7 . . . P–K4 is equally valid, but
less tested. Panno–Martz, Lone Pine
1976 continued: 8 Q–B1 (8 B–B5
is another thought; then Black might
try 8 . . . P–QR4, e.g. 9 N–B3
N–R3 10 B–QR3 N–N5.) 8 . . .
0–0 9 P–KR4!? (9 B–R6) 9 . . .
P–KR4 10 N–R3 R–K1 11 N–
KN5 P–QB3 12 0–0 N(1)–Q2

13 P–QN4 and one prefers White,
but there is much room for improvement.

B31
  7 . . .   N–B3
  8 B× Nch!
The critical continuation. 8 N–
B3 transposes back into B2.
  8 Q–Q2 N–Q5 9 R–B1 0–0
(9 . . . P–KR3 10 B× N!) 10 B–R6
B×B (or 10 . . . P –QB3!? and if
11 P–KR4, 11 . . . B×B 12 Q×B
N–B4 13 Q–Q2 P–KR4 Rivas–
Santos, Groningen 1977/8; and
here 14 N–K4! would have been
more challenging than 14 N–B3
N–Q5 15 N–K4 N×Nch 16 B×N
Q–Q5! =, as played.) 11 Q×B
P–QB3 12 N–B3 N×Nch 13 B×N
Q–Q5 14 P–KR4 (Byrne and
Mednis suggest 14 Q–B4 Q×Q
15 P×Q ±. This may be so, but
15 . . . B–B4!, stopping N–K4–B5
by virtue of 16 N–K4 B× N, puts
the burden of proof on White.)
14 . . . P–B3 15 P–R5 (15 Q–B4!?)
15 . . . P–N4 16 B–K4 R–B2
17 B×Pch? (17 P–K3! ∞) 17 . . .
R×B   18 Q–N6ch R–N2   19
Q–K8ch K–R2 20 P–R6 B–R6!
21 P–K3 Q–QN5   22 Q–R5
B–N5 23 P–R3 B×Q! 24 P×Q
B–B6 0–1 Matera–Martz, New York
1976.
  8 . . .   P× B
  9 Q–B1
(a) Benko suggests (and Byrne and
Mednis approve) 9 B–Q2 '!' and if
9 . . . N–Q4, 10 Q–R4 'when the
weakness of Black's QBP is highly
perceptible.' But after 10 . . . B–Q2
the pawn itself is also perceptible,
and though White may be better,

he still must worry about the enemy bishop pair, the half-open QN file, and weak squares around his king.

Actually, after 9 B–Q2, 9 . . . N–Q4 is not the only move; 9 . . . 0–0 is fine, and if 10 Q–B1, 10 . . . R–K1 11 B–R6 B–R1 12 P–KR4 P–K4 is B32, note (a), a tempo up for Black (!), or here 12 N–K4 R N1!. Moreover, (9 . . . 0–0) 10 R–B1 R–N1 11 N–B3 B–N5 or 11 P N3 N–Q4 looks full of promise for Black. 9 B–Q2 is plausible, but conceding one's g2 bishop and losing a tempo with the other is almost bound to give Black persistent dynamic chances.

(b) In Benko–Martz, Las Vegas 1976, the game which inspired this speculation, Benko tried 9 R–B1 instead: 9 . . . N–Q4 10 B–Q2 N× N! 11 B× N Q–Q4 12 N–B3 B× Bch 13 R× B Q× RP 14 Q–B1 QR–N1 and the game was soon drawn.

(c) 9 N–B3 N–Q4 10 B–Q2 0–0 11 Q–R4 R–N1 12 N–Q1! N–N3! 13 Q–R4?! (13 Q–B2 seems more thematic, yet with either 13 . . . B–N2 △ 14 0–0 P–QB4! or even 13 . . . P–QB4!? 14 Q× P B–N2 15 Q–K3 Q–Q2 16 0–0 P–K4!, Black is not submitting timidly to his 'positional doom'.) 13 . . . P–QB4 14 B–R6 B–N2! △ 15 N–N5 P–KB3! Langeweg–Ögaard, Dortmund 1975 (0-1, 39).

9 . . .   P–KR3

(a) 9 . . . 0-0. Now by 10 B–R6, White can initiate an attack by P–KR4–R5 (compare B32), or play against the doubled QBPs, e.g. 10 . . . P–K4 11 B× B K× B 12 N–B3 etc. This latter idea has more

effect when Black's KB–and consequently much of his counterplay, for instance against b2 and c3–has been eliminated. White's two knights will obviously be very strong in such a position.

(b) 9 . . . P–KR4 introduced the instructive game Smyslov–Robatsch, Sochi 1974: 10 N–B3 B–N5 11 N–KN5! (11 N–Q2 N–Q4 12 N× N P× N 13 P–Q4 0–0 14 P–B3 B–R6 15 N–N3 P–K4 ∞ L. Popov–Timman, Banja Luka 1974) 11 . . . N–Q4 12 N× N! Q× N 13 P–B3 R–QN1 14 R–QN1 B–Q2 15 P–N3 P–B3 (15 . . . Q–R4ch 16 K–B2 Q× RP 17 Q–B4 0–0 18 B–B5 ± –Smyslov) 16 N–K4 P–N4 17 K–B2 P–R4 18 N–B5 B–QB1 19 P–KR4 ± (19 Q–B3! was even stronger; 1–0, 36 anyway).

10 N–B3   B–R6
11 R–KN1!   B–N5
12 N–Q2 N–Q4 13 N× N! P× N 14 N–N3 Q–Q3 15 P–B3 B–Q2 16 P–Q4 R–QN1 17 K–B2 (Threatening 18 B–B4, whereas 17 . . . P–N4 meets with 18 Q–Q2 △ 19 QR–B1–Kavalek) 17 . . . P–KR4 18 B–B4 P–K4 19 P× P B× P 20 Q–K3 P–KB3 21 Q× RP 0–0 22 QR–QB1 KR–K1 23 B× B Q× B 24 R(N)–K1 R–R1 25 Q× BP Q–K6ch 26 K–N2 R–R2 27 Q–Q6 P–R5 28 P× P! B–K3 29 R–B3 Q–R3 30 P–QR3 and White won shortly, Petrosian–Schmidt, Skopje 1972. One of the great games of modern chess, which incidentally was responsible for the widespread replacement of 6 N–B3 by 6 P–Q3 B–N2 7 B–K3 on the international circuit.

B32

7 . . .   0–0

Black banks on quick development, but must brave a ferocious attack.

8 Q- B1 (8)

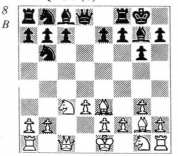

(a) **8 R—B1** led to obscure problems in Panno–Hort, Petropolis 1973: 8 . . . P–KR3 (8 . . . **P–K4** 9 Q–Q2 R–K1 10 B–R6 B–R1 11 P–KR4 N B3?! 12 Bx N Px B 13 N -B3 would be positionally much sounder than in the note to 8 . . . N(1)–Q2 below.) 9 Q–Q2 K–R2 10 P–B4!? P–KB4!? (10 . . . QN–Q2–Hort; 10 . . . P–K3 △ . . . N–Q4–Panno) 11 P–KR4! QN–Q2 12 P–R5 Px P 13 Rx P N–B3 14 R–R3 (14 R–R4!) 14 . . . P–B3 15 N–B3 N–N5 16 B–B5 R–K1 17 R–R4 K–N1 18 B–KR3 N–Q2 19 B–N1 N(2)–B3 20 N–K5 ± (but ½–½, 45). (a) **8 Q–Q2** is noteworthy, as White may wish to preserve the option of 0–0–0. Petrosian–Tukmakov, Three Team Event USSR 1973 saw 8 . . . **P–K4** 9 B–R6 N(1)–Q2   10   P–KR4   N–B3 11 Bx B (11 B–B3!?–Gufeld) 11 . . . Kx B 12 P–R5 Nx P 13 B–B3 Q–K2 14 Bx N Px B 15 Rx P P–KB3, and here 16 R–R4! would have preserved White's sig-

nificant advantage.

But 8 Q- Q2 may be less effective than 8 Q –B1 against **8 . . . N–B3(!)** because White's queen does not look down the QB file, e.g. 9 B(2)x N Px B 10 B –R6 P–QB4 11 Bx B Kx B 12 N–K4 B–N2 13 Q–B3ch Q–Q5; or 9 B–R6 N–Q5 10 R–B1 Bx B 11 Qx B P–QB3, as in Matera–Martz (B31 above).

8 . . .   N(1)–Q2

An important alternative is 8 . . . **R–K1!?**, which saves Black's bishop at the cost of a tempo. Then 9 B–R6 B–R1 10 P –KR4 N–B3 (Averbakh gives **10 . . . QN–Q2** 11 P–R5 N–B3, but then 12 Px P RPx P– *12 . . . BPx P 13 N–R3–*13 N–B3 is dangerous.) and now: (a) 11 Bx N Px B   12 N–B3 (12 P–R5 B–-B4! △ 13 . . . Px P) 12 . . . B–N5 13 N–KN5? (13 N–Q2! ∞) 13 . . . N–Q4 14 N(3)–K4 R–N1 15 R–QN1 R–N3!   16 P–B3 B–B4 ∓ Watson–Rohde, New York 1977; (b) 11 N–B3 (11 P–R5? B–B4!) 11 . . . P–K4? (11 . . . B–B4! looks better and =.) 12 P–R5 N–Q5 (now 12 . . . B–B4 13 N–KR4! ±) 13 Px P BPx P (**13 . . . RP**x P 14 N–K4 P–KB3   15 Nx N Px N 16 B–B8! **Rx B?**   17 Rx Bch! ±±; **16 . . . P–KN4** 17 B–QR3 ± – Averbakh) 14 N–K4 Q–K2 15 B–N5 Q–B2   16 B–K3! R–K2 17 N(3)–N5 Q–K1 18 Bx N Px B 19 P–R4! P–B3   20 N–Q6! ± Averbakh–Plachetka, Polanica Zdroj 1975.

9 B–R6   P–QB3

Probably **9 . . . N–B3** at once is preferable.

10 P–KR4   Bx B

11 Q×B N–K4 12 P–R5! N–N5
13 Q–Q2 Q–Q5 14 N–K4 B–B4
15 N–KB3 Q–N2 16 P×P BP×P
17 Q–N4! B×N? (17 . . . N–Q4!?)
18 Q×B Q×NP 19 0–0 ± (As often
happens, White's kingside threats
have forced positional concessions
from Black, in this case worth well
more than the pawn proferred.)
19 . . . N–B3 20 Q–K6ch K–N2
21 P–R4! KR–K1 22 P–R5
N(N)–Q2 23 QR–N1 ± Timman–
Jansa, Amsterdam 1974 (1–0, 32).

B33

7 . . .   **P–KR3**
Little tried; at least it avoids the
various attacks after B–R6 and
P–KR4–R5.

8 Q–B1
But now Black cannot castle.

8 . . .   N(1)–Q2
9 N–B3   N–B3
10 0–0   P–B3

Now we have transposed to
Simić–Bagirov, Vrnjacka Banja
1974, where 7 . . . P–QB3 8 Q–B1
P–KR3, etc. was played. That game
continued: **11 P–KR3?!** N(B)–Q4
12 B–Q2 B–K3 13 N–K4 N–Q2
14 R–Q1 Q–N3 = (though White
eventually won).

11 R–N1!

Obviously better than **11 P–
KR3?!**, as 11 . . . N–N5 threatens
only to decentralize Black's pieces.
Also **11 R–Q1** looks good △ **11** . . .
N–N5 12 B–B5! or **11 . . . N(B)–
Q4** 12 B–B5 N–Q2 13 B–QR3
P–QR4 14 N×N P×N 15 P–Q4
0–0 16 Q–K3 (or here 15 . . .
P–QN4 16 Q–B6 R–N1 17 B–B5
etc.).

11 . . .   P–QR4
12 P–N3   B–K3
13 N–QR4! ±

Miles–Tisdall, Lone Pine 1976.

CONCLUSION: Black has yet to
find a really convincing plan against
6 P–Q3 B–N2 7 B–K3. 7 . . .
N–B3!? is very shaky after 8 B×Nch.
Probably 7 . . . 0–0 and 8 . . .
R–K1!?, a risky but dynamic line,
should be considered; otherwise
Black seems to concede White basic
positional advantages without opening up a new front or beginning any
significant activity.

The variations after 5 . . . N×N
and 5 . . . N–N3 are classically logical, fighting for Black's share of the
board. To some extent, however,
they grant the player of 1 P–QB4
what he wants: a position free of
targets from which he can operate
down queenside files in conjunction
with his 'long artillery', the powerful KB.

2 GRÜNFELD-RELATED II:4 N–B3 P–KN3

1 P–QB4   N–KB3
2 N–QB3   P–Q4
3 P×P   N×P
4 N–B3

With 4 N–B3, White keeps his options open regarding the disposition of his king's bishop. On 4 . . . P–QB4, for example, he need not play 5 P–KN3 N–QB3 6 B–N2 N–B2 (*English III*, Chapter 5) but can try 5 P–K4, 5 P–Q4 or 5 P–K3 (*English III*, Chapter 7) 4 **P–K4**, seldom seen, can lead into:

(a) 4 . . . N×N 5 NP×N P–K4?!
(5 . . . P–QB4) 6 N–B3 B–Q3 7 P–Q4 Q–K2 8 B–QB4 P–KR3 9 0–0 0–0 10 P×P B×P 11 N×B Q×N 12 B–R3 R–K1 13 Q–N3 Q–B3 Landau–Thomas, England–Holland. 1937 and Schwarz suggests 14 QR–K1 △ P–B4 with 'clear advantage to White'. Perhaps not convincing after 14 . . . N–B3 e.g. 15 B–Q5 N–K4!, but White could not complain about his opening.
(b) 4 . . . N–N5 5 B–B4 (A surprising gambit is **5 P–Q4!?** Q×P 6 Q–K2!–*6 Q×Q?? N–B7ch*–*6 . . P–QB3* 7 P–B4 P–QN3 8 N–B3 Q–Q1 9 Q–KB2 P–K3 10 B–K3 N–Q6ch?–*10 . . . B–K2*–11 B×N Q×B 12 R–Q1 ± Shaposhnikov–Shamkovich, corres 1957; but **5 P–Q3?** is feeble: 5 . . . P–QB4 6 B–K2 P–KN3 7 B–K3 P–N3

8 P–B4 B–KN2 9 N–B3 N(5)–B3 ∓ Feuerstein–Bisguier, New York 1955) 5 . . . B–K3 (5 . . . **N–Q6ch** 6 K–K2 N–B5ch 7 K–B1 B–K3 8 B–N5ch B–Q2 9 P–Q4 B×Bch 10 N×B N–N3 11 P–KR4 P–KR4 12 B–N5 ± Reshko–Shamkovich, Four Teams, Moscow 1961.) 6 B×B P×B 7 KN–K2 (7 **N–B3?** Q–Q6!; 7 **P–Q4?** Q×P!) 7 . . . N–Q6ch 8 K–B1 N–B3 9 Q–N3 (9 **P–KN3** Q–Q2 10 K–N2 0–0–0 and 'Black stands excellently'–Taimanov) 9 . . . Q–Q2 10 Q×NP R–QN1 11 Q–R6 P–N3 12 P–KR4 R–N3 13 Q–R4 B–N2 14 R–R3 0–0 15 N–Q1? (15 P–B3) 15 . . . R–N5! 16 R×N Q×R 17 Q×N R×KP 18 N–K3 R×N 0–1 Mikenas–Goldenov, Tbilisi 1946.

4 . . .   P–KN3

In some cases (e.g. 5 P–Q4 B–N2), this will transpose to a Grünfeld Defence, but there is a variety of purely 'English' alternatives. These are mostly of recent vintage, and theory on them has not matured enough for definitive assessments. One observes nonetheless that very strong players have been willing to take both sides of:

A 5 Q–N3
B 5 Q–R4ch
C 5 P–K4

D 5 P–KN3

A

5 Q–N3
An attempt to dislodge the Black knight from d5.

  5 . . .   N–N3

5 . . . N×N? 6 Q×N makes no sense (6 . . . P–KB3 7 P–Q4), and 5 . . . **P–QB3**?! 6 P–K4 N–B2 7 P–Q4 also favours White.

  6 P–KN3

(a) **6 N–KN5**?! P–K3 7 P–Q3 ignores the centre: 7 . . . B–N2 8 P–N3 N–B3 9 B–N2 0–0 10 0–0 N–Q5 11 Q–Q1 P–K4 ∓ Shamkovich–Polugaevsky, 1968.
(b) **6 P–Q4** B–N2 is a Grünfeld e.g. 7 B–N5 P–KR3 8 B–R4, and now 8 . . . B–K3!? transposes to B, note (a) to 6 Q–B2 below.

  6 . . .   B–N2
  7 B–N2   0–0
  8 0–0

White does not benefit from delaying this: **8 P–Q3** N–B3 9 B–K3 P–K4 10 0–0 N–Q5 11 B×N P×B 12 N–K4 P–B3 ∓ O'Kelly–Polugayevsky, Havana 1967. Compare Chapter 1, where White's queen is better-placed.

  8 . . .   N–B3
  9 P–Q3   B–K3(?!)

9 . . . **P–KR3** or 9 . . . B–N5 is fully satisfactory, but not 9 . . . **P–K4**?! 10 B–N5! e.g. 10 . . . N–Q5 11 B×Q N×Q 12 P×N R×B 13 R–R5 ±.

  10 Q–N5!   P–KR3

Or **10** . . . **P–QR3** 11 Q–N5! △ Q–R4. **10** . . . **P–KR3** came from Bronstein–Taimanov, Vinkovci 1970: 11 B–K3 P–QR3 12 Q–QB5 N–Q2 13 Q–R3 P–QR4 14

Q–R4! ±. White again aims for h4!

B

5 Q–R4ch
Stein's move, attempting to cause disorder in Black's ranks.

  5 . . .   B–Q2 (9)

(a) **5** . . . **P–B3**? was Keres' move versus Stein in the stem game (Parnu 1971): 6 Q–Q4 N–B3 (**6** . . . **P–B3** 7 P–K4; and if 7 . . . P–K4, 8 N×P, etc.) 7 Q×Qch K×Q 8 P–K4 B–N2 9 P–Q4 R–B1 10 P–KR3 P–N3 11 P–KN4! P–KR4 12 P–N5 (or 12 P–K5 ± – Keene) 12 . . . N–K1 13 B–KB4 N–Q2 14 0–0–0 B–N2 15 P–KR4 N–B2 16 B–R3 ± (1–0, 30).
(b) **5** . . . **N–B3**!? may be playable: 6 N–K5 N(4)–N5! (**6** . . . **B–Q2** 7 N×B Q×N 8 P–KN3 ± –Minić) 7 P–QR3 B–N2 8 N×BP (**8** P×N B×N 9 P–N5 N–N1 10 P–N6ch N–B3 =) 8 . . . N–Q6ch! 9 P×N K×N 10 P–Q4 N×P 11 B–B4ch P–K3 12 0–0 R–B1 Kirov–Honfi, Maribor 1977. Difficult to assess!

  6 Q–B2   *

The current preference. White has tried no less than five moves from the diagram, of which (c) seems the most promising:
(a) **6 Q–N3** N–N3 7 P–Q4 B–N2

8 B–N5 P–KR3 9 B–R4 B–K3
10 Q–B2 0–0 (10 ... N–B3 11
R–Q1 0–0 12 P–K3–?! 12
P–KR3!–12 ... N–N5! 13 Q –N1
B–B4 14 P–K4 B–N5 15 P–Q5
P–N4 16 B–N3 P–KB4! with
good play. Furman–Savon, USSR
1970) 11 P–K4!? (11 R–Q1) 11
... Bx P 12 Nx B Qx N 13 Bx P
R–K1 14 B–R4 N–B3 =/∞
Gulko–Bagirov, USSR Ch 1973.
(b) **6 Q–Q4 N–KB3** 7 Q–KR4
B–N2 8 P–K4? (8 **P–Q3** P–KR3
9 B–Q2 = –Uhlmann) 8 ... P–KR3!
9 P–K5 N–N5! 10 Q–N3 (**10
P–Q4** P–QB4! 11 B–QB4 Q–B1 ∓
–Uhlmann) 10 ... N–QB3 11
P–Q4 N–N5 12 P–KR3 N–B7ch
13 K–Q1 Nx QP!! 14 Px N
B–R5ch! ∓∓ Andersson–Uhlmann,
Skopje 1972.
(c) **6 Q–R4** B–B3 (The best
solution, ceding no ground in the
centre. If now 7 P–Q4, 7 ... N–N5!.
By contrast **6 . . '. N–KB3?!** 7
P–Q4 P–KR3 8 P–K4 B–N2
9 N–K5 gave White the centre in
Dementiev–Vaiskov, Sochi 1977.)
7 Q–Q4 (**7 P–QR3** B–N2 8 Nx N
Qx N 9 P–K3 B–N4! ∓ Rytov–
Savon, USSR 1975; **7 P–KN3?!**
B–N2 8 B–N2 0–0 9 0–0 P–K4 ∓
Schmidt–Portisch, Skopje, 1972;
7 N–K5 B–N2 8 Nx B N(1)x N
9 Q–K4 P–K3 10 P–K3 0–0 =
Polugayevsky–Smejkal, Palma de
Mallorca 1972; Black's development
and centrally oriented pieces are
good value for the bishop pair.)
7 . . . P–B3 8 P–K3! (8 **P–K4**
Nx N?!–*8 ... P–K4! 9 Nx P Px N*
10 Qx Pch Q–K2 11 Qx R N–N5∞
–9 QPx N Qx Q 10 Nx Q P–K4
11 Nx B Nx N 12 B–QN5 ± –

Savon) 8 ... B–N2 9 B–K2 P–K4
10 Q–QB4 Nx N 11 Q–K6ch!
Q–K2 12 Qx Qch Kx Q 13 NPx N
R–Q1 14 P–Q4 N–Q2 15 0–0
P–QN3 16 P–QR4 ± Polugayevsky–
Mecking, Match (7) 1977.
(d) **6 Q–K4!?** Nx N?! (6 ... N–N3 =
–Bagirov) 7 Q–Q4 R–N1 8 Qx N
B–N2 9 P–Q4 P–QB4 10 Qx P
N–R3 11 Q–R3 Q–N3 12 B–Q2 ±
Chernev–Chaturian, USSR 1977.
6 ...   N–N3
7 P–Q4
7 P–KN3 B–N2 8 B–N2 N–B3
9 P–Q3 0–0 10 0–0 is a logical
choice, and on 10 . . . P–KR3,
White might choose a plan from
Chapter 12, e.g. 11 B–Q2 P–K4
12 QR–B1 B–K3 13 Q–N1! etc.
Andersson–Hartoch, Wijk an Zee
1973 saw instead 10 . . . N–B1!?
11 N–K4 (11 B–K3 N–Q3 13
B–B5!) 11 . . . N–Q3 12 N–B5
B–K1 13 B–Q2 P–N3 14 N–N3
R–B1 =.
7 ...   B–N2
7 . . . **B–N5** 8 Q–K4 Bx N
9 KPx B?! (9 Qx B ±) 9 ... P–QB3
10 P–QR4?! (**10 Q–K5** R–N1
11 B–K3 B–N2 = –Savon) 10 . . .
B–N2 11 P--R5 N–Q4 12 B–QB4
P–K3 ∓ Ornstein–Savon, Dortmund
1975.
8 P–K4   0–0
9 B–K3 B–N5?! (9 . . . **N–B3!** 10
P–Q5–*10 R–Q1 B–N5; 10 P–KR3
P –K4*–10 . . . N–K4 11 Nx N
Bx N 12 R–Q1 Q–B1 13 P–B4
B--N2 14 B–K2 P–QB3! = Benko–
Szabo, Hastings 1973/4) 10 N–K5
B–K3 11 R–Q1 Q–B1 12 N–B3
(12 P–B4!?) 12 . . . B–N5 13
B–K2 N–B3 14 P–Q5 N–K4?!
(Better 14 ... Bx N 15 Bx B N–K4

16 B−K2 P−QB3 17 Q−N3 ± −
Minić) 15 Nx N Bx B 16 Qx B Bx N
17 0−0 B−N2 18 R−B1 ± Jansson-
Jakobsen, Stockholm 1974. White
has more space and enduring
queenside pressure.

C

5 P−K4

A dangerous thrust; now **5 . . .
N−N5?** is easily answered by 6
P−Q4 (6 . . . B−N5? 7 Q−R4ch).
 5 . . .   Nx N
**5 . . . N−N3 6 P−Q4 B−N5
7 B−K2 B−N2 8 B−K3** gives White
a good centre, and **6 P−KR3** has
its merits too: 6 . . . P−QB4 7
P−Q4 ± △ 7 . . . Px P 8 Qx P!
 6 QPx N!?
This recapture has scored well,
but **6 NPx N** cannot be under-
estimated either: 6 . . . B−N2
(6 . . . P−QB4 7 Q−R4ch! B−Q2−
*7 . . . N−B3 8 B−R3−*8 Q−N3
Q−B2 9 B−B4 ±) 7 B−R3!
(7 P−Q4 P−QB4 = is an exchange
Grünfeld with White's knight on f3
7 Q−R4 ch!?−Larsen) and now:
(a) **7 . . . 0−0** 8 P−Q4 N−Q2
9 B−Q3 P−QB4 10 0−0 P−N3
11 Q−K2 B−N2 Averkin-Korchnoi,
USSR Ch 1973, a position in which
Rosenberg recommends **12 QR−Q1**
±. Judović mentions **12 P−K5!**,
which may be even better, e.g. 12
. . . **P−K3** 13 N−Q2 △ N−B4, while
12 . . . B−Q4 allows 13 N−N5!?
(13 . . . P−KR3 14 N−R3) or
13 B−K4 ±.
(b) 7 . . . **P−N3** 8 B−B4 0−0
9 0−0 N−B3 10 P−Q4 (10 B−Q5
B−Q2) 10 . . . N−R4 11 B−Q3
Q−Q2? (Premature, because the
queen may be better placed on c7.

11 . . . B−N2 is best, when Black
has in mind a sequence like 12
Q−K2 P−QB4 13 Px P Q−B2 14
Px P Px P etc.) 12 Q−K2 B−N2
13 QR−Q1 KR−Q1 14 P−Q5!
P−QB3 (15 B−N5 was threatened)
15 B−N4 Px P 16 Px P Bx QP 17
Bx N Px B 18 B−K4 Q−K3 19
N−N5 Q−K4 20 Rx B! Rx R 21
Nx BP! Kx N 22 Q−B3ch K−K3
23 P−B4 ± Korchnoi-Timman (6),
Leeuwarden 1976 (but ½−½, 28).
 6 . . .   Qx Qch
 7 Kx Q (10)

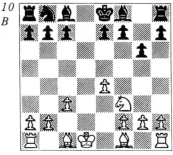

Black has had trouble equalizing
here; White's advantage consists in a
better hold on the centre and better
squares for his bishops.
 7 . . .   N−Q2
A noncommittal move which
also threatens . . . P−K4, e.g. 8
K−B2 P−K4 =. Black has two other
tries to neutralize White's pressure,
of which (a) is perhaps too casual,
but
(a) 7 . . . **B−N2?!** 8 K−B2 (or
similarly **8 B−KB4 P−QB3 9** K−B2
N−Q2 10 N−Q2 0−0 11 P−B3
R−K1 12 N−B4 ± Commons-
Mihalchishin, Primorsko 1976 (1−0,
33) 8 . . . N−Q2 9 B−KB4 P−QB3?!
(Black feels that his king's bishop
is misplaced for **9 . . . P−K4**, but he

could follow up with an early . . . B–KB1 and improve on what follows.) 10 N–Q2! (This idea of Hort's makes it hard for Black to develop.) 10 . . . 0–0 11 P–B3 (△ N–B4–R5!) 11 . . . P–KB4 12 B–KN5 B–B3 13 B×B N×B 14 B–B4ch K–N2 15 P–K5 N–K1 16 QR–Q1 ± Hort-Smejkal, Czechoslovakia 1973.

(b) 7 . . . P–KB3!? was Mecking's choice versus Najdorf in Wijk an Zee, 1978: 8 B–QB4 (insipid, but against Mecking, Najdorf was doubtless content to split the point.) 8 . . . P–K4 9 B–K3 N–Q2 10 K–K2 B–B4 11 KR–Q1 B×B 12 K×B N–N3 13 N–Q2 K–K2 14 B–N3 B–K3 15 B×B K×B 16 P–QN3 KR–Q1 (½–½, 43). If White wants to try for more, 8 P–K5!? is probably necessary e.g. 8 . . . B–N5 9 B–KB4 B×Nch?! (9 . . . P–KN4!? and if 10 B–K3, 10 . . . N–Q2!) 10 P×B and Black still has to fight off two rapacious bishops. Yet this is a good place to look for an equalizing sequence.

8 B–QB4

An instructive example of Black play was 8 B–KB4 N–B4! 9 N–Q2 P–QB3   10 B–K3 (10 P–B3 P–B4!?) 10 . . . P–K4 11 P–QN4 N–R5   12 K–B2 P–QN4! 13 P–QR3 B–K3 14 N–N3 P–QR3 15 B–K2 B–K2 (amusing . . .) 16 KR–Q1 P–KB4!?   17 P×P B×Pch 18 B–Q3 R–KN1 Larsen-Hübner, Biel 1977.

    8 . . .   B–N2
    8 . . . P–KB3?! 9 N–Q4! or
8 . . . P–K4? 9 N–N5
    9 R–K1   P–QB3
    10 K–B2   0–0

    11 B–K3

Less precise was 11 B–B4 N–B4 12 P–QN4 B–K3!?   13 B–QN3 (13 B–KB1 N–R5   14 N–Q4 P–QB4! is surprisingly strong.) 13 . . . N×B   14 P×N P–KR3 with only minimal White advantage, Palatnik–Mihalchishin, USSR 1976. The text move, preventing . . . N–B4, follows Romanishin–Grigorian, USSR Ch 1976: 11 . . . P–KR3 12 P–QR4 P–QR4 (Minev suggests 12 . . . R–K1 △ . . . N–B1–K3 ±.) 13 P–K5! P–K3   14 QR–Q1 R–K1 15 B–Q4 P–N3   16 B–K3! Black's last created definite queenside weaknesses which White was not long in exploiting (1–0, 35).

CONCLUSION: Of these three methods of probing Black's set-up with . . . P–KN3 and . . . P–Q4, 5 Q–N3 is the least convincing, and it is much too early to say whether 5 Q–R4ch leads to any tangible advantage (although it is certainly a safe move after e.g. 5 . . . B–Q2 6 Q–R4). The third try, 5 P–K4, puts Black in the discouraging position of being almost forced to play 5 . . . N×N, when 6 NP×N offers White dangerous attacking chances and 6 QP×N takes Black into an ending he has had trouble holding. Unless the defence improves (this is quite possible), 5 P–K4 may dissuade Black from the move order of this chapter.

D

    5 P–KN3   B–N2
(a) 5 . . . P–QB4 6 B–N2 B–N2 is the Symmetrical English again. White also has 6 Q–N3!?, but that runs into 6 . . . N–N5! and now

7 N–K4? (7 P–QR3 B–K3 8 Q–Q1
=) 7 . . . B–N2! 8 N×P N(1)–B3!
(Also 8 . . . Q–R4!? 9 P–QR3
N(5)–B3 proved hard to meet in
Polugayevsky–Bronstein,39th USSR
Ch 1972: 10 Q–B4?! P–QN4
11 Q–KR4 P–N5 12 N–Q3 N–R3
13 B–N2 B–Q2 14 0–0 R–QB1
15 N(Q)–K1 N–B4 16 N–B2
N–N6! ∓ Δ 17 P×P Q–QN4!) 9
P–QR3 Q–R4 10 N–QR4 B–K3!
(or 10 . . . B–B4!–Cvetković) 11
Q–Q1 (11 P×N B×Q 12 P×Q
N–N5 ∓∓) 11 . . . B–B4 12 P×N
N×P 13 P–K4 B×P 14 N–B3
Q×R 15 N×B 0–0 ∓ Vukić-
Bukal, Yugoslavia 1973.
(b) 5 . . . N×N 6 NP×N **B–N2**
7 B–N2 is a variation from Chapter 1, A2 (±). **6 . . . P–QB4** (instead of 6 . . . B–N2) allows
7 Q–R4ch N–Q2 (7 . . . **N–B3**
8 B–QR3 ± ; 7 . . . **B–Q2** 8 Q–QB4
±) 8 P–KR4 (Perhaps **8 R–QN1**
B–N2 9 B–KN2 0–0 10 P–B4
etc.) 8 . . . P–KR3 9 R–QN1
B–N2 10 B–KN2 0–0, which we
analyze (by transposition) in Chapter 1, A3.

6 B–N2
Now Black has two strategies
independent of . . . P–QB4, . . .
N×N, or . . . N–N3:
D1 6 . . . P–K4
D2 6 . . . 0–0 7 0–0 N–B3

D1
6 . . . P–K4 (11)
Korchnoi's move, sometimes
played after 6 . . . 0–0 7 0–0.
Black maximizes his guard on d4 by
means of . . . N–K2, . . . N(1)–B3
and possibly . . . N–KB4. 6 . . .
P–K4 may be considered an attempt

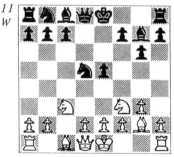

11
W

to transpose into Opocensky's 5 . . .
N–K2 line of *English I*, . . . *P–K4*
without allowing certain unfavour-
able variations (see (c) in the next
note). To avoid this, White can try:
7 N×N
(a) **7 Q–R4ch(!)** may be more
effective (and provides a case for
interposing 6 . . . 0–0 7 0–0 before
playing 7 . . . P–K4): 7 . . . P–B3
(7 . . . **N–B3**? 8 N×KP ±± ; 7 . . .
B–Q2 8 Q–N3 ± –Geller. 8 Q–R3!?
would also be interesting.) 8 N×N
Q×N 9 0–0 N–Q2 10 P–Q3
N–B4 (**10 . . . 0–0** 11 N–N5!
Δ 12 Q–R4) 11 Q–R3 (11 Q–R4!?)
11 . . . N–K3 12 B–K3 (**12 B–Q2**
Q–Q1 13 QR–B1 Q–K2 14
B–N4 ± –Geller) 12 . . . Q–Q1
13 QR–B1 Q–K2 14 Q–R5 Q–Q1
Podgayets–Tukmakov, E. Bloc
Armies Ch 1974, when by 15 Q×Qch
White maintained a slight advantage
(½–½, 46).
(b) **7 P–Q3** can be tried, because
7 . . . N×N 8 P×N P–K5?! 9
Q–R4ch K–B1 10 N–Q4 (or 10
B–R3ch and 11 N–Q4) is good for
White. Black probably responds by
7 . . . **N–K2**, when 8 0–0 N(1)–B3
is like the next note.
(c) **7 0–0** is critical. 7 . . . **0–0**
8 P–Q3 N–K2 (8 . . . N–QB3?!

9 N× P! ±: 8 . . . N× N 9 P× N P—K5
10 P× P B× P   11 R—N1 ±) transposes to an important but unclear
variation of 5 . . . N—K2 in an
Accelerated Fianchetto Reversed
(*English I*, Chapter 5). By this
order Black at least avoided the lines
of that chapter where White plays
an early P—QN4; worse, for example,
would be 7 . . . N—K2?! 8 P—QN4!
N(1)—B3 9 P—N5.

7 . . .	Q× N
8 0—0	0—0
9 P—Q3	N—B3

9 . . . Q—N4!? (compare D2!) 10
P—QR4 Q—R3   11 B—K3 N—B3
12 P—QN4 N—Q5 13 P—N5 Q—Q3
14 B× N (14 N—Q2) 14 . . . P× B
15 N—Q2 P—QR3 16 N—B4 Q—K2∞
Kushnir–Savereide, Haifa, 1976.

10 B—K3   Q—Q3!

10 . . . Q—Q1   11 P—QN4!
P—QR3 (**11 . . . P—K5?** 12 P× P
B× R 13 Q× B ±) 12 P—QR4 R—K1
13 R—N1 N—Q5 14 R—K1 P—QB3
15 N—N5 (Or 15 N× N P× N 16
B—B4 B—Q2?! 17 P—KR4 R—QB1
18 B—B3 B—B1 19 Q—Q2 ± Doda–
Korchnoi, Nice 1974) 15 . . . Q—K2
16 N—K4 ± Furman–Korchnoi, 3
Team Event, USSR 1973 (½–½, 33).

11 Q—R4

11 R—B1 N—Q5 12 P—QN4 is
plausible, although no plan is likely
to give a significant advantage at
this point.

11 . . .   N—Q5
12 N× N P× N   13 B—B4 Q—K2
14 KR—K1 P—QB3   15 P—QN4
P—QR3   16 Q—R5 (16 QR—B1)
16 . . . B—K3 17 Q—QB5 Q—Q2
Mecking–Korchnoi (10), 1974.
Black is holding the balance (½–½,
27).

D2

6 . . .	0—0
7 0—0	N—B3 (12)

7 . . . P—QB4 again transposes
to *English III*, Chapters 2 and 7, and
7 . . . N× N or 7 . . . N—N3 is Chapter
1. If White plays 8 P—Q4 in the diagrammed position we have a Neo-
Grünfeld. This may be his best
course (theory is in flux regarding
8 . . . N—N3), but there are also
the following 'English' (i.e. non-
P—Q4) ideas:

8 N× N

(a) **8 Q—N3?!** (a poor spot for the
queen, since . . . N—Q5 is always in
the air) 8 . . . N—N3 9 P—Q3
P—KR3 (9 . . . P—K4? 10 B—N5! ±)
10 B—K3 P—K4 11 B—B5 R—K1
(**11 . . . B—K3!** 12 Q—Q1 R—K1 or
12 Q—R3 R—K1 13 P—QN4 N—Q2
and Black has taken the initiative.)
12 KR—B1 N—Q5 (**12 . . . B—K3**
13 Q—Q1 P—QR4) 13 Q—Q1 B—N5
14 P—K3 N× Nch!? 15 B× N B× B
16 Q× B Q× P 17 Q× P P—K5! 18
R—Q1 Q—B7 19 QR—B1 Q× P 20
N× P Garcia Padron–Sigurjonsson,
Las Palmas 1976, and now 20 . . .
QR—Q1 (Gheorghiu) was equal.
(b) **8 Q—R4 N—N3 9 Q—R4** (not
much of an attack, really . . .) 9 . . .
P—B3 10 B—R3 (**10 P—Q4 P—KN4!**

Δ . . . P–N5 ∓) 10 . . . P–K3 (10
. . . B× B = –Byrne and Mednis)
11 P–Q4? **(11 P–Q3** Q–K1 12
Q–K4 = –Byrne and Mednis) 11 . . .
P–KN4! 12 B× P? P× B 13 N× P
P–KR3 14 B× Pch B× B 15 N× B
Q× Q 16 P× Q R –B2 ∓ R. Hernan-
dez–Rogoff, Las Palmas 1976.
(c) 8 **P–QR3**!? might be an alternative (just to keep the game complicated!). White intends 9 Q–B2, and
8 . . . **P–K4** 9 R N1 seems okay,
as 9 . . . **B–B4**, 9 . . . **P–KR3**, and
9 . . . **R–K1** are all answered by
10 P–Q3. Of course Black can still
play 8 . . . **N–N3**, leading after
9 P–Q3 P–K4 10 B –Q2 (or 10
R–N1) to a mutually acceptable
formation akin to Chapter 12, B.
Finally, 8 . . . **P–QR4** has two
replies: **9 Q–B2** Δ9 . . . B–N5 10
P K3 N–N3 11 P –Q4; and
9 P–Q4 N–N3 10 P–Q5!, trying
to improve on a normal Grünfeld
since 10 . . . N –QR4 is unavailable,
e.g. 10 . . . N –N1 11 P–K4 P–QB3
12 B–N5!? or 12 N–K1.

    8 . . .   Q× N
    9 P–Q3   Q–QN4(!)
Portisch has often played this, to
hamper White's queenside development and clear the open queen file
for Black's rooks. 9 . . . **P–K4**
would transpose to D1 above, and
9 . . . **Q–KR4**?! 10 Q–N3!? R –N1
11 B–K3 B–K3 12 Q–R3 is a little
in White's favour, e.g. 12 . . .
KR–Q1 13 QR–B1 R–Q4!? 14
B–Q2 (preventing . . . R–R4) 14 . . .
B–R6? (14 . . . R–QN4 ± –Marić)
15 R–B4! (Turnabout is fair play;

White threatens 16 R–KR4.) 15 . . .
B× B 16 K× B P–KN4 (else 17
P–KN4!) 17 P–KR3 ± Ribli–Honfi,
30th Hungarian Ch 1974.
    10 R–N1   P–QR4
    11 B –K3
Balashov gives 11 **B–B4** P–K4
12 B–K3 (=?); the similar **11
P–QR4** Q–R3 12 B–K3 P–K4
(12 . . . R–Q1!?) was played in
Valcarcel–Portisch, Las Palmas
1972: 13 Q–B1!? (13 N –Q2 or
13 N–N5) 13 . . . P–K5! 14 P× P
Q× P 15 R–Q1? (15 R–K1 = –
Portisch) 15 . . . B–K3 16 P–N3
KR–Q1 ∓.
    11 . . .   R–Q1
12 Q–B1? (12 Q–Q2 = –Balashov)
12 . . . B–K3 13 P–N3 N–N5 14
Q× P N× RP 15 N–N5 B–Q4 ∓
Notaras–Balashov, Novi Sad 1975.
Black has a queenside majority and
better-centralized pieces (0-1, 35).
CONCLUSION: 5 P–KN3 B–N2
6 B–N2 P–K4 has worked well
with Korchnoi supervising the Black
pieces. Whether it is actually equal
remains to be seen, and 7 0–0 0–0
8 P–Q3 N–K2, in *English I* should
be examined in this regard.
    The other sequence, 6 . . . 0–0
7 0–0 N–B3, has a reliable look to
it, and none of white's eighth moves
above seems to give better chances
than transposition to the Grünfeld
Defence by 8 P–Q4. I will recall
this point when discussing move
orders against a King's Indian
formation (Chapter 16, Introduction).

3 FLOHR-MIKENAS ATTACK: 3 P–K4

1 P–QB4	N–KB3
2 N–QB3	P–K3
3 P–K4 (13)	

13
B

A move that has alternated between popularity and obscurity several times since the 1920s! As Black's first two moves are fashionable in response to the English Opening, the variations introduced by 3 P–K4 are currently receiving a lot of attention. Both White's attacking ideas and Black's defensive resources have been strengthened, and lively games abound. The system initiated by 3 P–K4 was called the Flohr attack after the game Flohr–Kashdan, Folkestone 1933, but in some countries became known as the Mikenas System after its use by the Lithuanian master.

In its favour, 3 P–K4 threatens P–K5 and thereby discourages both

3 . . . B–N5 and 3 . . . P–QN3. White can also get promising play against 3 . . . P–Q4, though that move is far from refuted.

Since the 1940s, when Mikenas first played and analyzed 3 P–K4 extensively, the toughest counterplay has stemmed from 3 . . . P–B4, by which Black exploits his opponent's lack of control over d4 and prepares . . . P–Q4. After the consistent 4 P–K5 N–N1, White has gained time but overextended his KP, so he usually essays upon a speculative gambit (5 N–B3 N–QB3 6 P–Q4), the consequences of which are still unclear.

A variation rich in tactical ideas!

A 3 . . . P–Q4
B 3 . . . P–B4

The alternatives are dubious:

(a) 3 . . . B–N5?! 4 P–K5 N–N1 (4 . . . B× N 5 QP× B N–N1—*forced* — 6 Q–N4 K–B1 7 B–B4 △ 7 . . . P–Q3 8 R–Q1) 5 Q–N4 P–KN3 6 P–Q4 (or 6 N–B3, or 6 P–QR3) ±.

(b) 3 . . . N–B3 (Kevitz) is more troublesome. Schwarz gives 4 P–Q4 B–N5 5 B–N5 ±, but that assessment looks premature, and anyway, Black has 4 . . . P–Q4, when 5 BP× P P× P 6 P–K5 N–K5 7 B–QN5 B–QN5 8 Q–R4 0–0! 9 B× N B× Nch 10 P× B P× B 11 Q× P R–N1 gives Black the attack, and **5 P–K5 N–K5 6 N–B3 B–N5** is also undesirable. Compare A22 below.

After 3 . . . N–B3, **4 N–B3!** is best, and now **4 . . . B–N5 5 P–K5** favours White, while **4 . . . P–Q4 5 P–K5 N–K5 6 Q–B2!** transposes to A12 below (±), and here **5 . . . P–Q5? 6 PxN PxN 7 NPxP QxP 8 P–Q4** is clearly not to Black's liking.

(c) 3 . . . **P–K4**!? at least indicates that d4 is weak: **4 N–B3 (4 P–KN3 B–B4 5 B–N2 0–0 6 KN–K2 N–B3 7 0–0 P–Q3 8 P–Q3 B–KN5 9 P–KR3 BxN 10 NxB N–Q5 11 K–R2 =** Carls–Berndtsson, Hamburg, 1930) 4 . . . N–B3 (Now we are in Nimzowitsch's 4 P–K4 version of the 'Main Line' with White a tempo up! Compare *English I* Chapter 8, B.) 5 P–Q4 (By analogy, **5 P–QR3** is an idea, discouraging Black from 5 . . . B–N5 or 5 . . . B–B4. Best would be 5 . . . P–Q3. Naturally, **5 B–K2, 5 P–Q3,** and **5 P–KN3** are also reasonable.) 5 . . . PxP 6 NxP B–N5 '±', according to Schwarz. White plays 7 P–B3 and we have the kind of central bind where Black's knight on c6 would rather be somewhere else.

A

    3 . . .   P–Q4

'Mixing it'. White has two promising replies:
A1 4 P–K5 ➤
A2 4 BPxP

A1

    4 P–K5

Now it's Black's turn to decide between:
A11 4 . . . KN–Q2
A12 4 . . . N–K5
A13 4 . . . P–Q5

A11

    4 . . .   KN–Q2

Black attacks the KP and prepares the central thrust . . . P–QB4. By analogy with the French Defence, Steinitz Variation, White has potentially less control over his pawn chain (P–QB3 is not available), but more immediate pressure on d5. This central instability provides an explanation for the tactics which now explode.

White has two closely related moves (these subdivisions are not as confusing as they seem if you will bear with me):
A111 5 P–Q4
A112 5 PxP ➤

Other moves are worse:
(a) **5 N–B3?!** P–Q5! 6 NxP (6 N–QN5 N–QB3) 6 . . . NxP 7 N–B3 NxNch! 8 QxN N–B3 etc.
(b) **5 P–B4?** PxP! 6 N–B3 (6 BxP? NxP! 7 PxN Q–R5ch and 8 . . . QxB) 6 . . . N–N3 7 BxP NxB 8 Q–R4ch N–B3 9 QxN N–N5 10 0–0 P–QN3! ∓ Rabinovich–Levenfish, Leningrad Ch. 1936.

A111

    5 P–Q4   P–QB4

5 . . . PxP is rather passive, but playable, e.g. 6 BxP N–N3 7 B–Q3! (7 B–N3 P–QB4! 8 N–B3 –8 P–Q5 PxP 9 NxP P–B5! 10 NxN QxN–8 . . . N–B3 9 P–Q5 PxP 10 NxP B–N5) 7 . . . N–B3

(**7** . . . **P–QB4**   8 PxP BxP   9
N–B3 ±) 8 N–B3 N–N5 9 B–N1
B–Q2   10 0–0 B–B3   11 P–QR3
N(5)–Q4   12 N–K4 P–KR3
13 R–K1 ± Watson–Kaimo, New
York 1977.

   6 BPxP
   6 N–B3 BPxP 7 QxP N–QB3
8 Q–B4 (8 Q–K3 P–Q5! 9 NxP
N(2)xP) 8 . . . P–Q5! 9 N–QN5
B–N5ch (Shatskes).
          6 . . .   KPxP
          7 N–B3
(a) **7** NxP PxP   8 QxP? N–N3
9 B–QB4 B–K3 ∓∓ (Shatskes).
(b) **7 PxP!**? BxP 8 QxP Q–N3 is
very complicated: 9 B–QB4 (**9
B–KB4**?? QxP; **9 N–R3** N–QB3
10 P–B4 0–0 ∓, or here 10 P–K6
N–B3! 11 PxPch K–B1 with a
very strong attack) 9 . . . BxPch
10 K–B1 (**10 K–K2** 0–0   **11
N–B3** B–B4! and if 12 N–K4 or
12 N–QR4, 12 . . . Q–N3; or, in
this line, **11 N–R3** B–Q5!   12
N–R4 Q–N5   13 QxB N–QB3
14 Q–B4 N(2)xP   **15 B–N3**
Q–N4ch ∓∓ or **15 P–QN3** P–QN4!
16 B–Q2 Q–K2 etc.) 10 . . . 0–0
11 N–B3 B–B4 12 N–K4 N–R3!
13 N(4)–N5 N–B2   14 Q–K4
Q–N3, and Black is defending suc-
cessfully, according to Shatskes,
whose analysis this is.
          7 . . .   N–QB3 (14)
     7 . . . **PxP**   8 QxP N–N3 (8 . . .
N–QB3 9 QxQP N(2)xP?? 10
NxN) 9 B–KN5 N–B3 10 Q–Q2!
(Shatskes) ±.
     8 PxP!?
     8 B–QN5(!) is a direct transpos-
ition to A112 below, where White
gets a positional edge.
          8 . . .   BxP!

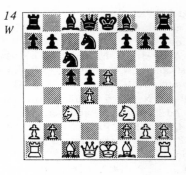

(a) **8** . . . **P–Q5?!** 9 NxP NxN
(9 . . . N(2)xP 10 B–K3!) 10 QxN
BxP 11 Q–Q5 Q–N3 12 B–QB4
BxPch 13 K–K2 0–0 14 N–K4
B–B4 15 R–B1 Q–N3 16 RxBP
RxR 17 N–N5 appears very strong,
although there may be improvements!
(b) **8** . . . **N(2)xKP?** 9 NxN NxN
10 Q–K2 Q–K2 11 NxP N–Q6ch
12 K–Q2 QxQch 13 BxQ ± Watson–
Hill, Calgary 1975.
          9 QxP   Q–N3
          10 B–QB4   BxPch
   A position hitherto unmentioned,
probably better for White than
note (b) to 7 N–B3. Though it
practically defies analysis, I offer
as a sample 11 K–B1!? 0–0 12
Q–K4!? N(2)xP! 13 N–Q5! Q–B4
14 NxN NxN   15 QxN QxBch
16 KxB P–B3, and White *may*
manage to consolidate, but it's not
simple.
CONCLUSION: As there are almost
endless tactical possibilities after
8 . . . BxP, 5 P–Q4 might be best
employed as a means of reaching
the position 5 . . . P–QB4 6 BPxP
KPxP 7 N–B3 N–QB3 8 B–QN5
(A112).

A112

5 P×P

This can lead to the same position as A111; but here we examine a different 8th move for White, and options on the way:

5 ...   P×P

For example, Black has the important alternative **5 . . . N×P(!)** 6 P–Q4 N–N3 and:

(a) **7 P×P** B×P 8 P–Q5 ('±' Smyslov, but Shatskes and Quinteros disagree) 8 . . . B–Q2 (or 8 . . . B–B1) **9 N–B3** (9 Q–N3 N–R3!–Shatskes) 9 . . . B–Q3 **10 B–K2** 0–0 11 0–0 R–K1; 'Fairly level' comments Shatskes; perhaps White has the tiniest of edges. He also had **9 Q–Q4!?** or, instead of 10 B–K2, **10 B–KN5!?** (△ 10 . . . P–KB3 11 B–K3 or 10 . . . B–K2 11 B–K3); but Black is only slightly cramped in such cases, and can prepare . . . P–QB3;

(b) **7 B–N5ch** P–B3 (7 . . . B–Q2? 8 P×P ±) 8 P×BP P×P (Or 8 . . . N×P!–Shatskes. Then 9 N–B3 B–K2 10 0–0 0–0 or 10 . . . B–Q2 is logical, giving a more-or-less normal isolated pawn position. After 11 R–K1, I suspect that White is better, but that may be a matter of taste.) 9 B–QB4 (**9 B–R4** B–K2 10 KN–K2–*10 N–B3 B–R3*–10 . . . 0–0–Shatskes; **9 B–K2** B–K2–Taimanov) 9 . . . B–K2 10 N–B3 0–0 11 0–0 and Black still faces the problem (perhaps not too oppressive) of trying to liquidate his QBP.

6 P–Q4

Schwarz suggests **6 P–B4** (?) P–QB4 7 N–B3, but 7 . . . N–QB3 and if **8 N×P**, 8 . . . N(2)×P!, or

8 P–Q4 P×P 9 N×P(4)? N(2)×P 10 P×N Q–R5ch, is good for Black. Should White try 8 P–KN3, 8 . . . B–K2 or 8 . . . N–N3 is fine.

6 ...   P–QB4
7 N–B3   N–QB3

Identical to A111 (diagram). This time we look at

8 B–QN5(!)   P–QR3

8 . . . P×P 9 N×P N(2)×P? 10 Q–K2! ±± Quinteros-Nunn, London 1977. But other ninth moves do not alleviate Black's plight, either.

9 B×N   P×B
10 0–0   B–K2
11 P×P   N×P
12 N–Q4   Q–N3?

Smyslov (who awards a '±' to 12 N–Q4) gives **12 . . . B–Q2** 13 B–K3 △ R–B1, P–B4 etc. True, but **12 . . . Q–B2** 13 P–B4 (or 13 Q–K2 N–K3 14 N–B5 B–N2) 13 . . . 0–0 △ . . . P–B3 would keep the bishops more active (±).

13 B–K3   0–0

Or 13 . . . Q×NP 14 N×BP Q×N 15 N×B etc. (Smyslov). The text, from Smyslov-Farago, Hastings 1976/7, concluded in fiasco: 14 R–B1 R–Q1 15 P–QN4! N–K5 16 N–R4 Q–N2 17 N×P 1-0.

CONCLUSION: Black seems unable to equalize after 4 . . . KN–Q2.

A12

4 ...   N–K5
5 N–B3

(a) **5 P×P** P×P is A2 below; here 5 . . . N×N 6 NP×N P×P looks =.

(b) **5 N×N** P×N 6 Q–N4 N–B3! (6 . . . **P–KB4**? 7 P×P e.p. Q×P 8 Q×KP B–B4 9 N–B3 N–B3 10 B–K2 B–Q2 11 0–0 0–0–0 12 P–Q3 ± Flohr-Thomas, Hastings

1931/2) 7 Q×KP Q–Q5 8 Q×Q
N×Q 9 B–Q3 (**9 K–Q1** B–Q2
10 P–Q3 0–0–0 11 B–K3 B–B3 ∞)
9 . . . B–B4 (or **9** . . . **B–Q2** 10
N–K2 N–B3 11 P–B4 B–B4 =/∞
Muratov-Noskov, Alma Ata 1967)
10 P–B4 0–0 11 N–K2 P–KB3!
12 P×P R×P 13 R–B1 B–Q2 14
B–K4 QR–KB1 15 N×N B×N 16
P–Q3 P–K4! with a fine game,
Sveshnikov-Klovan, USSR 1977.
(c) **5 Q–B2** (!) is a productive
move, roughly equivalent to the
text. Watson-Samuels, Las Cruces
1975, continued 5 . . . N×N (5 . . .
P–KB4   6 P×P e.p. ±) 6 QP×N
(This pawn structure favours White,
who has a wedge on e5, the queen-
file, and two active bishops.) 6 . . .
P×P   7 B×P Q–R5?   8 Q–K2
B–B4 9 N–B3 ±.
     5 . . .   P–QB4
     5 . . . **P–QN3**!? might be tried;
but **5** . . . **N –QB3** has led to trouble:
6 P–Q4 (Or **6 Q–B2!** P–KB4–
6 . . . *N×N*   7 *QP×N P–Q5   9
P–QR3!–* 7 P×P e.p. N×P 8 P–Q4
Watson–Carlson, Colorado 1975
and now 8 . . . P×P! 9 B–K3
N–QR4 10 B×P N×B 11 Q–R4ch
P–B3 12 Q×N N–Q4 with only a
slight inferiority was possible.) 6 . . .
B–K2 (6 . . . **B–N5**   7 Q–B2
P–B4!? e.g. 8 P×P e.p. Q×P   9
B–K3 0–0   10 P–QR3 B×Nch
11 P×B N–Q3 or 10 B–Q3 Q–N3
∞) 7 B–Q3 N×N   8 P×N P×P
9 B×P P–QN3   10 Q–K2 B–N2
11 0–0 0–0   12 R–Q1 N–QR4
13 B–Q3 Q–B1   14 N–N5 P–N3
15 P–KR4 with a strong attack,
Browne–Petursson, Reykjavik 1978
(1-0, 29).
     6 Q–B2!

Byvshev's idea, which shows up
the drawbacks of 5 . . . P–QB4.
What is Black to do? On 6 . . .
N×N   7 QP×N P–Q5 8 P×P P×P
9 P–QR3 △ B–B4, R–Q1, B–Q3
(or here 7 . . . N–B3 8 B–B4 B–K2
9 P×P P×P   10 P–KR3), Black is
still cramped.
In general, then, White gets the
edge after 4 . . . N–K5.

A13

     4 . . .   P–Q5
Long considered best by the
authorities; but there are many
pitfalls, and how Black should play
is not clear.
     5 P×N   P×N
Now we discuss two captures:
A131 6 P×NP
A132 6 NP×P
     6 QP×P? is worse: 6 . . . Q×P
(6 . . . Q×Qch =) 7 N–B3 P–KR3
8 Q–Q4 B–K2   9 B–K3 N–B3
10 Q–B4 P–K4   11 Q×Q B×Q ∓
Black has a nice pawn majority on
the kingside.

A131

     6 P×NP   P×Pch
     7 B×P
7 **Q×P** Q×Qch   8 B×Q B×P
9 0–0–0 N–B3   10 N–K2 (**10
N–B3** P–N3   11 P–KN3 B–N2
12 B–N2 0–0–0 = Paulsen-Van
Scheltinga) 10 . . . B–Q2 11 B–B3
B×B 12 N×B N–K4! △ . . . B–B3,
. . . N–N5 (Shatskes).
     7 . . .   B×P
     8 Q–B2   N–B3
8 . . . **P–QB4?** 9 N–B3 N–B3
10 0–0–0 (or **10 B–Q3** N–Q5
11 N×N B×N 12 0–0–0 ± Ragozin-
Sozin, Leningrad 1934) 10 . . .

Q–K2 11 B–Q3 P–KR3 12 B–B3
N–Q5 13 B×N P×B 14 Q–N3 ±
Ragozin-Dubinin, 11th USSR Ch
1939. In both cases, quick development outweighed control of d4.
 9 N–B3   Q–K2
(a) 9 . . . N–Q5?! 10 N×N Q×N
(10 . . . B×N 11 0–0–0 Q–B3
12 B–Q3 B–Q2 13 B×RP B×Pch
14 Q×B Q×Qch 15 K×Q R×B
16 B–N5 ± Sokolsky-Szuska, BSSR
1958) 11 0–0–0! Q×BP 12
Q–R4ch P–B3 13 Q–R3 B–Q2
14 B–Q3 B–Q5 15 KR–B1 Q×P
16 R×P! with a decisive attack
(16 . . . K×R 17 Q–Q6!) Sokolsky-
Abramov, corres 1953.
(b) 9 . . . B–Q2 10 B–Q3 Q–K2!
transposes, but 10 B–B3 is awkward
for Black.
 10 B–B3
 Or 10 0–0–0, but not 10 B–Q3
B–Q2 11 B×P? (11 P–QR3 0–0–0
12 0–0–0 N–Q5! 13 N×N B×N =
Roizman-Boleslavsky, Minsk 1957)
11 . . . 0–0–0 12 B–K4 P–B4!
13 B×N B×B 14 0–0–0 B–K5
15 B–N5? B–R3! 16 R×Rch R×R
17 B×B B×Q ∓∓ Dvorzinsky-Stein,
Poland 1966.
 10 . . .   B×Bch
 Simplest. 10 . . . P–K4 11 0–0–0
(also arising from 10 0–0–0)
11 . . . B–Q2 12 B–Q3 0–0–0
13 KR–K1 Q–B4 14 B–B5
N–Q5! = also suffices, Sokolsky-
Karev, USSR-Yugoslavia 1966.
 11 Q×B Q–N5 12 Q×Q N×Q
13 K–Q2! P–QB4! 14 P–QR3
N–B3 (Shatskes). The ending is
equal.

A132
        6 NP×P   Q×P

6 . . . P×P protects e5, but is
weakening: 7 N–B3 P–N3 (7 . . .
P–QB4 8 P–N3! P–N3 9 B–KN2
B–QN2 10 P–Q4 with White
better–Shatskes) 8 B–K2 (8
P–KN3!) 8 . . . B–QN2?! (8 . . .
P–QB4) 9 P–Q4 N–Q2 10 0–0
B–Q3 11 P–QR4 P–QR4 12
R–K1 Q–K2 13 P–Q5 ± Vuković–
Nedelković, Yugoslavia 1948.
 7 P–Q4 (15)

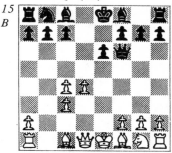

(a) 7 P–N3 B–Q2! 8 B–KN2
B–B3 9 N–B3 P–K4 (!) ∓ (Pachman).
(b) 7 N–B3 P–QN3 (7 . . . P–B4
8 P–N3 N–B3 9 B–KN2 B–Q3
10 0–0 0–0 11 P–Q4 Florian-
Estrin, Hungary 1966; 11 . . .
P–K4! =) 8 P–N3 (8 P–Q4 is
A1322 below, but White has
forfeited his chance to play B–K2–
B3.) 8 . . . B–N2 9 B–N2 N–Q2
10 P–Q4 B–Q3 = Eliskases-Becker,
Vienna 1933.
 The diagrammed position is
critical for the assessment of 3 . . .
P–Q4. White will have quicker
development and a bind on e5;
Black has (superficially, anyway)
the healthier pawn structure. This
is a crossroads:
A1321 7 . . . P–B4
A1322 7 . . . P–QN3

And these instructive options:
(a) **7 . . . P—K4** (An untested attempt to free both bishops) **8 N—B3!** (I feel this offers the best chances. The obvious **8 Q—K2** may be answered by **8 . . . B—K2!**— *or even 8 . . . B—K3—9* P× P Q—B3 10 B—B4 0—0 11 Q—B3 P—B3! etc. Or here **9** Q× P Q× Q 10 P× Q N—B3 affords strong counterplay e.g. **11 N—B3** B—KN5 or **11 P—B4** P—B3!, when White's extra queen bishop pawn hardly compensates for Black's attack in the centre.) **8 . . .** P× P (**8 . . . B—KN5** 9 B—K2 P× P 10 B—N5!) **9 B—N5** (Not **9** P× P? B—N5ch 10 B—Q2 B× Bch 11 Q× B P—B4 12 Q—K3ch B—K3 ∓) **9 . . .** Q—K3ch 10 B—K2. I believe that White is better after this move, since **10 . . . P—KB3** 11 N× P Q—B2 12 B—B4 yields a strong attack, and **10 . . . P—Q6?** 11 Q× P is still clearer: **11 . . .** B—K2 12 N—Q4 Q—Q2 13 Q—K3 P—KB3 14 B—R5ch etc.
(b) **7 . . . B—Q3** (? Evidently mistimed.) 8 N—B3 B—B5 (**8 . . . P—KR3** 9 B—Q3 0—0 10 Q—K2 R—K1 11 N—K5 ± Shatskes-Yurkov, Moscow 1967) 9 B—R3! P—QN3 10 B—K2 B—N2 11 0—0 N—Q2 12 Q—R4 Q—B4 13 P—Q5! P× P 14 P× P 0—0—0 15 N—Q4! Q× P 16 B—B3 N—B4 17 Q× RP ±± Mikenas-Furman, USSR Ch 1949.

A1321
7 . . .   P—B4
The move most often played, but perhaps somewhat wanting.
8 N—B3
(a) **8 P—N3?** P× P 9 P× P B—N5ch 10 B—Q2 B× Bch 11 Q× B N—B3 12 R—Q1 P—K4 (Shatskes).

(b) **8 P—QR3** (to prevent . . . B—N5ch after 8 . . . P× P) 8 . . . N—B3 9 N—B3 P—KR3 10 B—K2 B—Q3 11 B—K3 Q—K2! 12 N—Q2 0—0 13 P—Q5 P× P 14 P× P N—R4 Kostea-Aleksandrescu, Rumanian Ch. 1949.
With 8 N—B3, White threatens 9 B—KN5 and 10 B—Q3. Black can react by cautious development (A13211), or by heading for an ending (A13212).

A13211
8 . . .   P—KR3
9 B—Q3!
Even should this cost White a pawn, he achieves his aims:
(1) Black's . . . 0—0 may be met by Q—K2—K4; (2) the open king file can be used to prevent . . . P—K4. Neither of these purposes is served by 9 B—K2?!: 9 . . . B—Q3 (or **9 . . .** P× P 10 P× P B—N5ch 11 B—Q2 B× Bch 12 Q× B N—B3 13 0—0 0—0 14 Q—K3—*stopping . . . P—K4*—14 . . . P—QN3 15 B—Q3 B—N2 16 B—K4 KR—Q1 = /∞ Ulan Bator-Sverdlovsk, telegraph match 1956) 10 0—0 0—0 11 B—K3 N—B3 12 Q—N3 P—K4! 13 P× BP B—B2 14 N—Q2 Q—R5 15 P—N3 Q—K2 16 B—B3 B—R6 = Mikenas-Cherepkov, Leningrad 1954.
9 . . .   N—B3
The author has had fun against the alternatives:
(a) **9 . . .** P× P 10 P× P B—N5ch 11 K—B1! (**11 B—Q2** B× Bch 12 Q× B N—B3 13 B—K4 ± Ree-Radulov, Beverwijk 1974; 13 Q—K3!—Dvoretsky) 11 . . . N—B3 12 B—N2 0—0 13 Q—K2 Q—Q1 14 R—Q1 Q—R4 15 B—N1 R—Q1

16 Q−Q3 P−KN3   17 P−KR4
Q−R4 18 P−N4! QxNP 19 P−R5
P−K4 20 PxNP P−B4 21 P−Q5
P−K5 22 RxP K−B1 23 B−B6
B−K3 24 PxB QxNP 25 R−R8ch
1-0 Watson-Taylor, Vancouver 1977.
(b) **9 . . . B−Q3** 10 0−0 0−0 11
Q−K2 R−Q1   12 Q−K4 N−B3
(Still worse was **12 . . . Q−B4?**
13 Q−R4 Q−B3   14 QxQ±±
Dvoretsky-Langeweg, Wijk an Zee
1976.) 13 R−K1 PxP   14 PxP
B−N5   15 Q−R7ch K−B1   16
R−K4 B−Q3   17 R−N4 P−K4?
18 RxP±± Watson-Fowell, Los
Angeles 1974.
  10 0−0!   PxP
  10 . . . B−K2 11 Q−K2 0−0
12 R−N1 (12 R−K1 !? Δ Q−K4)
12 . . . R−Q1   13 R−Q1 B−B1
14 Q−K4 P−KN3 Ed.Lasker-Turim,
1952, and 15 B−B2 B−N2   16
B−K3 ± would have been correct
(Schwarz).
  11 PxP   NxP
  12 NxN   QxN
  13 R−N1
White has more than compensation for his pawn e.g. 13 . . . Q−Q1
14 Q−B3!? B−K2 15 R−Q1 Q−B2
16 R−N5! Dvoretsky-Agzamov,
Alma-Ata 1976 (1-0, 28). In later
analysis, Dvoretsky thought **14
B−N2!** even better, and if **14 . . .
Q−B2**, 15 R−K1 Δ B−K5; or on
14 . . . B−Q2, 15 B−K4!.
  I do not recommend 8 . . .
P−KR3.

A13212
  8 . . .   PxP
  In view of catastrophes such as
befell him above, Black seeks
simplification.

9 B−N5!
  This *zwischenzug* is important;.
otherwise: **9 PxP** B−N5ch   10
B−Q2 BxBch   11 QxB 0−0 (or
11 . . . N−B3) 12 B−Q3 (**12 B−K2**
R−Q1 already threatens . . . P−K4,
but **12 R−Q1!** N−B3   13 B−K2
R−Q1   14 Q−K3 holds out the
possibility of a minute edge.) 12 . . .
N−B3 13 0−0 R−Q1 14 KR−Q1
P−QN3   15 QR−N1 B−N2   16
P−B5 P−KN3   17 PxP NxP   18
NxN QxN   19 PxP RxP   20
Q−K2! ½−½ Rogoff−Gulko, Biel
1976.
  9 . . .   Q−B4
  9 . . . Q−N3? has two answers:
10 B−Q3 Q−R4 11 PxP B−N5ch
12 K−B1 and White gains still
more time with his threat of
Q−R4ch, or **10 PxP!** B−N5ch
11 B−Q2 BxBch   12 QxB 0−0
13 B−Q3!, which sets the old trap
13 . . . QxNP? (13 . . . Q−B3 ±) 14
R−KN1! QxN   15 RxPch KxR
16 Q−N5ch K−R1   17 Q−R6 1-0,
which was repeated as recently as
Fishman-Razmislovich, Riga 1977!
  10 PxP
  10 B−Q3?! Q−R4 11 0−0 PxP.
A position called '∓' by Schwarz,
'unclear' by Shatskes and 'very
hazardous' by Hort, who gives
12 R−K1. The burden of proof is
certainly on White here e.g. 12
R−K1 N−B3 or even 12 . . . N−Q2.
  10 . . .   B−N5ch
  Hort opines that **10 . . . N−B3**
is best because 'White has no useful
move', by which he means **11 B−Q3**
B−N5ch or **11 R−QN1** B−N5ch
12 B−Q2 BxBch (∓). Hort-Kovacs,
Stip 1977, went **11 B−K2** B−N5ch
12 B−Q2 Q−QR4   13 R−QN1

Bx Bch   14 QxB P–QN3! (Better
than the variations in the text below
because White's king's bishop is on
e2 instead of d3; from the latter
square it could reach e4.) 15 P–B5
Qx Qch 16 KxQ B–N2 17 KR–B1
0–0 18 B–Q3, and now 18 . . .
N–K2! (Hort) would be fully equal.
The crucial move here is 11
P–QR3!, which seems 'useful' indeed in its prevention of . . .
N–B5ch and threat of 12 B–Q3.
The retention of dark-squared
bishops may well favour the attacker
e.g. 11 . . . P–KR3 12 B–K3 B–K2
13 B–Q3 Q–R4ch 14 B–Q2
Q–Q1 15 B–B3 ±. To be tested!
    11 B–Q2   Q–QR4 (16)

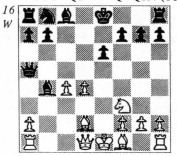
16
W

No one has quite found the key
to equality at this point:
(a) **11 . . . Bx Bch** 12 QxB N–B3
13 B–Q3 Q–QR4 **14 B–K4!** (Euwe)
14 . . . Qx Qch   15 KxQ B–Q2
16 QR–N1 ±. The well-known game
Ed. Lasker–Grünfeld, Vienna 1951,
saw White win a point by the inferior **14 P–Q5?!** PxP   15 QxQ
NxQ 16 PxP 0–0 17 0–0 P–QN3
18 KR–Q1 B–N2   19 P–Q6
QR Q1? (19 . . . BxN! 20 PxB
N–N2 ∓) 20 N–K5 KR–K1
21 P–B4 R–K3 22 BxPch! K–B1
23 B–B5! ±.

(b) **11 . . . N–B3?!** 12 BxB NxB
13 R–QN1! N–B3 (13 . . . N–B7ch
14 K–Q2 N–R6 15 R–N3 Q–R4ch
16 K–B1 ± -Minić) 14 B–Q3 Q–B3
15 B–K4 0–0   16 0–0 R–Q1
17 BxN PxB   18 Q–R4 (±) P–K4!
19 NxP RxP   20 R(N)–Q1! RxR
21 RxR ± Tal–Sonsonko, Wijk an Zee
1976.
    12 B–Q3   N–B3
    12 . . . Bx Bch 13 QxB QxQch
14 KxQ N–B3   15 QR–N1 0–0
16 B–K4 N–R4   17 K–B3?! (17
KR–B1!) 17 . . . R–N1 18 N–K5
P–QN3 19 P–B5 B–N2 = Muratov–
Klovan, Moscow 1967.
    13 R–N1   Bx Bch
    14 QxB   K–K2
Miles–Sonsonko, Tilburg 1977,
diverged from the text by 14 . . .
QxQch (?)   15 KxQ P–QN3
16 KR–B1 and Black must try
16 . . . B–N2 17 P–B5 ± rather
than **16 . . . B–R3?** 17 B–K4!
B–N2 18 P–B5 P–B4 19 BxNch
BxB   20 PxP BxN   21 P–N7! ±±.
    15 P–Q5!?
    15 B–K4 ± is also good. The
text is Reshko–Klaman, Leningrad
1967, which we follow a few more
moves: 15 . . . QxQch 16 KxQ
N–R4 17 KR–K1 ±.
    So White should be happy after
7 P–Q4 P–B4. Therefore:

A1322
    7 . . .   **P–QN3**
Quieter than 7 . . . P–B4 and in
my opinion more sensible. White
has two important ideas:
A13221 8 N–B3
A13222 8 B–K2
    I have toyed with the idea of
8 N–R3!? and if 8 . . . **P–KR3?!**

(to prevent 9 B-KN5), 9 Q-N4!
B-N2 10 B-B4 B-Q3 11 B-Q3 ±.
Simplest after 8 N-R3 is probably
8 ... **B-N2** (8 ... **P-K4** 9 Q-K2
Bx N 10 Px B B-K2 ∞) 9 B-N5
Q-B4, although White can still
try to confuse matters with 10
P-Q5!? e.**g**. 10 ... P-KR3! (10 ...
Px P 11 B-Q3 Q-K4ch 12 K-Q2!)
11 B-B4 (11 B-R4?? Q-K5ch)
11 ... Px P 12 B-Q3 Q-K3ch
13 K-Q2 B-K2 14 R-K1 Q-Q2
15 Px P. But such wildness is not
likely to succeed.

A13221
```
     8 N-B3      B-N2
     9 B-K2
```
9 B-Q3!? (Shatskes) tries to
spice things up: **9 ... N-Q2??**
10 B-N5 Bx N 11 Q-Q2 ±±, or
9 ... B-Q3? 10 B-N5 Bx N 11
Q-Q2 B-B5 12 Bx B Bx P 13
R-KN1 B-N2 14 B-K5 Q-B6
15 Bx NP etc. (This known trick
actually occurred in Miles-Sosonko,
Amsterdam 1977!).
   Critical after 9 B-Q3 is **9 ...**
BxN (!) 10 PxB, when Shatskes
claims that 'the threatened Q-K2-
K4 ties Black down.' But White's
two sets of doubled pawns can
cause him long-term difficulties.
A sample line: 10 ... B-Q3
11 Q-K2 Q-R5!? 12 Q-K4 (Else
White is tied down!) 12 ... QxQ
13 Px Q (13 Bx Q P-QB3 14 P-Q5
P-KB4 15 B-Q3 K-B2) 13 ...
P-K4 14 P-B4 P-KB3 ∞ or
similarly 10 ... N-Q2 11 Q-K2
Q-R5 12 B-K4 (12 P-Q5 N-B4
13 B-K4 0-0-0) 12 ... R-Q1
13 B-B6 B-Q3 14 P-Q5 0-0!
and White's lack of pawn mobility

is felt. Black's play looks satisfactory; nevertheless, this is only a
preliminary judgment and White's
bishops may be more annoying
than they seem.
   9 ...   B-Q3
(a) 9 ... P-KR3 is likely to be a
waste of time: 10 N-K5! B-Q3
(10 ... Bx P? 11 R-KN1 B-N2
12 B-R5 P-N3 13 Nx NP etc.-
Schwarz) 11 0-0! (11 Q-R4ch
K-K2! 12 B-B3 Bx B 13 Nx B
R-Q1 14 0-0 K-B1 ∓ Alexander-
Fine, Nottingham 1936.) 11 ...
0-0 (11 ... Bx N 12 Px B QxP
13 B-B3 P-QB3 14 B-R3! ± -
Alekhine; better 12 ... Q-Q1!
13 Q-Q4 Q-K2! 14 P-QR4
N-B3 15 Q-K3 N-R4 16 R-Q1 ±
Nei-Platonov, Otborchnii 1974.)
12 N-N4 (or 12 P-B4) 12 ...
Q-K2 (12 ... Q-B4 13 BxP!)
13 B-B3; 'advantage to White'
(Shatskes).
(b) 9 ... N-Q2 10 0-0 (10
Q-R4 P-B3 11 Q-B2 ∆ B-N5)
10 ... B-Q3 (10 ... P-KR3!?)
11 B-N5 Q-B4 12 Q-R4 P-B3
13 P-B5! Px P 14 Px P QxP
(14 ... Bx P 15 KR-Q1; 14 ...
Nx P 15 Q-Q4!) 15 KR-Q1
B-K2 16 Rx N! Kx R 17 B-K3
Q-R6 18 Q-Q4ch ±± Flohr-
Kashdan, Folkestone 1933.
   10 0-0
(a) 10 P-B5!? Px P 11 Q-R4ch
B-B3 12 B-QN5 Bx B 13 Qx Bch
N-Q2 14 0-0 Px P 15 B-N5
Q-N3! 16 KR-K1 Px P 17
QR-Q1 R-QN1 18 Q-B6 R-N3
19 Q-R4 R-N5 20 Q-R6 ½-½
Furman-Taimanov, USSR Ch 1955.
A textbook game!
(b) 10 B-N5 Q-N3 11 P-KR4

P–KR3 12 B–K3 N–Q2 13 Q–R4
K–K2! △ . . . P–QB4 (Shatskes).
  10 . . .   0–0
  11 B–K3 N–Q2   12 Q–R4
Q–K2 13 Q–N3 P–QB4 Mikenas-
Bondarevsky, USSR 1954. Perhaps
∓, since White has no constructive
plan and Black can prepare . . .
P–K4.

A13222
8 B–K2

Probably White's best move here,
although it has been neglected thus
far. White exchanges Black's powerful bishop and proceeds to tie up
his queenside.
      8 . . .   B–N2
      9 B–B3   B× B
  9 . . . P--B3 is self-restrictive.
Among other ideas, White has 10
N–R3 B–Q3   11 N–N5 △ N–K4.
     10 N× B   B–Q3
  Apparently best: **10 . . . P–B4?**
11 Q–R4ch N–Q2   12 B–N5
Q–B4 13 Q–B6 14 N–K5 ±±; or
10 . . . N–Q2 11 Q–R4 B–Q3?!
12 B–N5 Q–B4   13 Q--B6 ±
(Kevitz).
     11 Q–R4ch   P -B3
     12 B–N5   Q–B4
  Far more effective than 12 . . .
Q–N3, since now White must con-
tend with the possibility of . . .
·P–QN4.
     13 0 -0   0–0 (17)
  This position has not been ex-
amined by theory nor tested in
international contests, but it has
much to do with the viability of
3 . . . P–Q4. White has many
moves. **14 KR–K1 KR–B1!** (14
. . . P–QN4 15 Q–R5 ±) 15
QR–Q1 N–Q2 = was Watson-

Kane, San Francisco 1976, when
Black was ready for . . . P–QN4.
More heedful of reality was **14
QR–N1** (△ 15 R× NP) e.g. 14 . . .
Q–Q6 15 B–Q2 B–B2 16 R(N)–Q1
Q–B4 (**16 . . . P–QN4?!** 17 P× P
P× P 18 Q–N3), 17 B–N5! (△
B–R4–N3) and on 17 . . . KR–B1,
18 P–Q5! is strong. Of course
Black has other moves, and the
position may turn out to be objec-
tively equal, but 8 B–K2 strikes
me as White's most interesting
rejoinder to 7 . . . P–QN3.
  Thus 4 P–K5 has led to com-
plex and quite tactical play. White
can also try to reduce Black's
options with:

A2
4 BP× P

Freeing Black's light-squared
bishop, but also extending the range
of his own.
     4 . . .   P× P
     5 P–K5 and:
A21 5 . . . P–Q5
A22 5 . . . N–K5
(a) **5 . . . KN–Q2** 6 P–Q4 P–QB4
is A11 above.
(b) **5 . . . N–N5** (?!) 6 P–Q4 P--KN3
7 P–B4?! P–KR4 is an idea of
Vukovic's, which resembles the gur-

genidze System of the Caro–Kann.
It is to Black's advantage to have
his dark-squared bishop on its
original diagonal here. Of course
7 P–B4?! cuts off White's queen's
bishop and should be replaced by
7 N–B3, intending P–KR3 and
P –KN4. Then 7 . . . P–KR4 8
P–KR3 N–R3 9 B–N5 Q–Q2 10
P –KN4!? P× P 11 P× P ± (11 . . .
Q× P?? 12 R–R4! ± ±).

A21

    5 . . .   **P–Q5**
    6 P× N   P× N
    7 B–N5ch (?!)

7 Q–K2ch! looks good: 7 . . .
B –K3 8 QP× P N–Q2 (8 . . . Q× P
9 N–B3! ±, according to Partos.
That seems correct. **9 Q–N5ch** (?)
N –Q2 10 N –B3– *10 Q× P? Q –K4ch
11 B –K3 R –QN1 –Shatskes* –10 . . .
B–Q3 11 B –Q3 B –KN5 12 Q× P
0–0 13 Q–Q5 KR–K1ch 14 B–K3
B–QR6! =, quoted as Murei-
Sokolov (Moscow) 1964 by
Shatskes, is not so convincing.)
9 P× P B× P 10 N–B3 0–0 11
Q –B2 R –K1 12 B –K2 B–B5
13 B–K3 B× B 14 Q× B N–B3
15 0–0 N –N5 16 P–KR3 N× B
17 P× N R–K3? (17 . . . R–K5!–
Partos) 18 Q–KB2! Q–B3 19
QR–K1 QR–K1 20 N –R4 and
Black's pressure was petering out in
Korchnoi-Partos, Montreux 1977.
    7 . . .   N–B3!
    Better than 7 . . . **P–B3** 8
Q –K2ch B–K3 9 B–B4 Q× P
(9 . . . P× Pch 10 B× P Q× P 11
B –B3 Q–R3 12 N–B3 B–K2 13
B× B Q× B 14 Q× Q P× Q 15 B× P
R –N1 16 B–K5 Nei-Vainauskas.
Riga 1961; Black's KP was very

weak.) 10 QP× P B–K2 11 B× B
Q× B 12 Q× Q P× Q 13 N–B3
Pribyl-Novak, USSR 1970. White's
advantage is manifest (1–0, 48).
    8 Q –K2ch   B –K3
    9 QP× P   Q× P
    10 N–B3   B–Q3
11 N–Q4 0– 0 12 N× N (**12 N× B**
KR–K1   13 B–QB4 N–R4!–
Shatskes) 12 . . . P–QR3! 13 B–R4
KR–K1 14 B–K3 B–Q2 15
Q–Q3 (15 0–0 =) 15 . . . Q–R5
16 N–Q4 B× B 17 N–B5 Q–KN5
18 N× B QR–Q1 ∓ Chepukaitis-
Matsukevich, Trud, USSR 1964. In
this variation, **10 Q–K4** 0–0–0!
11 B× N P× B 12 Q× BP R–Q8ch!
13 K× R B–N5ch 14 Q–B3 B× Qch
leaves Black with a fearsome queen
(∓).
    So 7 Q–K2ch looks preferable
to 7 B–N5ch.

A22

    5 . . .   **N–K5!?**
    This and 5 . . . KN–Q2 are the
most reputable answers to 5 P–K5.
    6 N–B3
(a) **6 N× N** P× N 7 Q–R4ch N–B3
8 Q× P Q–Q5 (or 8 . . . B–K3!?
9 B–N5 B–Q4 10 Q–KN4 P–QR3
11 B× Nch B× B 12 N–K2 Q–Q4 ∓
Kuppe-Unzicker, Oldenburg 1949)
9 Q× Q N× Q 10 B–Q3 (10 K–Q1
B –KB4 11 P–Q3 0–0 12 B–K3
B–B4 = Drimer-Pogats, Budapest
1961) 10 . . . B–K3 11 N–K2
0–0–0   12 N–B4 (12 B–K4
Camin-Hobusch, W. German Ch
1978, 12 . . . B –QN5! =) 12 . . .
P–KN4! Borsky-Akimenko, USSR
1964.
(b) **6 P–Q4** B–QN5 7 Q–R4ch
N–B3 8 B–QN5 B–Q2 9 KN–K2

0–0! = Hort-Lengyel, Moscow 1971 (and Müller-Kollman, 1932!). Not **9 . . . N×N?** 10 P×N B–K2 11 N–B4 P–QR3 Hort-Unzicker, Siegen 1970, when 12 B×N! B×B 13 Q–N3 ± was best.

6 . . .   N–B3
(a) **6 . . . B -KB4 (!)** is loosening, but probably good: 7 Q–N3 (7 **P–Q4** B–QN5 =) 7 . . . N–B4! 8 Q×QP N–B3 9 B–N5 (9 P–Q4? N–N5!–Shatskes) 9 . . . Q×Q 10 N×Q 0–0–0 11 B×N?! P×B 12 N–N4 K–N2! Δ . . . P–QR4 ∓ Gipslis-Roizman, Moscow 1965.
(b) **6 . . . P–QB3** 7 P–Q3 N×N 8 P×N B–K2 (8 . . . **P–B3!?** 9 P–Q4 B–KB4 10 N–R4 B–K3 11 B–Q3 N–Q2 12 Q–R5ch B–B2 13 N–N6–Δ *P–K6*–13 . . . P×P 14 P×P P×N! 15 Q×R N×P with pressure for the exchange, Murei-Kaunas, USSR 1968) 9 P–Q4 B–KB4 10 B–Q3 B×B 11 Q×B N–R3! 12 0–0 0–0 13 B–K3 N–B2 14 N–Q2 P–KB4 = Reshko vs. Bonch-Osmolovsky, Moscow 1957.

7 B–N5   B–K2
8 Q–R4
The only move active enough to cause trouble.

8 . . .   N–B4!?
8 . . . N×N 9 B×Nch P×B 10 Q×Pch B–Q2 11 Q×N 0–0 ∞ –Shatskes. Perhaps ±, yet Black will have the initiative for a while.

9 B×Nch   K–B1
10 Q–B2 P×B 11 P–Q4 N–K3 12 0–0. White has been considered to have some advantage here (see e.g. Bobotsov-Kozma, Reggio Emilia 1967), but an interesting recent game, Diesen-Mednis, New York 1977, showed Black defending handily: 12 . . . B–Q2 13 B–K3 P–KR4!   14 N–K2 P–KN3 15 N–B4 N–N2 16 QR–B1 R–QN1 17 N–Q2 R–N3 18 N–N3 B–KB4 19 Q–K2 ½–½ (19 . . . Q–N1!?). Nevertheless, the defences in the notes to 6 . . . N–B3 look simpler.

CONCLUSION: 4 BP×P P×P 5 P–K5 is not only less exciting, but probably also less advantageous, than 4 P–K5. In particular, 5 . . . **P–Q5** is only minimally worse in one line (7 Q–K2ch), and 5 . . . **N–K5** seems reliably equal.

B
3 . . .   P–B4
4 P–K5
Else Black plays . . . N–QB3 and . . . P–Q4:
(a) **4 N–B3** N–B3 5 P–KR3! (Best: **5 P–K5?** N–KN5 6 Q–K2 P–Q3– *6 . . . Q–B2 7 P–Q4!?*–7 P×P B×P *–and here 7 . . . Q×P! covering d4, is excellent*–8 P–KN3 N–R3 9 B–N2 N–B4 10 0–0 0–0 ∓ Lysenko-Mikliayev, Riga 1968) 5 . . . P–Q4 6 BP×P P×P 7 P–K5 (The point of 5 P–KR3!: 5 . . . N–KN5 is prevented.) 7 . . . N–K5 8 B–N5 B–K2 9 Q–R4 N×N 10 B×Nch P×B 11 QP×N 0–0 = Ljubojevic-Gligorić, 1975.
(b) **4 P–B4** N–B3 5 N–B3 P–Q4 6 P–K5 (for 6 BP×P P×P 7 P–K5 N(3)–Q2, see A112 above, note to 6 P–Q4) N–KN5 (or 6 . . . P–Q5 !∓) 7 P×P P×P 8 Q–N3? (**8 P–Q4?** P×P 9 N×P N(5)×KP! 10 P×N Q–R5ch ∓; **8 B–N5**) 8 . . . N–N5! 9 P–QR3? P–B5 10 Q–R4ch B–Q2 11 Q–Q1 Q–N3 0–1, Model-Botvinnik, Leningrad 1938.

(c) **4 P–KN3 N–B3** (simplest, although 4 . . . **P–Q4**!, questioned by Schwarz, is also good: 5 BP×P– *5 P–K5 P–Q5 = –5* . . . P×P 6 P–K5 N–K5! 7 B–N2 N–QB3! 8 P–B4 B–B4 9 P–Q3 N×N 10 P×N Q–R4 11 N–K2 P–B5! 12 P–Q4 P–KR4 ∓ Etruk-Keres, Tallin 1969) 5 B–N2 P–Q4! 6 KP×P (**6 BP×P** P×P 7 N×P N×N 8 P×N N–N5 ∓) 6 . . . P×P 7 N×P (**7 P×P N–QN5** ∓) 7 . . . N×N 8 B×N N–N5 9 B–K4 P–B4! 10 B–N1 B–Q3 11 N–K2 0–0 12 P–Q4 P×P 13 Q×P R–K1 ∓ Vuković–Sokolov, Yugoslavia 1958.

4 . . . N–N1

Should White defend his advanced KP?

B1 5 P–Q4
B2 5 N–B3!?

Other moves are anti-positional:

(a) **5 P–B4** (doing nothing for the hole on d4) 5 . . . N–QB3 6 N–B3 P–Q3 7 P×P B×P (or 7 . . . Q×P) 8 P–Q4 N–B3! (8 . . . P×P? 9 N×P N–B3–*9* . . . *B×P 10 B×B N×N 11 B–K5 N–B4 12 Q×Qch K×Q 13 P–KN4 ± –Schwarz –* 10 N(4)–N5 B –N1?! 11 Q× Qch K× Q 12 B–K3 ± –Pachman) 9 P×P B×P 10 Q×Qch K×Q 11 B–Q2 ∓ (Alster). White's bishops are terrible.

(b) **5 P–QN4?!** is Reshko's mad plan to destroy Black's centre, but 5 . . . P×P 6 N–K4?! (**6 N–N5!?** ∆ 6 . . . P–QR3 7 Q–R4 is my only suggestion. From here on it looks bad:) 6 . . . P–Q4 7 P×P e.p. P–B4! 8 B–N2!? (Otherwise Black is positionally superior *and* a pawn up.) 8 . . . P×N 9 Q–R5ch K–Q2 10 P–B5 Q–K1 11 B–N5ch N–B3 12 Q–R4 Q–N3 13 N–K2 Reshko-

Alexandrovich, Leningrad 1966. Black is temporarily tied down, but one must agree with Shatskes and Taimanov that a piece is a piece (∓).

B1

5 P–Q4

Losing time but holding onto the KP, which White hopes will retard Black's development.

5 . . . P× P

(a) 5 . . . **P–Q4** 6 BP×P KP×P 7 P×P P–Q5 8 N–K4 B×P 9 B–N5ch B–Q2 10 Q–R4! ± (Schmid).

(b) 5 . . . **N–QB3** 6 P×P! (6 N–B3!? transposes directly to B2!) 6 . . . B×P (6 . . . N×P 7 B–K3 N–KB3 8 B–K2!–∆ 9 *N–N5–* 8 . . . P–QR3 9 N–B3 ± Mikenas-Kirillov, Riga 1954. 9 . . . N(4)–N5 10 B–Q4!) 7 N–B3 P–B4! (To stop 8 N–K4. 7 . . . **KN–K2** 8 B–Q3 N–N3 9 B×N! RP×N 10 N–K4 B–N5ch 11 B–Q2 Q–R4 12 P–QR3 B×Bch 13 Q×B Q×Qch 14 K×Q K–K2 15 K–B3! ± Nei-Klovan, Batumi 1954) 8 Q–K2 (8 P×P ep N×P 9 B–Q3 0–0 10 0–0 P–QN3 11 Q–K2–*11 B–N5 Q–K1!* 12 P–QR3 Q–R4 13 P–QN4 B–K2 = Sokolsky-Moiseyev, Moscow 1953–*11 . . . B–N2 12 N–K4 N–Q5 = Holmov-Gipslis, USSR 1955) 8 . . . Q–N3!? 9 B–Q2 Q×P (Else 10 N–QR4) 10 Q–Q1! Mikenas-Saigin, USSR 1954. White threatens R–QN1 and N–QN5. Yet it is not easy to refute Schwarz's 10 . . . N–Q5! e.g. 11 N×N B×N 12 R–QN1 Q–R6 13 N–N5 Q–B4 etc. So perhaps 5 . . . N–QB3 is playable!

6 Q×P N–QB3

7 Q—K4 (18)

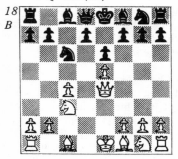

18
B

White prepares to support e5 with
P—B4 and/or N—KB3. Black has:
B11 7 ... P—B4
B12 7 ... P—Q3
B13 7 ... B—N5

B11
7 ...   **P—B4**
The riskiest and least advisable
of Black's moves here.
8 Q—K2
8 Q—K3 N—R3! threatens ...
N—KN5, and on 9 Q—N3 N—B2
10 P—B4, Schwarz gives 10 ...
B—K2 (!), presumable answering
11 Q×P with 11 ... N—N5 or
11 ... N—Q5 and ... P—Q3.
8 ...   **P—QR3**
Customarily given as best. Others:
(a) 8 ... **B—B4** 9 B—K3! B×B 10
Q×B N—R3 11 P—B4 0—0 12
N—B3 P—QR3 13 P—KR3 Q—R4
14 B—Q3 ± Mikenas-Hasin, Gorki
?F 22nd USSR Ch 1954.
(b) 8 ... **KN—K2** 9 N—B3 (Schwarz
is probably correct in recommend-
ing **9 P—B4** here. Compare similar
positions in the B12 and B13.)
9 ... N—N3 10 B—Q2 P—QR3
11 0—0—0 Q—B2 12 R—K1 B—N4
(12 ... **P—N4!?** 13 P×P P×P 14
N×P Q—N3 15 K—N1 B—B4 16

N—Q6ch ± Mikenas-Antoshin, USSR
1953)   13 K—N1 (**13 P—KR4?**
N—Q5 14 N×N B×N 15 P—B4
P—N4! ∓ Aronin-Smyslov, 17th
USSR Ch 1950) 13 ... N—Q5 14
N×N B×N 15 P—B4 P—N4!? (**15**
... B×N 16 B×B N×P 17 Q—K3
N—N3 18 P—KR4 ±—Schwarz)
16 P×P 0—0 17 B—K3 B×N 18
R—B1 ± Omeljchenko-Mikenas,
corres 1971 (1-0, 40).
(c) 8 ... **B—N5?!** 9 B—Q2 Q—R4
10 P—B4 N—R3 11 N—B3 N—B2
12 P—QR3 0—0 13 R—Q1 B×N
14 B×B Q—B2 15 Q—K3 ±
Sokolsky-Sorokin, Voroshilovgrad
1955. Black should not exchange
dark-squared bishops without compensation.
9 B—Q2
9 N—B3 is unclear: 9 ... Q—B2
(**9 ... Q—N3!?** 10 P—KN3 B—B4
11 B—N2 KN—K2? 12 0—0 N—Q5
13 Q—Q1! N×Nch 14 B×N Q—B2
15 N—R4 ± Pribyl-Hurme, Nice
1974 (1-0, 31). But Hort gives
11 ... N—Q5! =) 10 B—Q2 B—B4
(**10 ... P—KN3**—Shatskes—11
0—0—0 B—N2 12 B—B4 N—R3
13 P—KR4 N—B2 14 Q—K3 'better
for White', according to Taimanov,
probably because of the idea
N—Q5!) 11 0—0—0 KN—K2 (11 ...
P—QN4 12 P×P N—Q5 13 N×N
B×N 14 P—B4 P×P 15 K—N1
Q—R4—*15 ... Q—R2 16 P—QR3* ±
—16 Q×NP B×N 17 B×B Q×Pch
18 K—B2 ±—Schwarz) 12 K—N1
N—N3 (**12 ... 0—0** 13 N—QR4!
B—R2 14 B—K3 and White is
better) 13 R—K1 N—Q5 14 N×N
B×N 15 P—B4 P—N3 (**15 ...**
B×N 16 B×B N×P 17 Q—Q2
N—N3 18 B—N4 ± —Schwarz) 16

Q–Q3 B–B4 17 Q–N3! B–N2 18 P–KR4 ± Holmov-Averbach, USSR Ch 1954.
9 ... Q–B2
9 ... B–B4!? 10 P–B4 N–R3 11 0–0–0 N–KN5 12 N–R4 Bx N? (12 ... B–R2! and if 13 P–B5, 13 ... P–QN4 definitely looks better.) 13 Rx B P–QN4 14 P–KR3 N–R7 15 N–B3 Nx B 16 Qx N 0–0 17 B–K3 ± Korchnoi-Simagin, Leningrad 1957.
10 P–B4 N–R3 11 N–B3 N–B2 12 P–KN3 P–Q3 13 Px P Bx P 14 B–N2 0–0 15 0–0 B–Q2 16 QR–Q1 QR–K1 17 K–R1 P–K4 18 N–Q5 ± Bagirov-Abakorov, Baku 1959.
17 ... Q–N1 might have been better.

B12
7 ... P–Q3
The most obvious method of liquidating White's centre.
8 N–B3
Interesting although suspiciously slow is 8 P–B4, to keep a pawn on e5: 8 ... Px P (8 ... P–B4!? 9 Px Pep–*or 9 Q–K2–9* ... Nx P 10 Q–Q3 B–K2 11 N–B3 B–Q2 12 P–KN3 0–0 13 B–N2 Q–N3? 14 Q–K2–∆ *B–K3* ±–Schmid-Apking, corres 1948; 8 ... N–R3!? ∆ ... N–B4 looks logical.) 9 Px P P–B4 (or 9 ... B–N5 and ... P–B4) 10 Q–K2 KN–K2 11 N–B3 N–N3 12 B–N5 B–K2 13 Bx B N(N)x B 14 P–KN3 N–N3 15 B–N2 0–0 =/∞ Roizman-Boleslavsky, Minsk 1957. There are good alternatives for both sides.
8 ... Q–R4
The most frequent move, yet

quite as good seem
(a) 8 ... Px P 9 Nx P B–Q2! (9 ... N–B3 10 Nx N Nx Q–*or 10 ... Q–N3!? 11 Q–B3 Px N 12 B–K2 B–N2 13 0–0 P–B4 14 Q–R3 B–K2 15 B–B3 ± Korchnoi-Karpov (29), 1978*–11 Nx Q Nx N 12 Nx BP Kx N 13 Px N P–QN3 14 B–K3 B–R3 15 0–0–0 B–K2 16 P–B5! Bx B 17 KRx B Bx P 18 Bx B Px B 19 R–Q7ch ± Cafferty–Callaghan, corres 1972; 9 ... Nx N 10 Qx N Q–Q3 11 Q–N5ch Q–Q2 12 B–B4 ±– Euwe) 10 Nx B Qx N 11 B–N5 B–N5 (11 ... *N–B3* 12 Bx N Px B 13 R–Q1 Q–K2 Mikenas-Lilienthal, USSR 1948; 14 P–KN4! ±– Mikenas) 12 R–Q1 Q–B2 13 B–K2 (Extraordinary was 13 B–Q2? N–B3 14 N–Q5 0–0–0! 15 Nx N Rx B! 16 Rx R R–Q1 17 N–Q5 Px N 18 Q–B5ch K–N1 0–1 Bdobin-Korchisky, 1977.) 13 ... N–B3 14 Q–B3!? N–K4 15 Q–K3 Nx P 16 Q–Q4 R–QB1 17 0–0 ∞ Geller-Filip, Göteborg 1955.
(b) 8 ... Nx P 9 Nx N N–B3 10 Nx P! (10 Q–K2?! Px N 11 Qx P B–Q3 12 Q–N5 Q–Q2 = Petrosian-Rabar, Göteborg 1955. 12 ... B–Q2!? looks interesting.) 10 ... Nx Q 11 Nx Q Nx N 12 Nx NP Bx N 13 Px N ± (Shatskes).
9 Px P Bx P
10 B–Q3
Creating more problems than (a) 10 B–Q2 N–B3 11 Q–Q3 Q–Q1 12 0–0–0 (12 N–QN5!?) 12 ... 0–0 13 B–N5 B–K2 14 Q–N1 (14 Qx Q =) 14 ... Q–B2 15 B–Q3 P–KR3 16 B–R4 P–R3 17 P–KR3?! R–Q1 18 P–KN4 N–QR4 ∓ Pribyl-Andersson, Tallinn

1973 (0–1, 27); or

(b) **10 Q–N4 N–K4!** 11 N×N
(**11 Q×P??** N×Nch 12 P×N B–K4
∓∓) 11 ... B×N (or **11** ... **Q×Nch**
12 B–K3 P–B4) 12 B–Q2
P–QR3! ∓ (Schwarz).

10 ...   N–B3
11 Q–K2
11 Q–R4 N–K4   12 N×N
Q×Nch 13 B–K3 B–Q2!? (**13** ...
B–B4   14 Q–B4 = –Larsen) 14
0–0–0 B–B3 15 KR–K1 Q–QR4
16 B–B4 B×Bch 17 Q×B 0–0–0
18 P–B3? P–KR3   19 P–KR4
Q–QB4! ∓ Rajković–Larsen, Hastings 1972/3.

11 ...   B–Q2
Larsen gives **11 ... 0–0** as best.
After **11 ... B–Q2**, Pribyl–Adamski,
Bucharest 1975, went 12 B–Q2
Q–R4 (12 ... Q–Q1!?) 13 0–0–0
N–K4   14 N×N Q×N   15 Q×Q
B×Q 16 KR–K1. White has a lead
in development and some initiative
(1–0, 36).

B13
7 ...   B–N5
8 B–Q2   P–Q3
8 ... P–B4 9 Q–K3! N–R3
10 Q–N3 N–KN5 11 B–K2 0–0
12 P--B4 B–K2 13 N–B3 N–Q5
14 P–KR3! N×B 15 K×N N–R3
16 N–N5 N–B2   17 KR–Q1 ±
Chistiakov–Kan, USSR Team Ch
1954.

9 Q–N4!?
Rogoff, who incidentally awards
7 ... B–N5 and 8 ... P–Q3 exclamation marks, gives **9 N–B3**
P×P   10 N×P N–B3   11 N×N?
Q×Bch ∓∓, and **9 P–B4 P–B4!** ∓.
In the second case, 10 Q–K2 N–R3
11 N–B3 N–B2 is complex, but

certainly satisfactory for Black. The
text keeps a kind of balance, but
no more.

9 ...   N×P
10 Q×P   Q–B3
11 Q×Q (**11 B–R6?!** N–N5 or 11
... N–Q2–Rogoff) 11 ... N×Q
12 P–B4! N–N3 (12 ... N–B3!?)
13 N–B3 B–Q2 =/∞ Rogoff–Csom,
Biel 1976.
CONCLUSION: 5 P–Q4 P×P   6
Q×P N–QB3 7 Q–K4 is not very
challenging. Both 7 ... P–Q3 and
7 ... B–N5 appear to secure
equality without too much trouble,
although 7 ... P–B4 looks inferior.
Still, those averse to gambit play
might consider 5 P–Q4 as a sane alternative to:

B2
5 N–B3
At any rate more dynamic than
5 P–Q4. White intends a pawn
sacrifice whose consequences are
still being debated.
5 ...   N–QB3
5 ... P–Q3 6 P×P N–QB3 7
P–Q4 P×P 8 N×P N×N 9 Q×N ±
–Schwarz. Black evidently plays
9 ... Q×P when best seems the
modest 10 B–K3 P–QR3 11 Q×Q
B×Q 12 0–0–0 ±.
6 P–Q4
If White doesn't gambit, he tends
to get the worst of things:
(a) **6 P–KN3?** KN–K2 7 P–QN3
(else 7 ... N–N3 and 8 ... Q–B2)
7 ... N–N3 8 Q–K2 P–Q3 9 P×P
B×P ∓ Landau–Euwe, Match 1939.
White's QP remains backwards.
(b) **6 P–Q3** KN–K2   7 B–B4
N–N3   8 B–N3 P–Q3   9 P×P
B×P Ed. Lasker–van den Berg,

1953. Now 10 B×B Q×B 11
P–Q4! =. But even in this line,
7 . . . N–B4 tends to give Black
greater control over events.
(c) **6 B–K2** KN–K2 7 0-0 N–B4!
△ . . . P–Q3, as in Sokolsky-
Kottnauer, Moscow 1947. Here 7 . . .
N–N3!? 8 P–Q4! P×P 9 N×P
△ N(4)–N5, P–KB4–B5 might give
White attacking chances.

6 . . .   P×P
7 N×P (19)

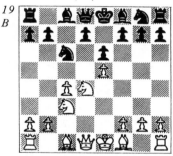

Not **7 N–QN5?** P–QR3 8 Q–R4
(8 N(5)×P N×P! 9 N×N Q–R4ch)
8 . . . P–Q3 9 P×P (9 N(5)×P
B–Q2 ∓ Mikenas-Abramian, Baku
1944) 9 . . . B×P 10 N(5)×P
B–N5ch ∓.

7 . . .   N×P
Consistently eliminating White's
vital KP. Critical but virtually un-
played is 'delayed' acceptance of
the gambit by
(a) **7 . . . Q–B2!?** 8 B–B4 (8 P–B4?
P–QR3 △ . . . P–Q3. *8 N×N* ±–Hort
but all recaputres look interesting.)
and:
a1) 8 . . . P–QR3!? is complex.
White might try 9 N×N!? Q×N
(9 . . . NP×N 10 P–QR3 ±; 9 . . .
QP×N!? and both **10 P–QR3**
P–KN4! and **10 Q–Q2** B–N5 are
obscure) 10 B–K2!? Q×NP 11 B–B3

Q–R6 12 N–K4 **P–B4** 13 P×P e.p.
N×P 14 N×Nch P×N 15 R–KN1!
with good chances. In this line,
12 . . . B–N5ch 13 K–K2! is like-
wise promising;
a2) 8 . . . N×P 9 B–N3 (Black was
threatening 9 . . . N–Q6ch!) 9 . . .
P–QR3 10 Q–R4! N–KB3 (Im-
portant is **10 . . . N–K2 (!)** 11
0–0–0 N(2)–B3, which is very
good for Black after, say, 12
N(4)–N5? Q–N1, or 12 B–K2
N×N 13 R×N B–B4 14 R–K4
P–B3. Probably White should try
12 N×N(!): now **12 . . . QP×N?**
13 N–K4–△ *P–B5*–13 . . . P–QN4
14 Q–B2 ±; or **12 . . . NP×N** 13
P–B5!? B×P 14 P–B4 N–N5
15 P–B5 N–K4 16 P×P BP×P,
and 17 Q–KB4, 17 Q–K4, and 17
N–K4 are all interesting. Very unclear!) 11 0–0–0 N–R4 12
N(4)–N5! Q–N1 13 B×N Q×B
14 B–K2? (Maric's 14 N–K4!
B–K2 15 N(5)–Q6ch K–B1 16
P–KN3 P–KN4! 17 P–KR4 P–N5
18 B–N2 P–B4 19 N×B R×N
20 N–B3 is clearly best, and
probably ±.) 14 . . . N–B3 15
R–Q2 B–B4 ∓ Pribyl-Darga,
Czechoslovakia 1970 (0–1, 27).
(b) **7 . . . N×N?!** 8 Q×N (This also
arises after 6 . . . N×QP 7 N×N
P×N 8 Q×N) 8 . . . N–K2 (8 . . .
P–Q3 9 B–B4 P×P 10 Q×Qch
K×Q 11 0–0–0ch B–Q2 12 B×P ±
N–B3 13 B–K2 R–QB1 14 B–B3
P–QN3 15 R–Q3 ±± Watson-
Herton, New York 1977) 9 B–B4
N–B3 10 Q–K3 (10 Q–Q2!? ±)
10 . . . P–QN3 11 B–K2 (11
0–0–0! △ N–K4) 11 . . . B–N2
12 0–0 B–K2 13 QR–Q1 0–0
Ree-Diez del Corral, Las Palmas

1973, and 14 R–Q2! would have kept the pressure on.

After 7 . . . Nx P, White has three ways to look for compensation for his pawn:

B21 8 B–B4
B22 8 N(4)–N5
B23 8 Q–R4

B21

8 B–B4

The old move, leading to some delicate situations.

8 . . .   N–N3

A strong reply, but there are other reasonable ideas:

(a) 8 . . . Q–B2 transposes to the complex note (a) to 7 . . . Nx P above.

(b) 8 . . . P–Q3 9 Q–Q2 (9 P–B5? P–QR3!–Schwarz) and:

b1) 9 . . . N–N3?! 10 B–N3̀P–QR3 (11 N(4)–N5 was a threat.) 11 0–0–0 N–B3 12 N–N3! P–K4 13 P–B5 P–Q4 14 B–QB4 B–K2 15 Nx P Nx N 16 Qx N Qx Q 17 Bx Q 0–0 18 K–N1 P–QR4 19 P–QR4! B–B4ch 20 K–R2 B–B7?! 21 R–QB1 Bx Nch 22 Kx B ± Korchnoi–Tal, Moscow 1956 (½ –½, 136!).

b2) 9 . . . B–Q2 10 0–0–0? (or 10 N(4)–N5? Bx N 11 Nx B P–QR3 and if 12 Bx N, 12 . . . Px B!, not 12 . . . Px N 13 B–N3 ∞; best might be 10 P–B5 Px P–*10 . . . P–QR3 11 Px P Bx P 12 N–B5–*11 Bx N Px N 12 N–N5 ∞) 10 . . . R–B1! 11 K–N1 P–QR3 12 N–N3 Nx P ∓ Hartoch–Donner, Amsterdam 1972.

(c) 8 . . . P–B3?! 9 Q–R4! (Promising-looking but ineffective was 9 Bx N Px B 10 Q–R5ch P–N3

11 Qx KP N–B3!!?–*or 11 . . . Q–B3* = Miles–Westerinen, *Reykjavik 1978*–12 R–Q1 Q–K2 13 N(4)–N5 K–B2 14 N–Q6ch K–N1 15 B–K2 B–N2 16 P–B5 N–K1 17 Q–K3 Nx N 18 Rx N P–N3! = 19 B–B3 Px P 20 Qx P R–N1 ∓ Watson–Westerinen, New York 1977.) 9 . . . K–B2 (9 . . . B–Q3? 10 B–N3 B–N1 11 0–0–0 K–B2 12 B–K2 N–K2 13 P–B5 ± Sokolsky–Roizman, Byelorussia Ch 1958; 9 . . . N–B3 10 N(4)–N5 P–K4 11 B–K3 B–K2 12 0–0–0 ± Sokolsky–Chernilov, USSR 1964) 10 0–0–0 Q–N3 11 P–QR3 P–Q3 12 N(4)–N5 B–Q2 13 Bx N Bx N (13 . . . BPx B 14 Nx Pch Qx B 15 Qx Bch etc.) 14 Qx B Qx Q 15 Nx Q BPx B 16 Nx Pch ± Sokolsky vs. Bonch–Osmolovsky, Moscow 1957.

9 B–N3   P–K4

Considered best, but other moves have done well:

(a) 9 . . . N–B3(!) 10 N(4)–N5 (10 Q–R4!?) 10 . . . P–K4 11 Q–R4 (11 N–Q6ch Bx N 12 Qx B Q–K2 ∓; 11 B–Q3 P–QR3–*or 11 . . . B–K2–*12 Q–R4 B–B4 13 0–0–0 0–0 14 Bx N BPx B! 15 Bx P? N–N5 16 B–Q6 Nx BP 17 Bx B Q–N4ch 18 K–N1 Qx B ∓ Miles–Zaltsman, Lone Pine 1978) 11 . . . B–K2 12 P–KR4?! (12 0–0–0) 12 . . . 0–0 13 0–0–0 Q–N3! (Very instructive! Not only is this a key defensive idea, but Black also avoids . . . P–QR3, a move which in many cases simply loses time and weakens his queenside.) 14 P–R5 N–B5 15 Bx N Px B 16 P–R6 P–N3 17 P–B5 Qx P 18 Qx BP P–Q3! ∓ Watson–

Zaltsman, New York 1977 (0-1, 37).

(b) **9 . . . P–QR3** (As indicated above, Black defense is often hurt by the inclusion of this move. After White's reply he must tread carefully.) 10 Q–R4! and now:
b1) **10 . . . P–KR4?!** 11 B–Q3 P–R5? 12 N×P!! P–QN4 (**12 . . . Q–K2** 13 0–0–0) 13 N×Q P×Q 14 B–B7 ± Reshko-Tolush, Leningrad Ch 1961;
b2) **10 . . . P–B4?!** 11 0–0–0 (**11 N×KP P–QN4!**) 11 . . . Q–N4ch 12 K–N1 K–B2 13 P–R4 Q–B3 14 P R5 N(3) K2 15 N–B3 N–B3 16 B–R4 P–KN4 17 N×Pch ±± Nei-Gipslis, USSR 1955;
b3) **10 . . . N–B3(!)** 11 N(4)–N5 (**11 0–0–0** N–R4! 12 B–K2 N×B 13 RP×N B–K2 14 P–B4 0–0 15 P–B5 P×P 16 N×P P–Q3 ∓ Sokolsky-Antoshin, USSR 1958) 11 . . . P K4! transposes back to the text;
b4) **10 . . . P–K4?!** 11 N–B3 N B3 12 0–0 0 B–B4 13 P KR4 0 0 14 P–R5 N–B5 15 P–R6 P–KN3 16 N×P N(5)–R4 17 B–R4 Q–B2 18 N–Q3 P QN4 19 P×P P×P 20 Q×R ±± Ree-Langeweg, Wijk an Zee 1968.

10 N(4) N5

In view of what follows **10 Q–K2!?** could be tried e.g. 10 . . . P–Q3? 11 0–0 0 P–QR3 12 P–B4 or 10 . . . B–N5 11 B×P B×Nch 12 P×B N×B 13 Q×Nch Q–K2 14 Q×Qch N×Q 15 N–N5.

10 . . .   P–QR3

11 Q–R4

11 N–Q6ch B×N 12 Q×B Q–K2 is thought to be in the second player's favour, although 13 Q–N6

is still interesting.

11 . . .   N–B3

Reaching a position that could have arisen via 9 . . . P–QR3 10 Q–R4 N B3 11 N(4)–N5 P–K4. The other move is 11 . . . **B–B4?!** 12 N–K4 P×N 13 Q×R B N5ch 14 N–B3 N(1)–K2 15 P B5? (15 P×P! ± –Matanović) 15 . . . Q–B2 16 R–B1 P–R4! 17 P–KR3 P–R5 18 B R2 0–0 19 B× NP N–Q4! ∞ Raicević–Matanović, Yugoslavia Ch 1975 (0-1, 51).

12 0–0–0

12 B–Q3 B–B4! 13 B× N BP× B! 14 B×P P×N 15 Q×R N–N5 16 B–N3 Q–K2ch and 17 . . . 0–0 with attack (Shatskes and Taimanov).

12 . . .   B–B4

12 . . . R–QN1?! encounters the wily 13 B–Q3! N–R4 (**13 . . . P× N?** 14 Q–R7) 14 B× N N× B 15 RP× N BP× B 16 Q–B2! (△ R×P) 16 . . . P–Q3 17 N×Pch! 1-0 Kopilov-Schlieder, corres 1968. If 17 . . . B× N, 18 Q×Pch! wins easily.

13 N Q6ch

Another try is **13 B–Q3** 0–0 14 B× N BP× B! 15 R(R)–K1 (**15 B×P N–N5!**–Taimanov) 15 . . . Q–N3! 16 B×P B×P 17 P–B5 (**17 B–Q4** would lead to equality.– Haag) 17 . . . P×N! 18 Q×R Q–B3 Behling-Haag, Solingen 1973, and 19 B–Q6! would be equal.

13 . . .   B× N

14 R×B 0–0 15 B–K2 Q–B2 16 KR–Q1 N–K1 17 R(6)–Q2 P–Q3 Reshko vs. Bonch-Osmolovsky, Moscow–Leningrad 1966. One prefers Black with his extra pawn and queenside play, although

as Shatskes points out, White may yet work up chances by P–KR4–R5.

CONCLUSION: 8 B–B4 has not been refuted, but Zaltsman's play in note (a) to 9 . . . P–K4 poses some real problems for White. To be investigated are the moves 9 . . . N–B3 10 Q–R4!? and, in the main text line, 9 . . . P–K4 10 Q–K2!?

B22

8 N(4)–N5 (20)

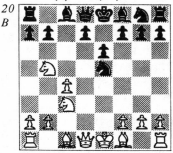

The current preference.

8 . . .   P–QR3

The most direct; others:

(a) 8 . . . **P–Q3?** and theory used to be

a1) **9 N–K4(?) P–Q4?** 10 PxP PxP 11 QxP QxQ 12 N–B7ch K–Q1 13 NxQ B–KB4, which Archives gives as equal, but is ± after 14 N–N3!. An improvement is 9 . . . **N–KB3!** 10 N(4)xPch BxN 11 QxB QxQ 12 NxBch K–K2 13 N–N5 B–Q2 14 B–B4 BxN! 15 BxN B–B3 Timofeyev-Astashin, Urozhai Ch Leningrad 1977 (0-1, 41). But all this has been turned around by

a2) **9 P–B5!** P–QR3 10 NxPch BxN 11 PxB N–KB3 12 B–KB4 N–N3 13 B–N3 B–Q2 14 P–KR4

P–KR4 15 B–Q3 and White's advantage was obvious, Timman-Najdorf, Haifa 1976. O'Kelly gives (after 9 P–B5) 9 . . . PxP 10 B–B4! ±± and 9 . . . **P–Q4** 10 B–KB4 P–QR3 11 BxN PxN 12 NxNP Q–R4ch 13 Q–Q2 QxQch 14 KxQ R–R5 15 N–Q6 ch BxN 16 BxNP ±±. Major improvements after 9 P–B5! are not likely to be found.

(b) 8 . . . **N–N3?!** looks bad after 9 N–K4! or 9 P–KR4!?. Ornstein-Harandi, Haifa 1976 saw instead 9 N–Q6ch?! BxN 10 QxB Q–K2 11 Q–N3 N–B3 12 P–KR4 Q–B4 13 B–K3Q–K4? (13 . . . Q–QR4!) 14 QxQ NxQ 15 N–N5 and White had a big advantage (although ½–½, 57).

(c) 8 . . . **P–B3** has been played often:

c1) **9 B–K3** P–QN3?! (Suspect. 9 . . . **P–QR3** 10 N–Q6ch BxN is the text.) 10 P–B4 N–B3 11 P–KB5! P–N3 (11 . . . **N–K4?** 12 Q–R5ch P–N3 13 PxP NxP 14 B–Q3 B–KN2 15 0–0! ±± Christiansen-Brasket, Lone Pine 1978) 12 PxKP PxP 13 QxQch KxQ 14 0–0–0ch K–K2 15 P–KN4! ± Miles-Flesch, Biel 1977;

c2) **9 P–B4!?** N–B2 10 P–KB5 (Keene) 'with a dangerous initiative' (Hort);

c3) **9 B–B4** is the 'traditional' move: 9 . . . **P–QR3** 10 BxN (Timman tried **10 N–Q6ch** BxN 11 QxB against Karpov, transposing to note (b) to 11 B–K3 below) 10 . . . PxN 11 B–N3 PxP (11 . . . **N–R3?** 12 Q–R5ch P–N3 13 QxNP N–B4 Keene-Furman, Bad Lauterberg 1977, and now 14

Q —N3 ±! —Keene) 12 Bx P P—Q4
13 B—Q3 B—N5 14 Q—R5ch K—B1
15 0—0 Bx N (?! 15 . . . N—K2 and
I prefer Black) 16 Px B N —K2
17 P —QB4 with good play, Liebert–
Zinn, E. Germany 1964. Here 13
B—N5ch B—Q2 14 Q—K2 has been
suggested, but 14 . . . K—B2! makes
it difficult for White to justify his
pawn minus.

9 N—Q6ch
9 B—B4? P—Q3! 10 Bx N Px B ∓;
9 Q—R4? R QN1!
  9 . . .   Bx N
  10 Qx B   P—B3
  10 . . . N—N3 11 B—K3! e.g.
11 . . . Q—K2 12 Q—N6 Q—Q1
13 Q—N4 △ N—K4, B—N6 (Soltis).
  11 B—K3
(a) 11 P—QN3!? N—K2 12 B—N2
0 0 13 0 0—0 N—B2 14 Q—N3
½ —½ Spassky–Hort (11) 1977. An
inauspicious beginning, but at least
11 P—QN3 keeps the pieces on!
(b) 11 B—B4 N—B2   12 Q—R3
N—K2 (12 . . . Q—K2? 13 Q—R5!–
Cvetković) 13 B K2 0—0 14 R—Q1
P—Q4   15 Px P Nx P   16 B—B3
(16 0—0 Nx N 17 Px N B—Q2 18
B—N4 R—K1 —Timman) 16 . . .
Q—K1! ∓ Timman–Karpov, Las
Palmas 1977 (½–½, 71).
  11 . . .   N—K2
  11 . . . N—B2 is plausible e.g.
12 Q—N3 N—K2! 13 Qx P N—B4
14 Q—N4 Nx B Keene–Partos, Montreux 1977, unclear; or 12 Q—N6
Qx Q 13 Bx Q is a slightly better
ending for Black than he gets in the
text. In my opinion, 12 Q—N4(!)
N—K2 13 0—0—0 N—B3 14 Q—N6
is a good sequence (despite the
apparent waste of time), and White's
dark-square pressure is hard to

shake.
  12 B—N6
  12 Q—R3!? 0—0 (12 . . . P—Q4
13 N—N5 ∞—Pytel) 13 B—B5 R—K1
14 N—R4 P—Q4! = was the course
of Pytel–Pokojwczyk, Poland 1977.
Here 13 0—0—0 needs a test.
  12 . . .   N—B4
  13 Bx Q   Nx Q
  14 B—B7   K—K2
  14 . . . N(3)x P? 15 P—B4; 14
. . . N(4)x P? 15 P—N3; 14 . . .
N(3)—B2? 15 N—R4.
  15 P—B5
  15 0—0—0? N(4)x P! △ 16
P—QN3 N—K1 ∓∓.
  15 . . .   N—K1 (21)

21
W

  16 B—N6
Despite initial successes for White
in this ending, it is probable that
Black has what winning chances
there are. White might therefore
consider 16 B—R5!?, so that after
16 . . . P—Q4 (16 . . . N—B3 17
B—N6) 17 Px P ep Nx P 18 B—N4,
the QB is more favourably placed
than in the note to White's 18th
below.
  16 . . .   P—Q4
  Or 16 . . . N—B2 17 0—0—0
P—Q4 transposing, but forfeiting
the possibility of . . . N(4)—B5 as in
the note to Black's 18th.

17 P×P e.p.   N×P!
17 . . . K×P led to these gamelets, in which Black simply couldn't hold the dark squares:
(a) **18 B–K2 K–K2** 19 0–0–0 P–B4(?) 20 B–Q4 N–QB3 21 B–B5ch K–B2 22 N–R4! P–QN4 23 B–B3 P×N 24 B×N R–QN1 25 R–Q8 R–N1 26 B–R7 1–0 Kavalek–Huss, Biel 1977.
(b) **18 P–B4 N–Q2** 19 B–Q8! N–B2 (19 . . . P–B4!?) 20 N–K4ch K–Q4 21 N×Pch P×N 22 B×N with a winning game, Gulko–Diesen, Polanica Zdroj 1977 (1–0, 29).
18 0–0–0
18 B–B5(!) is equivalent, but more forcing, as **18** . . . **N(4)–B2** (probably best) 19 0–0–0 does not allow the possibility of 18 . . . N(4)–B5!? in the next note. 18 . . . **P–QN3**!? (Miles) is universally recommended, but looks a shade less than equal after 19 B×P:
(a) **19** . . . **R–N1**?! 20 B–B5 △ 20 . . . R×P?? 21 0–0–0!;
(b) **19** . . . **B–N2** 20 B–B5 QR–QB1 21 B–R3 KR–Q1 22 0–0–0;
(c) **19** . . . **K–B2** 20 0–0–0 N(4)–B5 21 B–B5 N–N2 22 B–Q4 N(5)–Q3 23 P–B4.
Much worse was **18** . . . **N–Q2** 19 B–R3 P–QN3 20 0–0–0 N–B4 21 N–R4! ± Miles–L. Bronstein, Sao Paulo 1977.
18 . . .   N(4)–B2
(a) 18 . . . N(4)–B5! was Hübner's surprise for Miles at Tilburg 1977: 19 B×N (19 B–B5 P–QN3!; 19 B–B7 B–Q2 20 P–QN3 KR–QB1 etc.) 19 . . . N×B 20 B–B5ch K–B2 21 R–Q4 P–QN4 22 P–QN3 P–K4 23 R–Q5 N–R4 24 B–N6 N–N2 25 KR–Q1 ½–½.

But the final position seems at least ∓: 25 . . . R–K1! e.g. 26 N–K4 B–K3 27 R–Q7ch B×R 28 R×Bch R–K2 29 R×N R×R 30 N–Q6ch K–K3 31 N×R R–N1 32 N–B5 K–Q4 etc.
(b) **18** . . . **B–Q2**!? 19 B–B5 N–B2 20 N–K4 QR–QB1 21 K–N1 R–B3 22 B–K2 P–K4 23 B–R3 B–B4 Miles–Karpov, BBC 1977, about equal.
19 P–KN3
Critical is the untested **19 B–B5**!? Here are some ideas: **19** . . . **R–Q1** (19 . . . B–Q2 20 N–K4 is the preceding note (b)) 20 B–K2 (20 N–K4 P–QN3!) 20 . . . B–Q2 21 KR–K1 (**21 N–K4** B–B3 22 N×N N×N 23 R–Q2 B–Q4 or 23 . . . QR–B1; **21 R–Q2** QR–B1 22 B–R3 P–K4) 21 . . . QR–B1 22 B–R3 P–K4 23 P–B4 B–K3 24 P×P P×P 25 K–N1 K–K1 ∓ (26 B–B3? N–B5).
19 P–KN3 follows Miles–Polugayevsky, Reykjavik 1978: 19 . . . B–Q2 20 B–R3 KR–QB1 21 KR–K1 P–K4 (21 . . . P–B4!? △ . . . K–B1 at some point, is more ambitious.) 22 B–N2 B–B3 23 B–R3 ½–½.
CONCLUSION: 8 N(4)–N5 apparently gives White somewhat less than enough for a pawn, particularly in the ending following 12 B–N6. Theory is in flux, however; one is recommended to look around White's 12th and 16th moves for improvements.

B23
8 Q–R4 (22)
Waltzing to the edge of her court! This move of Murei's deserves

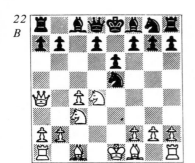

22
B

attention, if only because 8 B–B4 and 8 N(4)–N5 are getting rather played out. The idea is simple: White pins his opponent's QP, clears his back rank for 0–0–0, and guarantees a later N(4)–N5 (even after . . . P–QR3). The main drawbacks of 8 Q–R4 are reduced control of d6 and lack of immediate threats. We examine, by no means exhaustively, a few games and some sample ideas:

(a) **8 . . . N–QB3?!** (natural enough, but the move does nothing for Black's development) 9 N(4)–N5 and

a1) **9 . . . N–B3** 10 B–B4 P–K4 11 B–N5 B–K2 12 Bx N Bx B 13 N–Q6ch K–B1 14 P–B5 N–Q5 15 B–B4 ± Murei-Stetsko, USSR Central CC Ch 1972;

a2) **9 . . . P–QR3** 10 B–B4 P–K4 **11 N–Q5!** Px N 12 Qx R Px B 13 Px P etc. (Shatskes): **13 . . . Q–R4ch** 14 Qx Q Nx Q 15 P–QN4 or **13 . . . N(3)–K2** 14 R–B1. Actually, **11 B–N3** would also be good e.g. 11 . . . N–B3 12 0–0–0 P–Q3 13 P–B5 or here **12 . . . B–B4** 13 N–Q6ch Bx N 14 Rx B Q–B2 15 P–B5 P–QN3 16 Rx N(KB) Px R 17 N–Q5 etc.;

a3) **9 . . . P–Q3** 10 B–B4 P–K4

11 B–N3 B–K3 12 0–0–0 and **12 . . . P–QR3** 13 Nx Pch! or **12 . . . Q–N1** 13 N–K4.

(b) **8 . . . N–K2** ('!'–Haag) 9 B–N5 Q–N3 ('?'–Suetin, but he makes no suggestion. **9 . . . P–B3!?** is outrageous, e.g. **10 Nx P(?!)** Q–N3 11 N(3)–N5 Px N! 12 P–B5! (best) 12 . . . Q–B3 13 N–Q6ch K–Q1 14 B–N5! N–Q6ch! ∞–14 . . . Qx NP? 15 Q–R5ch!; or **10 0–0–0** Px B and now not **11 Nx P?** Q–N3 12 N(3)–N5 Px N, but **11 P–B5!!** with nothing fathomable in sight!) 10 0–0–0 N(2)–N3 (10 . . . N(2)–B3!?) 11 N(4)–N5 (or 11 P–B4) 11 . . . P–B4 (stopping 12 N–K4) 12 B–Q3! B–K2 13 Bx B Nx B 14 Q–R3 N–B2 15 KR–K1 P–QR3? (missing the point. 15 . . . Q–Q1!) 16 Qx Nch! Kx Q 17 N–Q5ch K–Q1 18 Nx Q Px N 19 Nx R 1–0 Murei-Kosenkov, RSFSR Spartakiada 1975.

(c) **8 . . . N–KB3** 9 N(4)–N5! (9 **B–B4** N–N3 10 B–N3 B–K2 11 N(4)–N5 P–K4–Shatskes, who doesn't consider 9 N(4)–N5) 9 . . . N–N3 10 P–KR4 P–KR4 11 B–Q3 (better than **11 B–N5?!** B–K2 12 0–0–0 0–0–0 13 N–Q6? Q–N3 14 Bx N Bx B 15 Q–B2 B–K4 ∓ Watson-Westerinen, Gausdal 1978) 11 . . . P–QR3 12 Bx N Px B 13 B–B4 K–B2 14 0–0–0 Q–N3 15 B–N3 Q–B3 16 N–Q4! Qx Q 17 Nx Q P–QN4 18 N–N6 winning a clear exchange, Heemsoth-Smit, corres (1–0, 46).

(d) **8 . . . Q–N3** 9 N(4)–N5 (9 **B–K3?** N–N5) 9 . . . P–QR3 (9 . . . **N–N5??** 10 P–B5 ±±; **9 . . . B–B4** 10 N–K4) 10 B–K3 Q–B3 11 B–Q4 P–B3 12 P–B4

(12 **Q–R5**? P–QN3!) 12 . . . N–B2
(12 . . . **N–N3** 13 P–B5 etc.)
13 B–K2! R–QN1 (13 . . . Q× **NP**
14 0–0–0 ±) 14 B–B3! P× N
15 N× P P–Q4 16 P× P P× P
17 B× QP with an overwhelming
attack.
(e) 8 . . . **N–N3** 9 N(4)–N5
P–QR3 (9 . . . N–B3 10 P–KR4 is
(c).) 10 N–K4 Q–N3 11 B–K3
Q–B3 12 0–0–0! ± .
(f) 8 . . . **B–B4** 9 N–N3 (9 **B–K3**
Q–N3! 10 0–0–0 N–N5;
9 N(4)–N5!?) 9 . . . B–K2 10 B–B4
N–N3 11 B–N3 N–B3 12 N–N5
P–K4 13 0–0–0 0–0 14 B–Q3
P–Q3 15 P–B5 ∞.
(g) 8 . . . **Q–B2!** (played against the
author by Rantanen in London,
1978. This move prevents 9 B–B4–
9 . . . *N–B6ch or* 9 . . . *N–Q6ch*–
and fights for control of d6 and e5:)
9 N(4)–N5!? (Hyperaggressive. The
alternative is **9 B–K2** e.g. 9 . . .
N–QB3 10 N(4)–N5 Q–N1 11
B–K3 P–QR3 12 N–Q4 with
some compensation, but a pawn is
a pawn is a . . .) 9 . . . Q–N1 10
P–B5 (The point. Now if **10 . . .
P–QR3**, 11 N–Q6ch B× N 12 P× B
Q× P 13 B–KB4 with a strong
attack.) 10 . . . B× P 11 N–K4
P–QR3 (11 . . . B–K2 12 B–KB4!
N–B6ch 13 P× N Q× B 14 R–Q1)
12 N× B P× N 13 Q–Q4 N(1)–K2!
14 B–KB4 N(2)–N3 15 B–N3

0–0 16 B× P. White maintained
pressure for some time, but 8 . . .
Q–B2 is obviously a major challenge
to Murei's idea.
CONCLUSION: 3 . . . P–B4 is still
a stumbling block to White's ambitions. 4 P–K5 N–N1 5 P–Q4
P× P 6 Q× P seems rather prospect-
less against precise defence; so most
interest has centered on 5 N–B3
N–QB3 6 P–Q4, the gambit line
which stands or falls on the outcome
of either 8 B–B4 (worthy of
further study), 8 N(4)–N5 (at
present looking about equal), or
the sanguine 8 Q–R4!? (enterprising
but a bit unlikely). At the time of
this writing, I believe that 3 . . .
P–B4 will stand up reliably to
future tests, although players of a
tactical bent may want to take
the White side in order to create
obscure situations. Then, too (as
the history of 3 P–K4 indicates),
the possibility of improvements in
any variation must not be ex-
cluded.

An overview of the Mikenas
System gives rise to this warning:
only the well-prepared may tread
here safely! For, whether one is
concerned with 3 . . . P–Q4 or
3 . . . P–B4, play tends to become
perilously sharp at an early stage,
and home analysis can single-
handedly win points.

4 NIMZO-AND QUEEN'S ENGLISH: 3 N–B3 B–N5

3 N–B3 P–QN3

1 P–QB4	N–KB3
2 N–QB3	P–K3
3 N–B3 (23)	

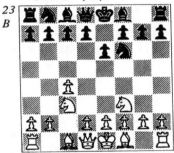

With the following variations:

A 3 . . . B–N5

B 3 . . . P–QN3

3 N–B3 brings us to a position whose resolution has decided the fate of some of the critical encounters in the last ten years of international chess. In particular, we associate the names of Karpov (playing the Black side), Uhlmann (playing the White side), Polugaevsky and Larsen (playing both sides), and Korchnoi (playing both sides and winning!) with the positions after 3 . . . B–N5 and 3 . . . P–QN3. From the 'earliest days' of this variation, furthermore, ex-world champion Smyslov has contributed many of the most important games and original ideas.

White may be playing 3 N–B3 on the grounds that after 3 P–Q4, he must face 3 . . . B–N5 (the Nimzo–Indian). That is a favourite weapon in the repertoire of almost all the world's leading players, against which no one seems to have found a reliable answer. Yet the alternative 3 P–K4, which we examined in Chapter 14, is risky and not to everyone's liking; while 3 P–KN3, seldom tried, transposes after 3 . . . P–Q4 4 P–Q4 to a Catalan where White's queen's knight has been committed rather early to c3. Otherwise 3 P–KN3 B–N5 is sometimes played, which can enter the lines of A2 below.

How to respond to 3 N–B3? 3 . . . B–N5 (The 'Nimzo–English') can only be called 'modern'. Until the early sixties the move was scarcely ventured upon; even then, Larsen, who later employed the move regularly, was suspicious of its efficacy. Taimanov, Shatskes, and Schwarz all speak cautiously of this bishop development, demeaning it in contrast with 3 . . . B–N5 in the Nimzo–Indian (where the knight is actually pinned, the c4 square weak, etc.). But if 3 . . . B–N5 is modern, 3 . . . P–QN3 is really avant garde! None of the above authors even mentions it, presumably assuming a transposition to the Queen's Indian Defence. 4 P–K4, however, gives the game an indisputably independent character, and White may also play with P–Q3 instead of P–Q4. I have dubbed this set of variations 'The Queen's English'.

Besides these third moves, Black has 3 . . . P–B4 (transposing into the Symmetrical English), and 3 . . . P–Q4, inviting a Queen's Gambit after 3 . . . P–Q4 4 P–Q4. Another idea (after 3 N–B3 P–Q4) is 4 P–K3 B–K2 (4 . . . P–B4 5 P–Q4 is a species of Queen's Gambit.) 5 P–QN3 0–0 6 B–N2 P–B4 7 PxP NxP (7 . . . PxP 8 P–Q4 N–B3 and 8 . . . N–K5!? are reasonable.) 8 NxN QxN (now 8 . . . PxN 9 P–Q4± and if 9 . . . PxP 10 QxP B–B3 11 Q–Q2) 9 B–B4 Q–Q1 (9 . . . Q–B4 10 N–K5 B–Q3? 11 B–Q3! Q–N4 12 P–B4! Q–R3? 13 N–N4 Q–R5ch 14 P–N3 Q–K2 15 N–B6ch! ±± Barshauskas–Roizman, USSR 1959) 10 N–K5 N–Q2 11 0–0 (Schwarz suggests 11 P–B4 as an improvement, giving 11 . . . NxN 12 PxN ±; however 12 . . . P–QN3 looks quite equal.) 11 . . . NxN 12 BxN B–B3 13 P–Q4 PxP 14 PxP B–Q2 15 Q–R5 B–B3 16 QR–Q1 Smyslov-Trifunović, Zagreb 1955, and 16 . . BxB 17 PxB Q–R4! (Euwe) was best (=). Most players will prefer 4 P–Q4.

A

3 . . .   **B–N5**

With the usual subdivision:
A1 4 P–QR3
A2 4 P–KN3
A3 4 Q–N3
A4 4 Q–B2

4 P–K3 is passive, but retains the option of some kind of Nimzo-Indian with a later P–Q4. Black may safely reply with almost any combination of moves like 4 . . . 0–0, 5 . . . P–B4, and 6 . . . P–Q4 or 4 . . . P–Q3, 5 . . . P–K4, and perhaps . . . BxN. Bobotsov-Korchnoi, Sochi 1966 saw 4 P–K3 0–0 5 B–K2 P–Q4 (a good time for 5 . . . BxN!) 6 0–0 P–QN3 7 P–Q4! B–N2 8 PxP PxP 9 B–Q2 P–QR3 10 N–K5 (or 10 R–B1) 10 . . . B–Q3 11 P–B4 P–B4 12 B–K1 ± (but 0-1, 39).

A1

4 P–QR3   BxN
5 NPxB

Taimanov and Shatskes dismiss 5 QPxB with notes that after 5 . . . P–Q3 and . . . P–K4 Black will equalize 'effortlessly.' Perhaps that depends on who Black is; but 5 . . . P–Q3 6 P–KN3 P–K4 7 B–N2 0–0 8 0–0 Q–K2 does leave White looking for a plan. In the game Karpenko-Murei, 1968, Black did not quite equalize after 5 QPxB P–QN3 6 P–KN3 B–N2 7 B–N2 N–B3?! 8 0–0 N–QR4 9 P–B5! PxP 10 Q–R4 N–B3 11 Q–N5 R–QN1 12 QxP.

5 . . .   0–0

5 . . . P–Q3 is Glatman-Bagirov, Riga 1968, analyzed by Shatskes: '6 P–KN3? (6 P–Q3! to answer 6 . . . P–K4 by 7 P–K4) 6 . . . P–K4 7 P–Q3 P–K5 (Excellent exploitation of the error committed by White at move 6. White is no longer allowed to get in P–K4,

and his pawn formation is therefore broken up.) 8 N-Q4 Q-K2 9 B-KN2 Px P 10 Qx P 0-0 . . . 11 0-0 N-R3! 12 R-K1 N-B4 13 Q-B2 B-K3 Black has the advantage.' Aside from 6 P-Q3!, better was **7 B-KN2** P-K5 8 N-Q4 0-0 9 0-0, a position from the 1 . . . P-K4 English, where White has equal chances.

6 P-N3	P-B4

6 . . . P-QN3 7 B-KN2 B-N2 8 P-Q3 P-Q3 9 P-K4 N-B3 (**9 . . . QN--Q2** 10 0-0 P-KR3 11 R-N1 P-QR4 12 N-Q4! N-B4 13 P-B4 ∓ Sliwa-Csom, Zinnowitz, 1967) 10 0-0 N-QR4 11 R-R2 N-Q2 12 R-K2 N-K4 13 N-Q4 ± Stein-Saharov, Kiev 1967.

7 B-KN2	N-B3
8 P-Q3	P-Q4

Stopping 9 P-K4.

9 Px P	Px P
10 0-0	R-K1

11 B-N5 (**11 N-Q2 B-N5!**; **11 P-KR3**-Taimanov) 11 . . . P-KR3 12 Bx N Qx B (This position, from Matulović-Korchnoi, Bucharest 1966, is usually given as equal, but Black has more space and well-coordinated pieces. The game continued:) 13 P-Q4 B-B4! 14 P-K3 QR-Q1 15 N-Q2 R-K2 16 Q-N3 B-Q6 17 KR-K1 P-B5 ∓.

A2

4 P-KN3 and:
A21 4 . . . P-QN3
A22 4 . . . 0-0

A21

4 . . .	P-QN3
5 B-N2	B-N2
6 0-0	

6 P-Q3 △ P-K4 is noteworthy; Black may try to cross White by **6 . . . P-Q4**, but then 7 Q-R4ch N-B3 8 N-K5 0-0 9 Nx N Bx Nch 10 Px B Q-Q2 11 Px P Px P 12 B-N5! Bx N 13 Q-Q4 ± (Olafsson). So **6 . . . 0-0** 7 P-K4 P-Q4 8 P-K5 N(3)-Q2 9 Px P Bx P 10 0-0 B(5)x N 11 Px B P-QB4 12 P-Q4 N-QB3 13 N-N5! P-KR3 14 Bx B Px B 15 N-R3 △ Q-N4 ± Olafsson-Timman, Reykjavik 1972 (1-0, 56).

6 . . .	0-0

Or **6 . . . B(5)x N!** 7 NPx B P-Q3 (Euwe); still, White could play 8 P-Q3 △ P-K4, N-R4, etc.

7 Q-B2	

(a) **7 Q-N3** Bx N?! (why not 7 . . . P-QR4! △ 8 P-QR3 Bx N 9 Qx B P-R5?) 8 Qx B P-Q3 9 P-N3 Q-K2 10 B-N2 P-B4 11 P-Q4 ± Smyslov-Reshevsky, Zurich 1953. (b) **7 P-Q3** P-Q4 8 Px P Px P 9 B-B4 B-Q3 10 Q-Q2 Pfleger-Mecking, Hastings 1971/2, and 10 . . . P-B4 = is Mecking's suggestion.

7 . . .	P-QR4
8 P-N3!	P-Q4
9 B-N2	QN-Q2 (24)

24
W

10 Px P	Px P
11 N-QN5!	B-R3

12 N(5)-Q4 B-B4 13 P-Q3 B-N2

14 QR—B1 R—K1   15 B—KR3!
P—N3 16 Q—B3 Bx N   17 Nx B
P—B4 18 P—K3! (Δ 18 . . . Px N
19 Qx P ±) ± Shamkovich—Saharov,
32nd USSR Ch 1964-5 (1-0, 31).

A22

4 . . .   0—0
5 B—N2   P—Q4!?

More consequent than, say,
5 . . . N—B3 6 0—0 Bx N 7 NPx B
P—Q3. A valid alternative is 5 . . .
P—B4 6 0—0 N—B3 7 N—QR4
(7 P—Q3 P—Q3 8 R—N1 Q—K2
9 P—QR3 B—R4 10 N—R2 P—Q4 =
Larsen—Matanović, Le Havre 1966;
or 7 . . . P—KR3!—Gheorghiu) 7 . . .
Q—K2 8 P—QR3 B—R4 9 P—Q4
P—Q3 10 R—N1 P—K4! 11 P—QN4
P—K5! (11 . . . Px NP 12 P—Q5)
12 N—KN5 Px NP 13 P—Q5 N—K4
14 Px P B—Q1 15 Q—B2 P—N4!
16 Px P B—B4∞ Ivkov—Gheorghiu,
1968.

6 P—QR3

For 6 Q—N3 N—B3! see A3,
note to 4 . . . P—B4.
(a) 6 Px P Px P 7 P—Q4 R—K1
8 0—0 P—QB3 9 B—B4 N(1)—Q2
10 P—QR3 B—B1 11 Q—N3? N—N3
12 QR—Q1 N—B5!   13 Q—B2
N—Q3 ∓ Darga—Lengyel, Amsterdam
1964; or here 7 0—0 R—K1! 8
P—QR3 B—B1 (8 . . . Bx N =) 9
P—QN4 P—QR4 (9 . . . P—Q5!?)
10 P—N5 N(1)—Q2   11 B—N2 ±
Geller—Lehman, Hamburg 1960.
(b) 6 0—0? Px P! 7 Q—R4 (7
N—K5? Q—Q5) 7 . . . N—R3 8
P—QR3 B—Q2 9 N—QN5?! Q—K1!
(∓∓) 10 N(3)—Q4 P—K4! 11 Bx P
Px N 12 Bx N B—R6! 13 Px B
Q—K5 14 B—N7 Qx B 15 P—B3
B—Q2 0-1 Bobotsov—Larsen, 1969.

6 . . .   B—K2
6 . . . Bx N!? 7 NPx B Px P
(7 . . . N—B3! looks best.) 8 N—K5
QN—Q2 9 Nx P N—N3 (9 . . .
P—B3   10 P—QR4! Δ B—QR3)
10 N—K3 ± (Schwarz).
7 P—Q4   P—B3
8 0—0   QN—Q2
9 P—N3!

Schwarz's improvement over 9
Q—Q3 P—QR4 10 B—B4 P—QN3 =
Uhlmann—Taimanov, USSR vs. The
Rest 1970.
9 . . .   P—QN3
10 B—N2 ±

With a slightly improved Catalan;
on 10 . . . B—R3?, 11 N—K5! ±.
CONCLUSION: 4 P—KN3 is not
especially dangerous after 4 . . .
0—0   5 B—N2 P—B4; but the
straightforward 5 . . . P—Q4 6
P—QR3! may be favourable for
White.

A3

4 Q—N3

Popular when 3 . . . B—N5 first
caught on, 4 Q—N3 has largely
given way to 4 Q—B2 (see A4
below). But the move has never
been thoroughly investigated, and
offers reasonable prospects to the
first player. White keeps an eye on
d5 and his QBP is protected.
4 . . .   P—B4

Most logical. 4 . . . N—B3 is
plausible, but White can reply
5 P—Q4 with Spielmann's variation of the Nimzo—Indian when
e.g. 5 . . . P—Q3? 6 P—Q5 Px P
7 Px P Bx Nch 8 Qx B ± or 5 . . .
P—Q4 6 B—N5 P—KR3 7 Bx N
Qx B 8 P—K3 Px P 9 Bx P 0—0
10 B—N5! (Soltis) 10 . . . B—Q2

11 0–0 B–Q3 12 N–K4 Q–K2 13 QR–B1 ± is possible. After 4 ... N–B3, however, 5 P–N3? does not impress: 5 ... P–Q4 6 B–N2 0–0 7 0–0 P–Q5 8 N–N1 P–QR4 9 P–Q3 P–K4 10 N–R3 N–Q2 11 Q–Q1 B –K2 12 N–B2 N–B4 13 P–QN3 B–N5 ∓ Langeweg–Bronstein, Beverwijk 1963.

5 P–QR3

A different approach characterized Ilivitsky–Osnos, Trud Ch 1975: **5 P–N3 0–0 6 B–N2 P–Q4 7 PxP PxP 8 P–Q4** (the point of leaving out 5 P–QR3 B–R4) **8 ... P–QN3 (?) 9 0–0 B–K3 10 R–Q1 QN–Q2 11 B–Q2?!** P–QR4 12 P–QR3 P–B5 13 Q–R4 BxN 14 BxB N–K5 =/∞ and ½–½, 41. Either 11 N–KN5 or 11 PxP PxP 12 N–KN5 would have given good play; but for the whole idea to be feasible, White must be able to answer 8 ... N–B3!, because 9 PxP? P–Q5 and 9 0–0 PxP 10 N–QN5 Q–N3 are insufficient. Black may also play without ... P–Q4, e.g. **6 P–QR3 B–R4 7 B–N2 P–QR3 8 0–0 N–B3 9 P–Q3 R–N1!** Tal–Lengyel, Moscow, 1971.

5 ...   B–R4 (25)

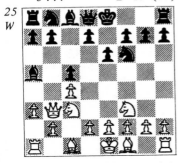

For 5 ... BxN, see A4 i.e. 4 Q–B2 P–B4 or 4 ... 0–0 5 P–QR3

BxN.

Karpov once called the exchange on c3 'necessary', but the situation after 5 ... B–R4 is murky indeed. White has:

A31 6 P–K3
A32 6 P–KN3

The author has toyed with 6 P–K4!?, emphasizing the increased influence over d5 that 4 Q–N3 gives. In reply, 6 ... BxN?! 7 QxB NxP? 8 QxP Q–B3 9 QxQ NxQ 10 P–QN4 is manifestly in White's favour, but 6 ... N–B3! 7 B–Q3 (7 P–K5?! N–KN5 8 N–QN5 0–0) 7 ... 0–0 8 0–0 P–Q3 can't be too bad for Black. Then White might try 9 B–N1 △ 9 ... P–K4 10 N–Q5 or 9 ... N–K4 10 N–K2, and although his pieces are not radiating strength, neither are Black's bishops. This idea at least avoids conceding the central control Black so often annexes after 3 ... B–N5.

A31

6 P–K3

This simple move is little-explored, but has the virtue of contesting the centre at once.

6 ...   0–0
7 B–K2   P–Q4
8 0–0   N–B3

8 ... P–Q5? 9 N–QR4. Black could try 8 ... BxN 9 QxB N–B3 △ 10 N–K5 Q–Q3!, but 10 P–Q4 would maintain some advantage.

9 N–QR4!

Now White threatens the QBP under more favourable circumstances than in many of the main (i.e. 6 P–N3) variations.

9 ...   Q–K2(?!)

Karpov claims that 'while Black's bishop is on a5 the move ... P–QN3 is not possible', but he does not give any analysis. **9** . . . **P–QN3** looks altogether possible; e.g. 10 Q–B2 P×P 11 Q×P B–Q2 (△ . . . P–QN4) 12 Q–B2 R–B1 or 10 P–Q4 B–R3! △ 11 P×BP P×P(5) 12 B×P P–QN4! or here 12 Q–B2 P–QN4 etc.

    10 Q–B2!   N–Q2

Now it's too late for **10** . . . **P–QN3?** 11 P×P and 12 P–QN4, and Karpov gives the following pretty variation: **10** . . . **P–Q5** 11 N×BP! P×P (**11** . . . **Q×N** 12 P–QN4 N×P 13 P×N B×P 14 P×P or **12** . . . **B×P** 13 P×B N×P 14 Q–N3 P×P 15 B–R3) 12 BP×P Q×N 13 P–QN4 N×P 14 P×N B×P 15 P–Q4 'and although White is a pawn down, his position is promising.'

    11 P–Q4   P×BP?

'. . . but this is an outright blunder. He could have played **11** . . . P×QP 12 KP×P P×P, but after 13 B×P White still has the advantage.' (Karpov)

    12 P×P   P–K4
13 P–K4 N–Q5   14 N×N P×N
15 B×P N–K4   16 P–QN4? (16 B–Q5–Karpov) 16 . . . B–B2 17 B–Q5 P–Q6? (**17** . . . **N–B6ch!** 18 P×N Q–R5 ∞–Karpov) 18 Q–Q1 B–N5 19 P–B3 B–KR4 20 R–R2 Karpov–Timman, Groningen 1968. White went on to win without much difficulty.

A32
6 P–N3

The normal move, but now Black can appropriate the centre to good effect.

    6 . . .   N–B3

An immediate **6** . . . **0–0** 7 B–N2 P–Q4 8 0–0 (8 N–QR4!?) 8 . . . B×N **9** Q×B P–Q5 is playable e.g. 10 Q–B2 N–B3 11 P–QN4?! P×P 12 P×P P–Q6!. But **9 QP×B** and if 9 . . . N–B3 (△ . . . N–QR4), 10 Q–N5! keeps Black under pressure. For most ideas involving . . . B×N (with Q×B), see A4.

    7 B–N2   P–Q4
    7 . . . 0–0 8 0–0 P–QR3 (8 . . . *Q–K2* 9 P–Q3 P–KR3 10 R–N1 P–R3?!–*10* . . . *R–N1–Hort*–11 N–R4 P–Q4 12 N–N6 B×N 13 Q×B P×P?–*13* . . . *P–Q5* ∞–*Hort* –14 P×P P–K4 15 B–K3! ± Hort-Sosonko, Portoroz 1977) 9 P–Q3 (?! 9 P–K3!?) 9 . . .R–N1 10 R–Q1 P–QN4 11 P×P P×P 12 N×P B–R3 13 P–QR4 B×N 14 P×B Q–N3 = Sofresky–Matanović, Škopje 1968.

    8 0–0

8 N–QR4!? is not especially appropriate here. Either 8 . . . **Q–K2** 9 P×P P×P 10 Q–B2 P–B5 or 8 . . . **P–QN3** 9 0–0 P×P 10 Q×P B–Q2! leaves Black comfortably placed.

    8 . . .   B×N

Or 8 . . . **0–0**, and if 9 N–QR4, Shatskes gives 9 . . . Q–K2 △ . . . B–B2. Then **10 Q–N5** P–QR3! is equal, and **10 P×P** N×P 11 Q–N5?! P–QN3! 12 Q×N B–Q2 13 Q–N7 QR–N1 is better for Black!

    9 Q×B   P–Q5
    10 Q–B2   P–QR4
11 P–Q3 0–0?! (**11** . . . **P–K4!** is quite equal.) 12 B–B4! Q–K2 13 N–K5 N×N 14 B×N N–R4? 15 P–K3 P–KB3 16 Q–K2 P–KN3

17 P–KN4! N–N2 18 B–N3
P–R5 19 Px P Px P 20 P–B4
Q–B4 21 B–K1! and White had a
winning advantage, Polugayevsky–
Korchnoi, Sochi 1966.
CONCLUSION: 4 Q–N3 merits
another look. True, 4 . . . P–B4
5 P–QR3 B–R4 6 P–N3 N–B3
gives Black fairly easy equality,
but 6 P–K3 claims more of the
centre and makes for a complicated
struggle.

A4

4 Q–B2
The principal continuation,
guarding c3, preparing P–QR3, and
introducing a great parting of ways:
A41 4 . . . P–Q4
A42 4 . . . P–B4
A43 4 . . . 0–0
4 . . . P–QN3 will usually transpose to A432. Seldom seen is
(a) 4 . . . N–B3. White has a reliable
response in 5 P–Q4, or he can play
as in Sakharov-Borisenko, 35th
USSR Ch 1967: **5 P–QR3** Bx N
6 Qx B P–QR4 7 P–QN3 0–0
8 B–N2 R–K1!? 9 P–Q3 P–Q4
10 P–KN4!? (**10 P–K3** P–K4
11 Px P ±) 10 . . . P–K4 11 P–N5
N–R4 12 R–KN1 P–Q5 13 Q–B2
B–B4 = (though 1–0, 38). Stranger
still was
(b) **4 . . . P–QR4**?! of Varnusz-
Nagy, Hungary 1973, when White
found a way to benefit from the
experiment by 5 P–Q4! P–Q4
(**5 . . . 0–0** 6 B–N5 is a good
Nimzo-Indian) 6 B–N5 0–0 7
P–K3 QN–Q2 8 B–Q3 P–R3 9
B–R4 (with a good Queen's Gambit.
White is ready for 0–0 and P–K4
or 0–0–0 and P–KN4.) 9 . . .
P–R5!? 10 0–0 Px P 11 Bx P
P–R6 12 Px P Bx P 13 P–K4! ±.

A41
4 . . . **P–Q4**
5 P–QR3 Bx N
5 . . . B–K2 6 Px P Px P 7 P–Q4
0–0 8 B–N5 B–KN5?! 9 N–K5
B–K3 10 P–K3 QN–Q2 and instead of 11 B–Q3 P–KR3 12
B–R4 P–B4 13 R–Q1 R–B1 =
(Pachman-Polugayevsky, Havana
1962), Pachman suggests 11 Nx N!
Nx N 12 Bx B Qx B 13 B–Q3
P–KR3 14 P–QN4! ±. The P–QR3
move should help White in most
lines of the Queen's Gambit Exchange Variation, as he can play
P–QN4 without lengthy preparation
or an exchange on f6.
6 Qx B 0–0
7 P–K3
7 P–Q4 is a thought.
7 . . . P–QR4
8 P–QN3 QN–Q2
9 B–N2 P–QN3
10 B–K2 B–N2 11 0–0 (Here
11 Px P was an option, and 11 . . .
Bx P 12 P–Q3 N–B4 13 P–K4!
B–N2 14 N–K5, or 11 . . . Px P
12 N–Q4!) 11 . . . Px P! 12 Bx P
N–B4 13 KR–Q1 (13 N–Q4?!)
13 . . . Q–Q3 14 Q–K5 B–R3! =
Furman-Makarichev, USSR Ch
1973.

A42
4 . . . **P–B4** and:
A421 5 P–KN3
A422 5 P–QR3

A421
5 P–KN3
There are two reasons to make

this move without a preliminary
5 P–QR3. One is that White wishes
to avoid 5 . . . B× N at the cost of a
tempo, after which he may no
longer have time for an effective
P–KN3 (compare A422). Moreover,
Black's KB may be better placed on
a5; indeed it often moves there un-
provoked, later shifting to c7.

    5 . . .   N–B3

Schwarz gives 5 . . . 0–0 6 B–N2
P–Q4 with the comment that the
White QBP is unprotected. He continues 7 P–N3 B× N 8 Q× B P–Q5
9 Q–B2 N–B3, and then hints that
the QBP is best left en prise, as in
A12, presumably via 7 P–QR3 B× N
8 NP× B (intending 8 . . . P× P
9 N–K5), but in that case 8 . . .
N–B3! equalizes, as 9 P× P P× P
activates Black's QB and opens his
king file. The reason why this move
order is seldom chosen is probably
7 N–QR4! threatening 8 P–QR3
and 9 N× P. After 7 N–QR4 P–QN3
(forced: 7 . . . Q–K2? 8 P–QR3
B–R4 9 P× P) 8 P–QR3 B–R4
9 0–0, both 9 . . . P× P? 10 N–N5
and 9 . . . N–B3? 10 P× P! △ P–N4
are ± ±. Even after the better 9 . . .
B–N2 10 P–Q3 White has a slight
edge, e.g. 10 . . . N–B3 11 P–K3
Q–K2 12 P–N3.

    6 B–N2   0–0
    7 0–0   Q–K2 (26)

    7 . . . P–Q4!? is playable here,
e.g. 8 N–QR4 Q–K2! 9 P–QR3
B–R4 10 P× P P× P 11 Q× P Q× P ∞.
Uhlmann gives instead 8 P× P P× P
9 P–Q3 ±. This threatens N–QR4
again, and 9 . . . Q–K2? 10 B–N5
B× N 11 Q× B! has little to recommend it. But 9 . . . B–N5! forces a
revision of Uhlmann's assessment;
White faces the immediate, and

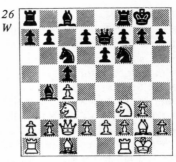

26
W

difficult to meet, threat 10 . . .
QB× N; also, moves such as . . .
Q–Q2, . . . R–K1, and in some
cases . . . P–Q5 are coming. To
avoid more serious disadvantage
White may have to try 10 B–KN5
QB× N 11 B× B N–Q5 12 Q–R4
N× Bch 13 P× N B× N 14 P× B
P–KR3 15 B–K3 ±. In my opinion,
the best answer to 7 . . . P–Q4 is
simply 8 P–Q3.

    7 . . . Q–K2 puts us at still
another crossroads! Now all three
White options have led to fascinating
games exemplary of modern chess
strategy:

A4211 8 P–Q3
A4212 8 R–Q1
A4213 8 P–K3

A4211

    8 P–Q3

Leading to positions that must
be handled gingerly, as these two
examples demonstrate:
(a) 8 . . . B–R4!? 9 N–KR4!
R–Q1?! 10 P–K4 P–Q3 11 P–B4
P–QR3 (11 . . . B–Q2 12 P–B5
N–Q5 13 Q–Q1 P× P 14 B–N5 ± –
Uhlmann; 12 . . . N–K1!?) 12
P–K5! (12 P–B5 N–Q2! ∞) 12 . . .
N–KN5! (12 . . . P× P 13 B× N
P× B 14 P× P N–Q2 15 N–B3
P–R3 16 P–KR4!–Uhlmann;

White will overprotect e5 to the hilt and then exploit Black's vulnerable pawns and passive pieces.) 13 Q—K2 N—R3 14 B×N P×B 15 N—K4 (**15 B—K3 P—Q4 16 N—R4 ±— —Uhlman**) 15 . . . P—Q4 16 N—Q6 (**16 N—N5!**) 16 . . . B—B2 17 N×B R(R)×N 18 B—K3 ± Uhlmann-Hübner, Leningrad 1973 (½—½, 74). (b) **8 . . . P—KR3** 9 P—K4 (Now if **9 N—KR4** as above, 9 . . . P—Q4! and White cannot play B—KN5; yet **9 P—K3!**, as in Lombardy-Polugayevsky of A422, holds forth the promise of a lasting advantage.) 9 . . . P—Q3 10 N—KR4 R—N1! 11 P—B4 B—Q2 (What a difference from (a)! Black's king's rook defends his kingside, c6 is guarded by a piece, and there exists a definite plan of attack on the queenside via . . . P—QR3. White should now choose **12 N—B3**, for 12 P—B5 N—Q5 13 Q—Q1 P×P favours Black. Instead:) **12 P—KR3?** N—Q5 13 Q—B2 P—QN4 14 B—K3 P×P 15 P×P B—B3! 16 QR—K1 Q—N2 (Black mounts pressure on White's centre and queen's wing.) 17 B—B1 Q—R3 18 P—K5 P×P 19 P×P N—R2! 20 B×B Q×B 21 R—K3 N—N4 22 Q—N2 Q—R3 23 P—N3 N×Pch! 24 Q×N B×N and Black scored the full point in Hübner-Tal, Biel 1976.

A4212
8 R—Q1 B×N!
8 . . . P—Q3 9 P—Q4 ± (Romanishin).
9 Q×B P—K4
Consistent, preventing P—Q4 and making the rook on d1 look as

though it should have stayed home. If **9 . . . P—Q4**, 10 P—Q4! BP×P 11 N×P N×N 12 Q×N P—K4 13 Q—KR4 seems good. Then on **13 . . . P—Q5**, 14 B—N5; or on **13 . . . P×P**, 14 Q×P △ 14 . . . B—K3 15 Q—N5 or 14 . . . P—KR3 15 B—K3. An instructive position for the use of two bishops.
10 P—Q3
10 P—K3 is dubious after **10 . . . P—Q4** 11 P—Q4 KP×P 12 KP×P B—N5! or even **10 . . . P—K5** 11 N—K1 (11 N—N5 P—KR3 12 N—R3 P—Q4!) 11 . . . P—Q3.
10 . . . **P—KR3**
Here **10 . . . P—Q4** 11 P×P N×P appears to save a tempo but Black may have feared 12 Q—B4 N—N3 13 B—N5! Q—Q3 14 Q—B1 ∞ or **12 . . . B—K3** 13 N—N5 N—N3 14 Q—KR4 P—KR3 15 N×B ±.
11 P—N3 **P—Q4**
12 P×P **N×P**
13 Q—Q2 **B—N5**
Romanishin proposes **13 . . . R—Q1!** 14 B—QR3 P—QN3 15 QR—B1 B—N2. In this line **15 P—K3**, threatening 16 P—Q4, would only be weakening after 15 . . . Q—B3! △ 16 . . . B—N5. This position is noteworthy: White's set-up is similar to Bellon's . . . P—QN3 against the Maroczy Bind and therefore also to White's position in *English III*, Chapter 5. The difference here is that Black has traded his black-squared bishop for one of White's knights. The exchange in itself is beneficial, for the bishop would be 'bad' here; moreover, general principle urges that such exchanges clarify the second player's space advantage. White's development is certainly a little faster than in the above

openings; but if Black can consolidate (e.g. 13 . . . R–Q1!), he will hold what advantage there is.

14 P–KR3   B–R4
15 B–R3 QR–Q1   16 Q–B1! P–QN3 17 Q–B4 (Now we see the drawback of 13 . . . B–N5: Black's bishop is missed in the centre.) 17 . . . Q–K3 18 P–KN4 (18 QR–B1 gives Black time ·for 18 . . . N–Q5 19 Nx N KPx N ∓.) 18 . . . B–N3 19 N–R4 N–R4 20 Q–B2 N–KB5 21 K–R2 Nx B 22 Kx N B–R2   23 P–K4! Vaganian–Romanishin, USSR Ch 1975. White was holding the balance (½–½, 80).

A4213

8 P–K3 (27)

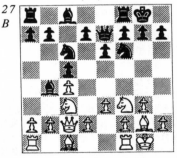

27
B

Uhlmann's attempt at improving the line for White, who now fights directly for the centre.

8 . . .   Bx N?!

Black wants to play . . . P–K4, but 8 . . . P–K4? 9 N–Q5! is naturally not to his liking. Other stories from the diagram:

(a) 8 . . . P–QN3!?, as in Balashov–Romanishin, USSR Ch 1976, makes sense. In the game, 9 N–K5 was not tried, but we may assume that Romanishin intended 9 . . . Nx N! 10 Bx R and either 10 . . . P–Q4

11 Px P B–R3   12 P–Q6 Qx P ∞ or 10 . . . B–R3 11 B–N2 Bx BP which, although not as clear, offers better winning chances. On 8 . . . P--QN3, Balashov responded instead with 9 P–N3 P–Q4, and his 10 B–N2 provoked the incredible blunder 10 . . . Px P?? 11 N–KN5! ±± (White is threatening both 12 Bx N and 12 N–Q5! Px N 13 Bx N.). However, either 10 . . . R–Q1 11 P–Q3 B–N2 or 10 . . . B–N2 might have maintained a dynamic equilibrium.

(b) 8 . . . P–Q4 can be met by 9 P–N3, or by 9 N–QR4 Px P 10 Qx P R–N1 11 Q–B2 P–QN4 12 N–B3 B–Q2 13 P–N3 KR–B1 = Korchnoi–Polugayevsky (13), 1977. Yielding a double-edged initiative was 10 P–QR3! B–R4 11 Qx P N–Q2 12 P–Q4 Px P 13 Px P, but Korchnoi needed only a draw.

(c) 8 . . . P–Q3 9 P–N3 P–KR3 (probably unnecessary. 9 . . . B–Q2!?) 10 B–N2 B–Q2 11 P–QR3 B–R4 12 P–Q4 Px P 13 Px P Bx N?! (trying to saddle White with a bad QB, but 13 . . . P–Q4 ± was better) 14 Bx B P–Q4 15 P–QN4! P–QR4 16 P–N5! N–Q1 17 P–QR4 Px P 18 B–N2 ± Ftacnik–Romanishin, Kiev 1978 (1-0, 43).

9 Qx B   P–K4
10 P–N3   P–Q3

Uhlmann points out 10 . . . P–Q4 11 P–Q4! ±, after which pawn exchanges merely pry the position open for White's bishops, while . . . N–K5 reduces Black's hold on the centre after Q–N2!.

11 B–N2   P–KR3

12 P–Q4?!

But this proves to be a misjudgment. After the next few moves, White's pawns lack the necessary flexibility to attack Black's position. **12 P–Q3!** is much better; on 12 . . . B–B4, for example, White could play 13 P–QR3 P–QR4 14 QR–K1! intending 15 N–R4 and P–KB4.

12 . . .	P–K5
13 N–Q2 B–B4	14 P–B3 Px BP
15 Rx P B–N3	16 QR–KB1

KR–K1 17 P–QR3 P–QR4 with a dynamically equal game. This was demonstrated convincingly when the struggle was brought to a conclusion by a 16-move *forced* drawing combination! Uhlmann-Balashov, Halle 1976.

CONCLUSION: 5 P–KN3 initiates a complex manoeuvring game, and offers interesting prospects from both sides of the board. Against precise play by White, Black is the one who must work for equality; but with proper defence, he will just about get it.

A422

| 5 P–QR3 | B–R4 (28) |

28
W

In lieu of this retreat, given '?' by Shatskes, 5 . . . Bx N is often

recommended. In spite of this, most masters prefer to capture via 4 . . . 0–0 5 P–QR3 Bx N, and after 6 Qx B, we note that 6 . . . P–B4 (see A431) is rarely seen. So 5 . . . B–R4 is crucial.

6 P–KN3

More frequently played than 6 P–K3, which nevertheless holds forth good chances for an initiative in the centre:

(a) **6 . . . P–Q4?** 7 N–QR4 P–QN3 8 R–QN1 N–R3 (forced!) 9 Px P Nx P 10 B–N5ch ± Smyslov-Matanović, Monte Carlo 1967.

(b) **6 . . . 0–0** 7 P–Q4 P–QN3 8 B–Q3 B–N2 9 0–0 B(4)x N 10 Qx B B–K5 11 B–K2 N–B3 (11 . . . P–QR4) 12 Px P Px P 13 P–QN4 R–B1 14 P–N5 ± Korchnoi-Panno, Wijk an Zee 1978. White has two bishops and strong queenside pawns.

(c) **6 . . . N–B3** 7 P–Q4 P–Q3 8 B–Q3 P–K4!? (8 . . . 0–0 9 0–0 Q–K2, 'cramped but solid' is the comment of Taimanov. White can play for a slight pull with 10 R–N1 e.g. 10 . . . B–Q2 11 P–QN4!?– *or 11 N–R2–*11 . . . Px P 12 N–R2 △ 12 . . . P–N6 13 Rx P ±.) 9 Px KP Nx P 10 Nx N Px N 11 0–0 Bx N 12 Qx B 0–0 13 P–QN3 R–K1 14 B–N2 P–QN3 15 QR–Q1 Q–K2 16 B–B2 B–N2 17 P–B3! P–K5 18 P–KB4 QR–Q1? (18 . . . **KR–Q1!** △ 19 P–R3 N–K1 was correct–Larsen) 19 P–R3 Rx R 20 Rx R R–Q1 21 Rx Rch Qx R 22 Q–K5! K–B1 23 B–B3 N–K1 24 P–QN4! ± Larsen-Gheorghiu, Lugano 1968.

| 6 . . . | 0–0 |
| 7 B–N2 | N–B3 |

7 . . . P–Q4 is apparently worse: (a) **8 0–0?!** B×N! 9 NP×B **(9 Q×B** P–Q5 10 Q–B2 P–K4 =) **9 . . . P–QN3?!** 10 P–QR4! (or **10** P×P P×P 11 P–B4) 10 . . . B–R3 11 P–R5! B×P 12 P×P Q×P 13 P–Q3 B–R3 14 B–B4 with plenty for a pawn, Nikolayevsky–Sakharov, Irkutsk 1966. But **8 . . .** B×N! makes sense; Black should answer 9 NP×B with **9 ·. . . N–B3!** as in A12, threatening 10 . . . P×P; if White continues 10 P×P P×P, Black has space and his pieces become active (∓).

(b) **8 N–QR4!** QN–Q2 (**8 . . . P–QN3** 9 0–0 △ 10 P–Q4) 9 0–0 **(9** P×P P×P 10 N×P N×N 11· O×N R–K1 ±–Razuvayev) **9 . . .** P×P 10 Q×P Q–K2 11 P–Q4 P×P 12 P–QN4 B–Q1 13 Q×QP P–K4 14 Q–B3 P–K5 15 N–Q4 N–N3 16 N–QB5 R–K1 (**16 . . . N(N)–Q4** 17 Q–B4 △ 18 N×P ± –Razuvayev) 17 B–N2 B–Q2 18 Q–N3! (clearer than 18 N×NP) 18 . . . R–B1 19 QR–B1 R–B2 20 P–QR4 P–QR3 21 P–R5 N–B1 22 KR–Q1 ± Razuvayev– G. Garcia, Cienfuegos 1976. An aesthetically appealing demonstration of White's opportunities in this variation!

8 0–0   Q–K2

As in A421; otherwise Black usually tries to expand on the queenside:

(a) **8 . . . P–QR3.** This is a logical move analogous to the Symmetrical Variation. Polugayevsky–Csom, RSFSR vs. Hungary 1968, proceeded **9 R–Q1** Q–K2 10 P–Q4 P×P 11 N×P N×N 12 R×N R–N1 13 P–QN4 B–B2 14 B–N2

P–QN4? 15 P×P P×P 16 R–R4 B–K4?? 17 N–K4! 1–0. Korchnoi– Andersson, Palma de Mallorca 1972, varied with **9 P–N3?!** R–N1 10 N–R2 P–Q3?! (**10 . . . Q–K2!** 11 B–N2 P–QN4 12 P×P? P×P 13 QR–B1 B–N3 ∓–Korchnoi) 11 R–N1 B–B2?! 12 P–QN4 ±. In his notes to the game, Korchnoi analyzes '9 R–Q1! N–Q5 10 N×N P×N 11 N–K4 ±'. This was tested in Furman–Kuindzhi, Tbilisi 1973, when Black selected 11 . . . N–K1? (the spirited **11 . . . P–Q4!** was recommended instead): 1̇2 P–QN4 B–N3 13 B–N2 P–Q3 14 P–B5 P×P 15 N×P B×N 16 Q×B P–Q6 17 P–K3 ±. A better version of this plan was

(b) **8 . . . P–Q3 9 P–Q3** P–QR3 as in Larsen–Darga, Winnipeg 1967, when 10 R–N1 should have been countered by 11 . . . R–N1! =. The more assertive **9 P–K3** was tried in Evans–Rossolimo, USA 1968: 9 . . . B–Q2 10 P–Q4 B×N 11 Q×B P×P 12 N×P N×N 13 Q×N B–B3 14 P–K4 ±. Here 9 . . . P–K4 10 P–Q4!? (**10 P–Q3** or **10 P–N3!?**) 10 . . . KP×P 11 P×P B–KN5 (**11 . . .** P×P? 12 N–QN5) 12 P×P QB×N? 13 B×B N–Q5 14 Q–Q1 P×P 15 B–N2 was ± in Pytel– Tiller, Gausdal 1978. Better **12 . . . P×P =.**

The text (**8 . . . Q–K2**) is perhaps the most logical, in that it covers b4, supports . . . P–K4, and retains the option of . . . P–Q4 in one step.

9 P–Q3

9 P–K3 is possible; compare A421. **9 R–Q1** was the stem game, Pachman–Matanović,   Vrnjacka

Banja 1967. Black pushed **9** . . .
P–K4 and after **10 P–Q3 P–Q3
11 B–N5 B×N 12 P×B P–KR3
13 B×N Q×B 14 N–Q2! Q–Q1
15 N–B1 B–K3 16 N–K3 R–N1
17 QR–N1** White had a slight edge.
Against 9 R–Q1, however, .Tal's
analysis of **9** . . . **B×N!** spoils the
fun: .10 Q×B P–K4 and if **11
P–QN4,** 11 . . . P–K5 12 N–K1
N–Q5 ∓ or **11 P–Q3**.**P–Q4!**, again
similar to A421.

     9 . . .   **P–KR3?!**
Probably unnecessary, since
B–KN5 is not yet a threat. As the
text game shows, Black should not
allow White to build up too casually.
Polugayevsky–Hübner, Palma de
Mallorca 1970 saw **9** . . . **P–QR3(!)**
10 R–N1 and now **10** . . . **B–B2!**
was suggested, preparing 11 . . .
R–N1 and 12 . . . P–QN4. Instead,
Hübner played **10** . . . **R–N1?!**
11 B–B4! P–Q3 12 N–R2 B–B2
13 P–QN4 P–QN3 14 P–K4 ±,
but managed to draw in 20, anyway.

     9 . . . **P –Q3** has some of the same
handicaps as the text e.g. 10 R–N1
(10 P–K4 or **10 P–N3** ±) 10 . . .
P–KR3 11 N–R2 P–Q4 12
P–QN4! B–N3 **(12** . . . **P×NP**
13 P×NP N×P? 14 B–QR3 N×Q
15 B×Q R–K1 16 B×N P×B 17
R(B)–B1–Tal) Tal–Polugayevsky,
USSR Ch 1975, and now, as Tal
later indicated, a good move was
13 P–K3! ± △ 13 . . . R–Q1 14
B–N2 or 13 . . . P–K4 14 P× QP
N× QP 15 P×P B×P 16 N×KP!
N×N 17 P–Q4 etc. (Tal).

     10 P –K3   P–Q3
Lombardy gives these instructive alternatives:
(a) **10** . . . **P–Q4** 11 P×P P×P

(**11** . . . N×P 12 N–QR4 ±) 12
N–QR4 N–Q2 13 N–Q2 Q–Q3
14 N–N3 B–N3 15 P–K4 ±;
(b) **10** . . . **R–Q1** 11 P–Q4 (or
11 P–N3 P–Q4 12 B–N2 e.g.
12 . . . P–Q5 13 P×P P×P 14
N–N1 P–K4 15 N(1)–Q2 △
P–QN4) 11 . . . P×P 12 P×P
P–Q4 13 P–QN4 ± △ P–B5 P–N5.
If such central action is forbidden
the second player, he must stand
worse due to the misplaced bishop
on a5.

     11 P–N3   B–Q2
     11 . . . **B×N** 12 Q×B P–K4
(12 . . . B–Q2!? ±) **13 N–K1** △
N–B2, P–Q4; or here **13 N–R4**
△ P–B4 (Lombardy).
     12 B–N2   QR–N1
13 P–Q4! P×P?! (**13** . . . **KR–B1**
14 P–Q5 or 14 QR–Q1 ±) 14
P×P KR–B1 15 P–QN4 B–Q1
16 KR–K1 Q–B1 17 Q–Q3 ±
Lombardy–Polugayevsky, Reykjavik
1978. White has a spatial preponderance and can prepare P–Q5.
CONCLUSION: The retreat 5 . . .
B–R4 has by no means been refuted, although both 6 P–K3 and
6 P–KN3 confer upon the careful
White player a persistent superiority.

A43

     4 . . .   **0–0**
     5 P–QR3
     5 P–KN3 and **5 P–K3** are trans-
positions; recent praxis has seen
two original notions:
(a) **5 P–K4 P–K4!?** (**5** . . . **P–B4**)
6 P–QR3 B×N 7 QP×B P–QN3
(**7** . . . **P–KR3**) 8 B–N5 P–Q3
9 B–K2 B–N2 10 N–Q2 QN–Q2
11 P–B3 N–B4 12 N–B1! △

N–K3 ± Hort–Sosonko, Portoroz 1977.
(b) **5 P–QN3 P–B4** (or **5 . . . P–QN3** 6 B–N2 B–N2 7 P–K3 P–Q4 8 B–K2 Q–K2 9 P×P P×P 10 0–0 QN–Q2 11 QR–B1 P–QR3! Smejkal–Tal, Leningrad 1977) 6 B–N2 Q–K2 7 P–K3 N–B3 8 B–K2 P–Q3 9 0–0 B×N 10 B×B P–K4 11 P–QR3 B–N5 12 KR–K1 P–QR4 13 P–Q4 with some initiative, Petrosian–Balashov, USSR Ch 1977.

    5 . . .   B× N
    6 Q× B

Black's strategy at this point must take into account the potential of White's bishop pair:
A431 6 . . . P–Q3
A432 6 . . . P–QN3

A forceful advance was chosen by Makarichev against Podgayets in the USSR Championship of 1973: **6 . . . P–B4** and now **7 P–QN4 P–Q4!** 8 NP×P N–K5 9 Q–B2 N×QBP **10 B–N2** P–QN3 11 P×P P×P 12 P–K3 B–R3! 13 B×B N(1)×B 14 0–0 Q–K2 15 P–Q3 KR–K1 =. Here **10 P–N3** might have left more play e.g. 10 . . . N–B3 11 B- KN2 P–Q5 12 P–Q3 P–K4 13 0–0 P–KR3 14 B–N2 P–B4 15 QR–Q1 Q–K2 16 P–K3; another improvement in that game was (after 10 B–N2) 10 . . . N–B3.

Theoretically, the position after 6 . . . P–B4 is trebly important, as it can be reached by 4 Q–B2 P–B4 5 P–QR3 B×N 6 Q×B 0–0 or even 4 Q–N3 P–B4 5 P–QR3 B×N etc. White should also consider **7 P–K3** e.g. 7 . . . P–QN3 8 B–K2 B–N2 9 P–QN3! P–Q3 10 B–N2 QN–Q2 11 0–0 P–K4

12 P–Q4 R–K1 13 P× KP P×P 14 QR–Q1 Q–B2 15 N–R4 P–K5!? 16 N–B5 R–K4 17 P–KN4 B–B3 19 R–Q2 with pressure, Sydor–Goichberg, Gausdal 1978. There are few examples of 6 . . . P–B4; one tends to prefer White because of his two bishops and still-flexible pawn configuration, but a good fight may be anticipated.

A431
    6 . . .   P–Q3 (29)

Often played, but perhaps not aggressive enough in the centre. Black will play . . . P–K4 and defend e5 to the hilt.
    7 P–KN3

Again the most frequent, but not necessarily best, continuation. (a) **7 P–K3** was not especially effective in Hartoch–Keene, Amsterdam, 1973: 7 . . . P–K4 8 B–K2 P–QR4 9 P–QN4 P×P 10 P×P R×R 11 Q×R N–B3 12 B–R3 P–K5 =; but
(b) **7 P–QN4**, seizing territory on the queenside, is more assertive: 7 . . . P–K4 8 B–N2 N–B3 (8 . . . **P–QR4** 9 P–K3 QN–Q2 10 B–K2 N–N3! 11 Q–B2 B–N5 12 0–0 R–K1 13 P–Q3 Q–Q2! was Furman–Holmov, 40th USSR

Ch 1972. Black has stationed his pieces productively, and after 14 KR—Q1 Q—R5 15 Q—B3 Q—Q2 16 Q—B2 Q—R5 could have split the point—Furman. This disposition of Black's forces appears plausible and deserves another try.) 9 P—K3 N—K5 10 Q—B2 P—B4 11 B—K2 P—QR4 12 P—Q3 N—B3 13 P—N5 N—K2 14 P—B5! P—N3! 15 P×QP P×P 16 R—QB1 B—N2 17 0—0 R—B1 ± Portisch-Larsen, Las Palmas 1976. White makes no inroads on the QB file, and the situation borders on equality. Yet an end-game tends to favour White's two bishops, and Portisch exploited this fact to take home the point. (c) 7 P—Q4! has obvious merits, and may well be best: 7 ... P—QN3 (7 ... QN—Q2—Uhlmann) 8 P—KN3 B—N2 9 B—N2 QN—Q2 10 0—0 Q—K2 11 P—N3 P—K4?! (11 ... N—K5 12 Q—B2 P—KB4 13 N—KN5 N(2)—B3 ∞—Bukić. Preferable seems 13 N—K1 or 13 B—N2 △ N—K1 ±.) 12 P—Q5! P—QR4 13 N—R4 N—B4 14 B—N2 KR—K1 15 Q—B2 P—QN4 16 N—B5 Q—B1 17 P—B4 ± Uhlmann-Larsen, Hastings 1972/3.

7 ...   P—K4

7 ... P—QN3, Queen's Indian style, allows 8 P—Q4 transposing into the last note (c), or 8 B—N2 B—N2 9 0—0 P—B4 10 P—QN4 N—B3 (After 10 ... QN—Q2 11 P—Q4, the Black QP may become vulnerable. 10 ... Q—K2!?) 11 P—Q3 R—K1 12 P—N5 N—K2 13 P—QR4 P—QR4 14 B—N2 P—Q4 (14 ... P—K4 15 P—K4 ±) 15 Q—B2 N—N3 16 N—Q2 R—QB1 17 P—K4 and White has pressure à

la Reti, Petrosian-Larsen, Vinkovci 1970 (though ½—½, 42).

8 B—N2   N—B3

8 ... R—K1 (!) waits for White: 9 0—0 P—QR4 (9 ... P—B4?!—*If there is any 'rule' in these positions, it might be that Black should not commit himself to an inflexible pawn formation when White has yet to advance his pawns*—10 P—Q3 N—B3 11 P—K3 P—QR4 12 P—N3 R—N1 13 B—N2 P—QN4 14 P×P R×P 15 N—Q2 N—K2 16 P—B4! ± Najdorf-Panno, Mar del Plata 1971. A pleasing and instructive build-up! If 16 ... P×P, 17 N—K4! N(2)—Q4 18 N×Nch N×N 19 B—B6 R—N3 20 B×R Q×B 21 QR—K1!) 10 P—Q3?! (10 P—N3!) 10 ... N—B3! (△ 11 .. ... B—N5) 11 P—KR3 P—R5 = Lein-Lengyel, Sochi 1967.

9 P—QN4

Forthright. 9 0—0 B—N5! threatens ... P—K5. Or 9 P—Q3!? P—QR4 10 P—N3 B—N5! 11 B—N2 N—Q2 (Hecht gives also 11 ... B×N 12 B×B N—Q5 13 B—KN2 R—K1 14 P—K3 N—N5!? —*an enterprising foray, but 14 ... P—B3 and 14 ... Q—B1 are not bad* —15 P—R3 N×BP 16 K×N Q—B3ch 17 K—K1 Q—N4 ∞) 12 P—K3 N—B4 ≅ Jakobsen-Hecht, Amsterdam II 1973.

9 ...   B—N5
10 P—R3   B—R4

11 P—N5 N—N1 12 0—0 N(1)—Q2 13 B—N2 R—K1 14 P—QR4 P—R4 15 P—Q4!? P—K5 16 N—Q2 B×P 17 R—K1 B—Q6 18 P—B3 P—Q4 19 P×QP N×P 20 Q—N3 N—N5? (20 ... P×P! ∞) 21 P×P Ree-Timman, IBM 1973. White was manifestly better.

A432

6 ...   P−QN3 (30)

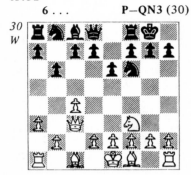

30
W

The informed choice, in many ways more active than 6 . . . P−Q3 or 6 . . . P−B4. Black is not so intent on . . : P−K4 or . . . P−QB4; he may opt for . . . P−Q4 with spritely piece play, a strategy Korchnoi employs in the text.

7 P−KN3?!
Apparently too sedate. The alternatives are therefore theoretically crucial:
(a) **7 P−K3** B−N2 8 B−K2. A safe set-up, if not immediately challenging:
a1) 8 . . . **P−Q3** 9 P−QN4 (9 P−Q3 !?) 9 . . . N−K5 10 Q−B2 N−N4! 11 B−N2 N−Q2 12 Q−Q1 P−K4 ∞ Polugaevsky−Larsen, Busum 1969;
a2) 8 . . . **N−K5** 9 Q−B2 N−N4 (9 . . . **P−KB4**!? 10 P−QN3 P−Q3 11 B−N2 N−Q2 12 P−Q3 N−N4 13 0−0−0!?) 10 P−QN3 (**10 P−KR4**!? Nx Nch 11 Px N Q−B3 12 R−R3 ± Marović−Barle, Maribor 1977; White can calmly build up on the kingside.) 10 . . . Nx Nch 11 Px N Q−R5! 12 B−N2 P−Q3 13 R−N1 P−KN3 14 0−0−0 Qx BP 15 P−KR4!!? (15 B−Q3!?) 15 . . . Qx B 16 P−R5 P−KB4 17 Px P P−KR3 ∞! Isaksen−Barle,

Esbjerg 1977 (½−½, 27); .
a3) 8 . . . **P−B4** 9 P−QN4 (**9 P−QN3**!? compare A431) 9 . . . P−Q3 10 B−N2 QN−Q2 11 0−0 (For **11 P−Q4** see '(b)') 11 . . . P−K4?! **(11 . . . R−B1** 12 P−Q3 P−Q4 13 P−N5 R−K1 14 P−QR4 P−K4 15 Px P Nx P 16 Q−N3 ± Portisch−Najdorf, Wijk an Zee 1978. White plans P−R5, Px P, etc.) 12 P−Q3 Q−K2 13 N−Q2? P−Q4! ∓ Ree−Euwe, Holland 1973.
(b) **7 P−QN4!** is more to the point if White wants such positions, because . . . N−K5−N4 is no problem e.g. 7 . . . B−N2 8 B−N2 P−Q3 9 P−K3 (or **9 P−KN3**!? *P−K4−9 . . . QN−Q2 is the note to 8 . . . P−Q4 in the text*−10 B−N2 P−B4 11 0−0 N−B3 12 P−K3 ± Tiller−Iskov, Gausdal 1978) 9 . . . QN−Q2 **(9 . . . P−K4** 10 P−Q3 N−N5!? is commendably adventurous, yet a bit neglectful of the centre: 11 P−R3 N−KR3 12 P−Q4! P−KB3 13 Px P BPx P 14 P−B5! NPx P 15 Px P Bx N! 16 Px B N−Q2 17 0−0−0 ± Suba−Tal, Sochi 1977) **10 B−K2** P−B4 **(10 . . . P−K4**!?), reaching note (a) by a different route, and now, instead of Ree's 11 0−0, **11 P−Q4**!? Q−K2 12 0−0 N−K5 13 Q−B2 P−B4 14 QPx P NPx P **(14 . . . QPx P** 15 QR−Q1− Shamkovich) 15 P−N5 N(2)−B3 16 N−Q2 QR−Q1 17 P−B3 N−N4!? (17 . . . Nx N!?) 18 KR−Q1 ± Shamkovich−Holmov, USSR Ch 1972 (1−0, 59).
(c) **7 P−QN3** B−N2 8 P−N3 P−Q4 9 B−KN2 (related to the text; see note to 9 P−Q4) 9 . . . P−Q5 (9 . . . P−B4) 10 Q−N2!

P–B4 11 0–0 N–B3 12 P–Q3
Q–K2 13 P–QN4! KR–Q1 14
Px P Qx P 15 P–QR4 P–KR3
16 B–B4 N–KR4 17 B–Q2
QR–N1 18 Q–N5! ± Uhlmann-
Augustin, Decin 1977.

7 ...   B–N2
8 B–N2   P–Q4!
8 ... **P–Q3?!** 9 0–0 QN–Q2
10 P–QN4 Q–K2 11 B–N2 P–B4
12 P–Q3 P–Q4! (12 ... **P–K4?**
13 N–R4! Bx B 14 Kx B △ P–K4,
P–B4–Szmetan. Again, Black's
pawns should not be so inflexible.)
13 Px QP Bx P 14 P–N5 Szmetan-
Christiansen, Wijk an Zee II 1977.
White is to be preferred, although
Black is hardly lost.

The text lays bare the light-
square weaknesses of White's queenside:

9 P–Q4?!
9 Px P improves on the text,
but holds out few prospects for
advantage: 9 ... Nx P 10 Q–B2
P–QB4 11 0–0 N–QB3 =.

9 ...   Px P
10 Qx P   B–Q4
Against Vaganian in Moscow
1975, Korchnoi chose the seemingly
more binding:
(a) **10 ... B–K5,** but after 11 0–0
N–QB3!? 12 P–QN4 P–QR4!?
13 P–N5 B–Q4 14 Q–Q3 B–K5
15 Q–B4 B–Q4 16 Q–B3! N–R2
17 P–QR4 P–B3 18 B–QR3 R–K1
19 Px P Nx P 20 KR–Q1, White
was ready to mobilize his centre
pawns (± ; 1–0, 40). However,
(b) **10 ... N–B3!** looks excellent:
11 0–0 (11 P–QN4? Nx QP!) 11
... N–QR4 12 Q–B3 N–K5 13
Q–B2 B–Q4 14 P–QN4 N–N6
15 R–N1 Nx B 16 KRx N N–Q3! ∓

de Roode-van der Wiel, Netherlands Junior Ch 1977.
11 Q–B3   N(1)–Q2
12 P–QN4?
Black threatened ... P–QB4,
but here it was better to allow it.
12 ...   P–QR4!
13 P–N5
13 Px P Rx P 14 0–0 P–B4
△ ...˙Q–R1 (Kovacević).
13 ...   P–B3
14 Px P R–B1 15 0–0 (At last,
but Black has an extra rook in play
in comparison with Vaganian-
Korchnoi, and White lacks P–QR4
and B–QR3!) 15 ... Rx P 16
Q–K3 Q–R1! 17 B–Q2 P–QN4
18 KR–N1? (**18 QR–N1** ±–Korchnoi) 18 ... R–N1 19 N–K1 Bx B
20 Nx B N–K5! (31)

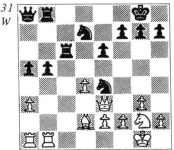
31
W

(Things look black for White! If
21 Qx N? 21 ... R–B8ch.) 21
Q–Q3 R–Q3! 22 B–K3 N–K4
23 Q–B2 R–QB1! 24 Q–N3
N–B5 25 R–QB1 R(3)–B3 26
Qx NP Nx RP 27 Q–R4 N–B7!
28 QR–N1 R–B5 0–1 Langeweg-
Korchnoi, Amsterdam 1976.
CONCLUSION: 4 ... 0–0 5 P–QR3
Bx N 6 Qx B is rather complex.
Black should probably opt for the
plan beginning with 6 ... P–QN3,
since 6 ... P–Q3 leads to difficul-

ties after 7 P−QN4 or 7 P−Q4. After 6 . . . P−QN3, White's best formations stem from 7 P−QN4.

3 . . . B−N5 remains a staunch, active weapon for the Black player who is not averse to prolonged positional play frequently involving the surrender of his bishop pair.

B

3 . . .   P−QN3 (32)

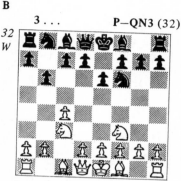

32
W

A move that world champion Karpov did much to popularize. Smyslov defended this position (via 2 . . . P−QN3) in the 1960s, but not until the 1970s did 3 . . . P−QN3 burst into prominence.

We examine:

B1 4 P−KN3
B2 4 P−K4

4 P−Q4 will lead to a Queen's or Nimzo−Indian Defence.

B1

    4 P−KN3   B−N2

Interestingly, **4 . . . B−N5** switches back to Section A in a position where White has committed himself to P−KN3 (instead of, say, P−K3 and B−K2).

    5 B−N2   B−K2

Now **6 P−Q4** is a Queen's Indian Defence. To avoid this, or to attempt to enter the corresponding variations of the Symmetrical English, . . . P−B4 is often played on either the fifth, sixth, or seventh moves. In this section, we discuss lines where Black eschews an early . . . P−B4.

    6 0−0

6 P−Q3 0−0 7 P−K4 achieves White's goal in B11 below, but Black can also reply with **6 . . . P−Q4**, when 7 0−0 and 7 N−K5 are the next note.

    6 . . .   0−0

On **6 . . . P−Q4**, **7 P×P N×P** and **7 Q−R4ch Q−Q2** are harmless, while **7 N−K5(!) 0−0 8 P−Q4** is a normal Queen's Indian variation (8 . . . Q−B1!?). Finally, the modest **7 P−Q3!?** deserves attention, since both **7 . . . P×P 8 P×P 0−0 9 Q−B2** and **7 . . . P−Q5 8 N−QN5 P−B4 9 B−B4** give White fair prospects. Leoni−Scorza, corres, continued, by transposition: **7 . . . P−B4 8 B−B4 QN−Q2?!** (8 . . . 0−0) **9 P−K4! P×KP 10 P×P N×P 11 N×N B×N 12 Q−R4! B−KB3!?** 13 QR−Q1 K−K2 14 KR−K1 B×N 15 B×B B−Q5 16 Q−B6 R−QB1 17 Q−Q6ch K−K1 18 B−N7 R−QN1 19 B−B6 R−QB1 20 R×Pch! 1−0.

After 6 . . . 0−0, the play divides into:

B11 7 P−Q3
B12 7 R−K1

Both moves intend P−K4, but 4 P−K4 B−N2 5 P−Q3 (see B21 below) may be a better way to achieve that pawn structure because of the difficulties which follow:

B11

7 P–Q3   P–Q4

7 ... **P–B4** transposes to *English III*, Chapter 10. The restrained approach is 7 ... **P–Q3** 8 P–K4 QN–Q2 9 N–K1 N–K1 10 P–Q4 P–QB4 (Essential. **10 ... P–N3?** 11 B–R6 N–N2 12 N–Q3 and White's space advantage dominated the play, Reti-Muffang, London 1927!) 11 P–Q5!? (11 N–B2! ±) 11 ... B–KB3 12 P×P (12 Q–B2) 12 ... P×P 13 P–B4 P–QR3! 14 B–Q2 P–QN4! 15 Q–N3 Q–N3 16 N–B2 B–B3   17 N–K3 P–N5 18 N–K2 P–QR4 ∓ Shamkovich-Garcia-Palermo, Lone Pine, 1978 (½–½, 51).

8 P×P

(a) **8 Q–B2!?** P–Q5 9 N–QR4 (**9 N–QN5** P–B4   10 P–K4 ∞) 9 ... P–B4 10 P–QR3 QN–Q2 11 P–QN4 P–K4   12 R–N1 P–K5 13 N–R4 P×QP 14 P×QP B×B 15 K×B Q–B2 =/∞ Schmidt-Unzicker, European Team Ch, 1973.

(b) **8 N–K5** QN–Q2 (8...**Q–B1** = Pytel) 9 P–Q4 (9 P–B4) 9 ... P–B4 10 B–B4 R–B1 11 P×QP N×N? (11 ... N×P = –Pytel) 12 P–Q6! ± Pytel-Liebert, Polanica Zdroj, 1972 (½–½, 19).

8 ...   P×P!?

8 ... **N×P** is safer: 9 N×N B×N 10 B–Q2 P–QB4 11 B–B3 N–Q2 12 R–K1 (△ P–K4, P–Q4) 12 ... B–KB3 13 P–QR4 (13 P–K4!?) 13 ... Q–B2 = Schmidt-Saṛen, Helsinki, 1972.

9 N–Q4!?   Q–B1?

We are following Schmidt-Jakobsen, Helsinki 1972: 10 P–K4! P×P 11 P×P R–Q1   12 N–B5 B–KB1

13 Q–B3 QN–Q2 (13 ... Q–K3 14 B–R3!) 14 B–N5 R–K1   15 Q–B4 ± (1–0, 28).

Also inadequate was **9 ... R–K1?** 10 N–B5 B–KB1   11 Q–R4! QN–Q2   12 Q–R4 P–KR3 13 P–KN4 P–B3   14 P–N5 N–R2 15 P–B4 N–B4   16 Q–N3 ± Forintos-Matanović,   Bordeaux 1964.

But after the correct 9 ... **P–N3!** (Schmidt), White has less to be happy about, since ... P–QB4 will drive his active knight from the centre. Best seems 10 B–R6 R–K1   11 P–K3 QN–Q2 with a tough positional struggle ahead.

B12

7 R–K1

The purpose of this move is to meet 7 ... P–B4(?) by 8 P–K4 P–Q3   9 P–Q4, and White has gained a tempo on a normal line of *English III*, Chapter 10.

7 ...   P–Q4!

The obvious retort. 7 ... **N–K5** also kept the balance after 8 N×N B×N   9 P–Q3 B–N2   **10 P–Q4** B–K5! 11 P–Q5 P×P   12 P×P B–B3 13 N–Q2 B×B   14 K×B R–K1 Petrosian-Portisch Match (11), 1974. **10 P–K4** would have more bite e.g. 10 ... P–Q4 11 BP×P P×P   12 P–K5 P–Q5 13 B–B4 etc.

8 P×P   N×P

The opening of Petrosian-Gulko, 43rd USSR Ch Top L, 1975 was a mini-masterpiece: 9 ... P×P 9 P–Q4 **QN–Q2** 10 Q–N3! P–B4 11 P×P N×P   12 Q–Q1 N–K3?! 13 N–QN5 B–N5 14 B–Q2 B–B4 15 P–K3 N–K5 16 B–B3!! P–QR3

17 N(5)–Q4 N×B 18 P×N Q–B2
19 Q–Q3 and White's pieces are
clearly better than their Black
counterparts. Wonderful!

An attempted improvement was
9 . . . N–R3 10 B–N5 (**10 B–B4**
P–B4 11 Q–R4 N–K5 was only
minimally ± in Suba–Darga, Eur.
Team Ch., 1977) 10 . . . P–B4
11 P×P N×P **12 N–Q4** Q–Q2
Portisch–Hübner, Biel 1976 (½–½,
33). Forintos suggests **10 R–QB1**,
keeping more tension; **12 N–QN5**,
as in the Petrosian game, was
another interesting option.

$\quad$ 9 N×N $\qquad$ P×N

Ceding ground in the centre was
9 . . . B×N?! 10 P–Q4 P–QB4
11 P–K4 B–N2 12 P–Q5! P×P
13 P×P B–KB3 14 N–K5 ±
Dementiev–Vasulivev, Saratov 1977.

9 . . . P×N is Portisch–Karpov
(3), 1975: 10 P–Q4 N–Q2 11
B–B4 P–QB4 12 P×P (**12 P–N3!?**
R–B1 13 R–B1–Minev. And
after 13 . ●. R–K1 . . . ?) 12 . . .
P×P 12 N–Q2 P–QR4! 14 R–B1
R–R2! 15 N–N1 N–N3 16 P–N3
P–Q5 17 P–K4! (preventing . . .
N–Q4) = (½–½, 30).

CONCLUSION: 7 . . . P–Q4! is a
good answer to both 7 P–Q3 and
7 R–K1.

B2

$\qquad$ **4 P–K4**

Directed against . . . P–Q4. This
is the current preference, after
which Black's task is not easy!

$\qquad$ 4 . . . $\qquad$ B–N2 (33)

Black attacks White's KP, which
White can defend in three interesting ways:

B21 5 P–Q3

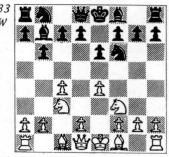

33
W

B22 5 Q–K2
B23 5 B–Q3

$\quad$ **5 P–K5** is innocuous after 5
. . . N–K5 e.g. 6 B–Q3 (**6 N–QN1** !?
N–N4! 7 N–Q4 P–KB4 △ . . .
N–B2–Cafferty) 6 . . . N×N (or
6 . . . N–N4) 7 QP×N **B–K2** 'with
an excellent position' –Cafferty.
Here not 7 . . . **P–Q3?** 8 N–N5!
P×P? **9 N×BP!** ±± De Veauce–
Cafferty, Birmingham 1974.

B21

$\qquad$ **5 P–Q3**

Apparently unambitious, but
posing certain difficulties. Now
5 . . . P–Q4? 6 BP×P P×P 7 P–K5
KN–Q2 8 P–Q4 is good for White,
and **5 . . . P–Q3** 6 P–KN3 B–K2
7 B–N2 0–0 8 0–0 P–B4 transposes to *English III*, Chapter 10.
The independent try is:

$\qquad$ 5 . . . $\qquad$ P–B4
$\qquad$ 6 P–K5!?

$\quad$ **6 P–KN3 B–K2** 7 B–N2 0–0
8 0–0 P–Q3, again a Symmetrical
English, has been the usual continuation. 6 P–KN3 **P–Q4?!** $\quad$ 7
BP×P P×P 8 P–K5 N(3)–Q2
(8 . . . **P–Q5?** 9 P×N P×N 10
Q–K2ch) 9 P–Q4 P×P? (The only
chance to justify Black's strategy is
Boleslavsky's **9 . . . B–K2** 10

B–N2 N–R3 11 0–0 N–B2)
10 N×P N×P (What else?) 11
B–N5ch N(1)–Q2 12 Q–K2
Q–K2 13 0–0 0–0–0 14 B–KB4
P–N4 15 B×Nch N×B 16 QR–B1
Q×Q 17 N(3)×Qch B–B4 18
B×P ±± Platonov–Grigorian, USSR
Ch. 1971.

  6 ...   N–N1
  7 P–Q4   P×P
  8 N×P   N–QB3

8 ... **P–QR3** is passive (9 B–B4),
but preferable.

  9 N(4)–N5! P–QR3
  9 ... N×P· 10 B–B4 P–Q3
11 Q–R4 B–B3 12 0–0–0(Florian).
  10 N–Q6ch B×N
  11 P×B!   N–B3?!

11 ... **P–B4** would guard more
central squares, although after 12
B–K3 White obviously has the
upper hand. After 11 ... N–B3,
Portisch–Larsen, Milan 1975, went
12 B–K2 0–0 13 0–0 R–B1 14
B–K3 N–QR4 15 Q–R4! and
White was well on the way to victory.

B22

  5 Q–K2

This curious move was another
Portisch discovery. White threatens
P–K5, since the Black knight cannot come to e4. Also, 5 ... P–Q4
is directly prevented, so Black
chooses from:

B221 5 ... P–B4
B222 5 ... P–Q3
B223 5 ... B–N5

B221

  5 ...   P–B4
  6 P–K5

6 P–KN3 N–B3 7 B–N2 **B–K2**
8 0–0 0–0 9 R–Q1 ∆ P–Q4 is
complex. Instead 7 ... N–Q5?

came out badly in Uhlmann–
Spassov, Cienfuegos 1973: 8 N×N
P×N 9 N–N5 P–K4 10 0–0 B–K2
11 P–Q3 0–0 12 P–B4 P–Q3
13 B–Q2 N–Q2 14 R–B2! B–QB3
15 QR–KB1 N–B4 and now 16
B–R3! was strong, according to
Uhlmann, who kept the advantage
anyway and went on to win.

  6 ...   N–N1
  6 ... N–N5? 7 P–Q4! ±
  7 P–Q4   B×N?!
  7 ... P×P 8 N×P N–QB3 is
probably best, and on 9 N(4)–N5
P–QR3 10 N–Q6ch B×N 11 P×B
N–B3, Black is better off than in
B21 (Portisch–Larsen) due to
White's poor queen position. Even
so, '±' is a fair assessment. A mistake
in this line is 9 N×N?: 9 ... B×N
10 B–Q2 N–K2 11 0–0–0 Q–B2
12 K–N1 N–B4 ∓ Portisch–Matanović, Erevan 1965.

  8 Q×B   N–QB3
  9 P–Q5!   N×P
  9 ... N–Q5 10 Q–Q1 P–Q3
(Geller), is well met by 11 B–B4;
perhaps 10 ... N–K2!?
  10 Q–N3   P–Q3
  11 B–B4   N–N3

White's two bishops and central
pressure are decisive e.g. 11 ...
N–KB3 12 B×N P×B 13 0–0–0!
Q–N1 14 P×P P×P 15 B–Q3
∆ B–K4 (Archives)
  12 P×P   P×P
  13 0–0–0   N×B
14 Q×N P–KN3 (14 ... N–B3
15 P–KN3! B–K2 16 B–N2
R–QB1 17 KR–K1 ± –Korchnoi)
15 Q–K4 N–B3 16 Q×Pch Q–K2
17 R×P Korchnoi–Petrosian (3),
1974. White's extra pawn proved
sufficient for the win.

B222

    5 ...   P–Q3 (?!)
    6 P–Q4   B–K2
    7 P–KN3!?

Plausible, but **7 Q–B2!** (Rogoff) casts doubt on 5 . . . P–Q3. White intends simply B–K2, 0–0, etc. with a comfortable spatial plus; on 7 . . . P–B4 8 P–Q5 P×P, he can recapture by either 9 KP×P or 9 BP×P and keep a clear advantage.

    7 ...   0–0
    8 B–N2   P–B4
    9 P–K5?!

9 0–0 seems preferable, as 9 . . . N–B3 10 P–Q5 N–Q5? 11 N×N P×N 12 N–N5 reminds one of Uhlmann–Spassov (B221), and 9 . . . P×P 10 N×P grants White a familiar edge in the centre.

After **9 P–K5**, Vaganian–Polugayevsky, USSR Ch 1974 went 9 . . . N(3)–Q2! 10 P×QP B×P 11 N–K4 B–K2 12 0–0 N–KB3 13 N×Nch B×N 14 P×P P×P 15 B–K3 Q–K2! = .

B223

    5 ...   B–N5

This developing move has the side benefit of preventing 6 P–KN3 by an immediate attack on White's KP.

    6 P–K5   N–N1
    7 P–Q4   N–K2!

7 . . . P–Q3 8 B–Q2 (**8 P–QR3** B×Nch 9 P×B N–K2 10 P–KR4 N–Q2 11 P–R5! B×N?!–*11 . . . P–KR3!*–12 Q×B P×P 13 P–R6 P×RP 14 B×P P×P?–*14 . . . N–KB4 ±*–15 B–N7 R–KN1 16 R×P N–KB4 17 B×P P–B4 18 P–N4! ± Stein–Smyslov, Moscow 1972) 8 . . . P×P 9 P×P N–QR3 10 0–0–0 Q–K2 11 P–KN3 0--0–0 12 B–N2 N–B4 13 B–N5 P–B3 14 R×Rch Q×R 15 R–Q1 Q–K1 16 P×P P×P 17 B–Q2 N–K2 18 N–K4! ± Korchnoi–Karpov (1), 1974 (½–½, 38).

    8 Q–Q3

8 B–Q2 0–0 9 0–0–0 P–Q4! 10 P–KR4?! (**10 BP×P** B–R3! 11 Q–K4! ∞) 10 . . . BP×N 11 B×B P×P 12 Q×P B–R3 13 Q–R4 B×B and Black owned the central light squares in Korchnoi–Karpov (3), 1974. With the text (8 Q–Q3), White plans to recapture on c3 with his queen, posting his queen's bishop more aggressively than he did in this example.

    8 . . .   P–Q4
    9 P×P e.p.   P×P
    10 P–QR3   B×Nch
    11 Q×B   N–Q2!

In the meantime, Black rapidly develops his queenside. **11 . . . 0–0?!** 12 P–QN4 N–Q2 13 B–K2 R–B1 was slower in Korchnoi–Karpov (7), 1974 and White might have tried Uhlmann's idea of 14 P–QR4!, intending P–N5 and B–QR3.

After **11 . . . N–Q2**, 12 P–QN4 is still best; 12 B–K2?! R–B1 13 0–0 0–0 14 B–N5?! P–KR3 15 B–R4 Q–K1! (△ . . . N–B4) was to Black's advantage in Uhlmann–Karpov, Skopje 1976 (0–1, 51).

CONCLUSION: 5 Q–K2 is strong versus 5 . . . P–B4, but an effective answer to 5 . . . B–N5 has not yet been found.

B23

    5 B–Q3 (34)

Romanishin's move, all the rage

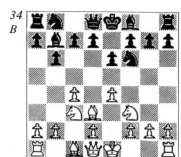

34
B

at the time of this writing. White intends B–B2 and P–Q4. In response, Black can create immediate tactics in the centre or play it quietly, although things do not usually remain quiet for very long:

B231 5 . . . P–Q4
B232 5 . . . N–B3
B233 5 . . . P–B4
B234 5 . . . P–Q3

An oddity is 5 . . . B–N5: 6 P–K5 N–N1 7 B–K4 B× B 8 N× B P–Q4 9 P× P e.p. B× P 10 0–0 N–KB3 11 N× Nch Q× N 12 Q–R4ch! P–B3 13 P–Q4 ± Korchnoi–Kraidman, Beersheva 1978 (1–0, 40).

B231

5 . . .   P–Q4

Often denigrated, this thrust is certainly risky, but unrefuted.

6 BP× P   P× P
7 P–K5   KN–Q2

7 . . . N–K5 may be practicable: 8 B–B2 (For 8 0–0 N–B4 9 B–N5ch, see the following note) 8 . . . B–K2 9 0–0 0–0 10 P–Q4 N× N (Cafferty) definitely favours White: Black's queen's bishop is misplaced, and White has strong attacking prospects. But 10 . . .

P–KB4! is harder to assess, e.g. 11 P× P e.p. B× P 12 B–B4 N–Q2 ∞
8 B–B2

An original approach was 8 0–0!? N–B4 9 B–N5ch P–B3 10 P–Q4, Chekhov–A. Ivanov, USSR Young Masters Ch 1978, when Black played warily with 10 . . . N–K3?! 11 B–R4 B–K2 12 R–K1 0–0 13 B–B2 ±. 10 . . . P× B 11 P× N P× P was more enterprising e.g. 12 N× NP B–K2 or 12˙ B–N5 B–K2 (12 . . . Q–Q2? 13 P–K6!) 13 N× NP 0–0 14 N–Q6 B–QB3.

8 . . .   P–Q5
9 B–K4!?

(a) 9 N× P N× P 10 Q–K2! (10 N–B5 N–Q6ch 11 K–B1 B–R3!? or 11 . . . N–B5 looks fine for Black) 10 . . . P–KB3 (10 . . . Q–K2 11 N–B5 Q–K3 12 N–N5 N–R3 13 N(N)–Q4 ±±; 10 . . . Q× N 11 N–N5 ±± –Smejkal) 11 N–K6 (11 N–B5 B–R3!?; 11 P–B4 Q× N 12 N–N5 Q× BP ∞) 11 . . . Q–Q2 (11 . . . Q–K2 12 B–R4ch △ N–Q5) with obscure complications.
(b) 9 P–K6 P× P! (9 . . . P× N 10 P× Pch! K× P 11 B–N3ch K–K1 12 0–0 ∞) 10 N–QN5 (10 N× P Q–N4!) 10 . . . N–QB3 and White seems short of compensation for the pawn.

9 . . .   B× B!?

9 . . . P–QB3!? is a hazardous but important alternative. White can reply 10 N× P N× P = or 10 N–K2? N–B4, but Black has easy play in both cases. Critical is 10 P–K6!?, and now 10 . . . P× P 11 N× P △ Q–R5ch, N× KP, evidently favours White. So 10 . . . P× N 11 P× Pch (11 P× Nch =) 11 . . . K× P

12 Q–N3ch (12 QP×P!?) 12 ...
K–K1 13 P–Q4 (13 0–0 N–B4).
Unclear! For example, 13 ... Q–K2
14 0–0 or 13 ... B–R3 14 B–N5
B–K2 15 P–KR4!?

10 N×B   N–B4

10 ... N×P 11 N×N Q–Q4
12 0–0 Q×N(4) 13 R–K1 is always
mentioned in the notes, but 13 ...
B–K2 defends against immediate
threats.

11 N×N   B×N
12 0–0   0–0
13 P–Q3   Q–Q4
14 R–K1   N–B3
15 R–K4!

The remarkable feature of this
position is the strength of White's
pawn on e5, which, though easily
enough blockaded, brought home
the point very quickly in two encounters:

(a) 15 ... KR–K1 16 Q–K2 R–K3
17 B–B4 P–KR3 18 P–QR3 B–B1
19 P–KR4 QR–K1 20 R–K1
P–N3 (weakening, but otherwise
White may play P–R5 and N–R4)
21 Q–Q2 P–KR4 (21 ... K–R2
22 P–R5 P–KN4 23 B×P!) 22
B–N5! B–N2 (22 ... N×P 23 N×P
R–Q3 24 B–B4 B–N2 25 B–N3
–Polugayevsky) 23 B–B6! B×B
24 P×B Q–B4 25 N–N5! R×R
26 N×R N–Q1 27 Q–R6 N–K3
28 N–Q6! 1–0 Polugayevsky–Gulko,
USSR Ch 1975. A classic perform-
ance.

(b) With the moves P–QR3 and
... P–QR4 included: 16 ... P–R5
17 B–B4!? N–Q1 (this time Black
constructs the ideal blockade with
his knight ...) 18 N–R4 N–K3
19 B–N3 (... but White's majority
proves dangerously mobile. Now

Black must prepare for P–B4–B5.)
19 ... P–N3! 20 P–B4 N–N2
21 Q–B3 B–K2? (21 ... P–B4!
22 P×P e.p. and of course not
22 ... R×P?? 23 R–K8ch, but
22 ... N–R4 seems satisfactory.
The possibility of such moves
tends to make one prefer 17 Q–K2,
as in the Polugayevsky game. Then
after 17 ... N–Q1 18 N–R4,
White's pawns are not obstructed
by his bishop.) 22 P–B5! B×N
23 B×B N×P 24 B–B6 Q–N6
25 P–N4 N–N2 26 R–KB1
N–K3 27 Q–R3 QR–K1 28
R–K2 (△ R–Q2, R–B3, Q×Pch)
28 ... P–KN4 29 R–B5 Q–Q8ch
30 K–B2 1–0 Magerramos–Ivanov,
Alma Ata 1977.

CONCLUSION: Black should look
into the notes to his 7th and 9th
(or even 10th !?) if he wants to
redeem 5 ... P–Q4.

B232
5 ...   N–B3

Black aims to slow things down
some with 6 ... P–K4.

6 B–B2
6 P–K5 N–KN5 7 B–K4
(7 Q–K2 P–Q3 8 P×P B×P =)
7 ... P–Q3 (7 ... P–B4!?) 8 P×P
B×P 9 P–Q4 apparently grants
some central preponderance, but
this could use tests.

6 ...   P–K4
7 P–Q4   P×P

7 ... N×QP 8 N×N P×N
9 Q×P B–B4 10 Q–K5ch Q–K2
11 Q×Qch K×Q favours White
slightly, e.g. 12 P–B3 K–Q1 13
B–Q2 R–K1 14 0–0–0 ±
Gheorghiu–Unzicker, Eur.Team Ch.
1977 (but ½–½, 39).

8 N×P   B–B4

9 B–K3   N–K4

We are following Reshevsky–Garcia–Palermo, Lone pine 1978: 10 N–B5 (10 Q–K2 N(3)–N5) 10 . . . 0–0 11 Q–K2 Bx B 12 Nx B R–K1 13 0–0. White has a bind on the centre, but Black's pieces are well placed and he has some hopes of an early . . . P–Q4. Best now would have been 13 . . . N–N3 14 P–B3 Q–K2 Δ . . . QR–Q1.

5 . . . N–B3 is still in the experimental stage.

B233

5 . . .   **P–B4**
6 P–K5!?

The last word has not been spoken here, either:

(a) **6 B–B2** N–B3 (! 6 . . . **P–Q3** transposes to B234) 7P–Q4 (7 **0–0** N–Q5! =, Cvetković–Kluger, Varna II 1976) 7 . . . Px P 8 Nx P Nx N 9 Qx N and now 9 . . . B–B4! (9 . . . **N–N5!?** 10 P–KR3–or *10 P–B3! Q–R5ch 11 P–N3 Q–R6 12 Q–Q2! N–K4 13 Q–K2 ± –*Nei–10 . . . Q–R5 11 P–KN3 Q–B3 12 Qx Q Nx Q 13 B–Q2 ± Nei–Kärner, Tallin 1977) 10 Q–Q1 (Else 10 . . . N–N5 e.g. **10 Q–Q2** N–N5 11 0–0 Q–R5 12 P–KR3 P–KR4 13 Q–B4 P–KN4!) 10 . . . B–N5! (**10 . . . P–KR4!?** 11 P–KR3 P–Q4 12 BPx P Px P 13 P–K5 N–K5 ∞ Smejkal–Makarichev, Vrbas 1977; or **10 . . . Q–B2** 11 0–0 P–KR4!? ∞ Uhlmann–Gulko, Nikšić 1978.) 11 Q–K2 and Smejkal gives 11 . . . Bx N 12 Px B ±, but 11 . . . 0–0 (Δ 12 P–K5 N–K1) will not be easy for either side.

(b) **6 0–0** N–B3 (6 . . . P–Q3) 7 P–K5 N–KN5 8 B–K4 P–B4!? 9 Px P e.p. Nx P(3) 10 Bx N Bx B 11 P–Q4 Px P 12 Nx P B–N2 13 B–B4 (13 Q–R4!–Keene–± !) 13 . . . B–K2 14 N(3)–N5 0–0 15 B–B7 Q–B1 16 B–Q6 Q–Q1 = Korchnoi–Polugayevsky (9) 1977.

6 . . .   N–N5
7 P–KR3!

The most enterprising continuation, since **7 0–0** P–Q3 8 B–K4 (8 Px P Qx P!) 8 . . . Bx B 9 Nx B N–QB3! equalizes: **10 P–Q4!** Px QP 11 Nx P(4) Nx N (11 . . . N(5)x P 12 B–B4) 12 Qx N(Q4) Px P 13 Q–B3 = (analysis by Smejkal). Here **10 Q–R4?** Q–Q2 11 Px P N(5)–K4! 12 Nx N Nx N 13 Q–N3 was Smejkal–Gulko, Erevan 1976, and 13 . . . N–B3! would have kept a considerable advantage for Black.

7 . . .   Bx N
8 Qx B   Nx KP
9 Qx R   Nx Bch
10 K–K2   N–B5ch

Black has a pawn for the exchange and certain possibilities because of White's king position and backward QP. But this move is part of a plan to exchange queens, after which White's king can be useful in the centre. What else can Black try?

Smejkal's suggestion
(a) **10 . . . N–K4!?** appears insufficient after 11 P–Q3 (Mednis mentions **11 Q–K4**, but 11 . . . N(1)–B3 12 P–Q3 P–B4! 13 Q–K3 Q–R5! is unclear.) 11 . . . N(4)–B3 (11 . . . N(1)–B3 12 Qx Qch ±) 12 B–B4 or 12 B–K3, but:

(b) **10 . . . N—N5!?** is a determined attacking attempt, when **11 Q×RP?!** N(1)—B3 12 Q—R4 can be answered wildly by **12 . . . Q—R5!?** 13 Q—R8ch K—K2 ∆ . . . Q×P(5)ch, . . . N—Q5ch, or more simply by **12 . . . N—B7!** 13 R—QN1 N(7)—Q5ch and 14 . . . B—Q3. Less obliging after 10 . . . N—N5 is **11 P—Q3**, intending 12 B—B4, although White's problems do not diminish much after 11 . . . B—Q3! 12 N—N5 Q—K2, e.g. 13 N×Bch Q×·N 14 Q—K4 (14 Q—B3?? N—B7) 14 . . . N(1)—B3! with awkward threats.

Such lines may, in White's eyes, detract from the appeal of 6 P—K5!?, but the ending which follows shouldn't, for all the chances are his.

> 11 K—B1   N—B3

12 P—Q4 was a threat, as well as 12 Q—K4.

> 12 Q×Qch   K×Q
> 13 P—QN3!   N—Q6
> 14 P—KR4!   B—K2
> 15 R—R3   N×B
> 16 R×N ±

Korchnoi–Polugayevsky   (1), 1977. (1–0, 60).

B234

> 5 . . .   P—Q3
> 6 B—B2

6 0—0 QN—Q2 (6 . . . B—K2 7 B—B2 P—B4 transposes) 7 B—B2 N—K4?! 8 P—Q4! N×BP (8 . . . N×Nch 9 Q×N P—K4 Pytel) 9 Q—K2 P—Q4 10 P×P B×P 11 N×B Q×N 12 B—N5 N—Q3 14 KR—K1 B—K2 15 B—N3 Q—N4 16 P—Q5! ± Pytel–Szumilo, Polish Ch 1976 (1–0, 30).

> 6 . . .   P—B4
> 7 P—Q4   P×P
> 8 N×P   P—QR3

In many games, 8 . . . B—K2 is played, but that allows the irksome 9 B—R4ch(!), which seems better than the lack of an example would indicate e.g. 9 . . . N(3)—Q2 10 N(4)—N5 or 9 . . . N(1)—Q2 10 N—B6 Q—B2 11 N×B K×N 12 Q—K2 ±.

> 9 P—QN3

After **9 0—0 (9 B—R4ch?** N(1)—Q2 10 N—B6 Q—B2), White may have to worry about 9 . . . Q—B2 e.g. 10 P—QN3? P—QN4 or 10 Q—K2, which commits his queen before he knows the best square for her (d3 is sometimes preferable).

> 9 . . .   B—K2
> 10 0—0   0—0

10 . . . QN—Q2 encourages White to attack by K—R1, P—B4, Q—K2, N—KB3 and P—K5 or P—KB5, the standard plan against Black's same set-up of the Kan/Paulsen Sicilian. See also next note.

> 11 B—N2   N—B3

Again, **11 . . . QN—Q2** can be met by **12 K—R1** or **12 Q—K2** (see the preceding note), or by:
(a) **12 R—K1 R—B1** 13 P—QR4!? N—K4 14 Q—Q2 Q—B2 15 P—B4 N—B3 16 N×N B×N 17 Q—Q3 P—N3 (**17 . . . KR—Q1?** 18 N—Q5!) 18 R—K2 KR—Q1 19 N—Q5!? (**19 R(1)—K1** P—Q4! = —Peters) 19 . . . P×N 20 KP×P N—R4! 21 R×B! ≅ Christiansen–Peters, Phoenix 1976 (0–1, 44).
(b) **12 Q—Q2 R—B1** 13 QR—K1 P—KN3! 14 K—R1 P—K4 15

N(4)–K2 N–B4 16 P–B3 B–B3
17 P–QN4 N(4)–Q2 18 B–Q3
N–R4 (Δ . . . B–KN4!) ∞ R. Rod-
riguez–Dzhindzhihashvili, Haifa
1976.
(c) **12 P–B4 N–B4 13
R–K1 P–K4!?** 14 PxP PxP 15
N–B5 N–K3 16 N–Q5 (Peters).
This looks ±, so 12 . . . R–K1 and
12 . . . R–N1 must be examined.
12 K–R1 (35)

Not **12 P–B4?** NxN 13 QxN
P–Q4; but **12 NxN** BxN 13 Q–K2
is a straightforward alternative.

The diagrammed position has
received a considerable amount of
attention without any clear verdict.
White can attack on the kingside by
a variety of methods (e.g. NxN,
Q–Q3, QR–K1 and N–Q5; P–B4
and P–K5; P–B4, R–B3), whereas
Black's play usually stems from an
early . . . P–QN4 or a timely break
in the centre by, say, . . . R–K1
and . . . P–Q4 or P–K4. Black's
12th is crucial:
(a) **12 . . . Q–B2** 13 P–B4 QR–Q1
14 R–B1 Q–N1? (**14** . . . NxN
15 QxN Q–B4 = –Romanishin)
15 R–B3! P–N3 16 N–Q5! PxN
Romanishin–Petrosian, USSR Ch.
1975, and instead of **17 KPxP?**
which won the game unsoundly,

objectively best was **17 N–B5!!**
PxN 18 KPxQP KR–K1 19
R–N3ch ±± (**19** . . . **K–R1** 20
PxN BxP 21 BxP R–N1 22
Q–R5 or **19** . . . **K–B1** 20 BxP!
B–B1 21 BxP! etc.) –Romanishin.
(b) **12 . . . Q–N1** 13 P–B4 P–QN4?!
14 P–K5! QPxP 15 NxN BxN
16 PxKP N–Q2 17 N–Q5! PxN
18 PxQP B–N2 (**18** . . . **BxP**
19 QxB N–B4 20 B–B5! Q–N2
21 QxQ ± –Bagirov) 19 P–Q6 (In
Informant #22, Bagirov shows that
19 P–K6! leads to a win) 19 . . .
B–N4 20 Q–R5? (And here **20
Q–N4!** is decisive) 20 . . . P–KR3
21 P–KR4 Q–B1! = (Δ 22 . . .
QxB or 22 . . . N–B3! 23 PxN
Q–R6ch!) Polugayevsky–Gheorghiu,
Manila 1976 (1–0, 31, after mis-
takes).
(c) **12 . . . Q–Q2!?** 13 NxN (**13
P–B3!?** P–QN4 14 PxP NxN
15 QxN PxP 16 P–QR3 would be
a typical sequence) 13 . . . BxN
14 Q–Q3 (Δ 15 N–Q5) 14 . . .
P–QN4 15 PxP (Not **15 N–Q5?**
PxN 16 KPxP PxP 17 PxP B–R5!
∓∓) 15 . . . BxNP 16 NxB QxN
17 QR–B1?! (In Reykjavik, 1978,
Smejkal tested Bagirov's suggestion
of **17 Q–Q4** against Petursson:
17 . . . KR–Q1? 18 B–Q3 Q–K4
19 QxQ PxQ 20 KR–Q1. Black
has weak pawns and lost in 39
moves. Better would be **17 . . .
P–QR4** Δ 18 B–Q3 Q–R4 or even
18 . . . Q–N5, although White must
be preferred in view of his bishop
pair.) 17 . . . KR–Q1 18 P–B3
N–Q2! 19 B–N1 B–B3 20 BxB
NxB 21 KR–Q1 K–B1! 22 R–B7
N–K1 = Mecking–Polugayevsky
(12), 1977. White could not make
progress.

(d) **12 . . . P—QN4!?** (Zaitsev) looks wanting after 13 P×P N×N 14 Q×N P×P 15 N×P. 13 . . . N—K4!?
(e) **12 . . . R—N1!?** (Peters), deserves to be tried, to be followed in many cases by . . . P—QN4 and/or . . . Q—Q2.

CONCLUSION: 3 . . . P—QN3 is a topical line with intriguing possibilities. 4 P—KN3 B—N2 5 B—N2 B—K2 seems too slow for 'a White advantage, but 4 P—K4 is crucial and unclear. After 4 . . . B—N2, 5 P—Q3 will usually lead to a line of the Symmetrical English (only minimally ±) and 5 Q—K2 is rather well met by 5 . . . B—N5. So theory presently hinges on an assessment of 5 B—Q3, which tends to lead into highly charged tactical situations. At this point, the audacious moves 5 . . . P—Q4 and 5 . . . P—B4 (especially the latter) look quite as good as the 'solider' 5 . . . P—Q3, which keeps getting mated! Nevertheless, this last move yields a vital, Sicilian-like formation and may yet prove to be a dynamic counter-attacking weapon if the theoretical 'details' can be worked out.

All very exciting!

5 KING'S INDIAN I:
5 N–B3 P–Q3 6 0–0 P–K4 7 P–Q3 N–B3

1 P–QB4	N–KB3
2 N–QB3	P–KN3
3 P–KN3	B–N2
4 B–N2	0–0
5 N–B3	P–Q3
6 0–0	P–K4
7 P–Q3	N–B3 (36)

36
W

In this chapter we scrutinize an important variation which we call, because of its move order, 'King's Indian I'. It may be described as a reversed Closed Sicilian, since Black's knight comes to c6 and both sides fianchetto their king's bishops; but the diagrammed position will not normally arise after 1 P–QB4 P–K4 2 N–QB3 N–QB3 3 P–KN3 P–KN3 for reasons described in the Closed English, Chapter 1 of *English I*.

An alternate sequence which legitimately (i.e. without inferior moves) leads to this chapter is 1 P–QB4 P–K4 2 N–QB3 N–KB3 3 N–B3 N–B3   4 P–Q3 P–Q3 5 P–KN3 P–KN3 6 B–N2 B–N2 7 0–0 0–0.

Facing a King's Indian Defence formation poses a dilemma for the player of 1 P–QB4 who doesn't like to play 2 P–Q4 or 3 P–Q4. The order of moves presented here might be used by those who are willing to play the 'Classical Fianchetto' system as White, but prefer not to deal with the ever-popular Panno and Simagin variations (otherwise 5 P–Q4 should be considered). After 6 0–0 P–K4, White can play 7 P–Q4 and his threat to Black's KP eliminates the latter possibilities (on 7 . . . N–B3, 8 P–Q5 is the Uhlmann Variation of the K.I.D., held to be somewhat in White's favour).

Yet 5 N–B3 introduces further questions about move order. For one thing, developing the knight to f3 allows 5 . . . P–Q4 6 Px P Nx P 7 0–0 N–QB3 or 5 . . . N–B3 6 0–0 P–Q4, introducing the Grünfeld-related positions discussed in Chapter 13, D2. On e.g. 8 P–Q4 N–N3 (Neo–Grünfeld), Black's piece play is pitted against White's potentially strong centre, and theory has pronounced no clear verdict.

The second question deserves some analysis, for it remains within the scope of the English 'proper'. After the move 6 0–0, Black can forego 6 . . . **P–K4** for the immediate 6 . . . **N–B3**. Then **7 P–Q4** allows 7 . . . **P–QR3** (Panno), 7 . . . **B–N5** (Simagin), or 7 . . . **R–N1** (a currently popular Panno sub-variant). Against 6 . . . N–B3, White could choose **7 R–N1!?**, although 7 . . . **B–B4!?** 8 P–Q3 Q–Q2 may be unappealing to him. Moreover, the sequence 7 R–N1 **P–K4** 8 P–QN4? (8 P–Q3) is incautious: 8 . . . P–K5! 9 N–K1 B–B4 10 P–Q3 P–Q4! 11 P–N5 N–K2 12 BP×P N(2)×P 13 B–N2 N×N 14 B×N R–K1 ∓ Petrosian-Tal, Curaçao 1962.

So White may wish to respond to 6 . . . N–B3 by **7 P–Q3**, when 7 . . . P–K4 transposes to this chapter. Black's main alternative to 7 . . . P–K4 in that case is Boleslavky's 7 . . . **N–KR4!?**, the clever point of which is demonstrated in Andersson-Tal, Sochi 1973: 8 **R–N1 (?)** P–B4! 9 B–Q2 (Due to Black's 8th, 9 P–QN4?? drops a knight; but now Tal is able to transpose into main line A below with White having played the passive B–Q2 instead of B–QN2 or B–QR3:) 9 . . . P–B5 10 P–QN4 P–K4 11 Q–N3 B–N5 12 N–K4 K–R1 (or 12 . . . B×N △ . . . N–Q5) 13 P–N5 N–Q5 14 N×N P×N 15 QR–K1 B–K4 16 B–N4 P–N3. Black is indisputably better (though ½–½, 34).

Most masters feel that the drawback to 7 . . . N–KR4 is 8 **P–Q4!**, advancing in the 'neglected' centre. Although this has received no theoretical attention, it must be considered critical. The natural move, 8 . . . **P–K4**, can be met by 9 P–Q5 N–K2 10 P–K4, when 10 . . . **P–KB4** 11 P×P P×P 12 N–N5 N–KB3 13 P–B4 P–K5 14 P–KR3!? (or 14 B–K3 P–KR3 15 N–R3 △ N–B2) 14 . . . P–KR3 15 N–K6 is promising for White, and 10 . . . **P–KR3?** 11 N–K1! △ N–Q3 is still worse for the second player, who can no longer get in . . . P–KB4 quickly. But Black should not despair of finding an answer to 8 P–Q4; among other possibilities is 8 . . . **P–B4!?** 9 P–Q5 N–K4 10 N×N P×N, a Leningrad Dutch (!) where Black has gained the move . . . N–KR4 at the expense of White's P–Q3–Q4. Nevertheless, this may not be a desirable tempo against White's 11 P–B5. Also 8 . . . **P–B4!?** 9 P–Q5 N–R4, even though it puts two knights on the rim, creates interesting problems.

Returning to the main line (6 . . . **P–K4**), **7 P–Q3** is still less popular than **7 P–Q4** (the King's Indian Defence) in international chess, partly because Black may reply with moves like 7 . . . **P–B3** and 7 . . . **R–K1**, which (along with 7 . . . **QN–Q2**, 7 . . . **N–KR4**, etc.) are the subject of Chapter 6.

The position of the diagram, all these preliminaries notwithstanding, crops up often. White has gained a tempo on a standard Black position from the Closed Sicilian, and, considering the fine record of the Black side of that opening, one might expect things to be rather easy for the first player here. However, the particular formation White has 'chosen', with his knight on f3, is hardly one of the more aggressive Black schemas, and in fact the second player has scored nowhere near so well with a knight on f6 as in those lines with . . . KN—K2. White's advantage here, if he has any, is based on his extra tempo; consequently, forthright play is required:

8 R—N1

Surely the most accurate move, hurrying to gain ground on the queenside. White rarely plays otherwise. The game Korchmar—Maresov, USSR 1968, featured **8 B—Q2** and, while it does not indicate the value of 8 B—Q2, we witness the actualization of a White idea Black seldom allows in these variations: 8 . . . N—Q5 (Obviously the 'normal' 8 . . . B—Q2, 8 . . . R—K1, and 8 . . . P—KR3(!) cannot be bad here.) 9 R—N1 N×Nch (obligingly increasing the scope of White's KB. 9 . . . P—B3!) 10 B×N B—R6!? 11 B×P! B×R 12 K×B!? R—N1 13 B—N2 (White has control over the light squares, a target in the enemy QRP, and two bishops versus Black's lone bad one; in short, good value for the exchange.) 13 . . . Q—Q2 14 P—QN4 P—B3 15 Q—R4 KR—B1 16 R—N3 R—B2 17 P—N5! P—B4. After great complications, and with some luck, White won.

Also virtually unanalyzed is **8 P—QR3**, but that move is more significant, because in the line 1 P—QB4 P—K4 2 N—QB3 N—KB3 3 N—B3 N—B3 4 P—QR3 (Chapter 8, D), Black's 4 . . . P—KN3 will sometimes lead, via 5 P—KN3

B—N2 6 B—N2 0—0 7 0—0 P—Q3 8 P—Q3, to this position. Comparing Black's defensive methods below (A through G), one finds that 8 P—QR3 works about as well as 8 R—N1 against the moves 8 . . . N—Q5, 8 . . . B—B4, and 8 . . . R—K1, but not so well (often losing a tempo) against 8 . . . B—Q2, 8 . . . N—KR4 (!), or simply 8 . . . P—KR3 △ . . . B—K3, when White's rook is exposed on the long diagonal and a3 will not be available for the bishop until P—QR4 is played. See also Chapter 8, D2.

If one were to recommend an irregular variation here, it would not be 8 B—Q2 or 8 P—QR3, but something like **8 B—N5 P—KR3 9 B×N B×B 10 R—N1**, emphasizing control of the central light squares (compare G63), or **8 N—K1!?**, intending to meet a later . . . P—KB4 with P—KB4 and meanwhile planning N—B2 (supporting P—QN4) and considering a further knight's trek, perhaps to d5 via e3 or b4. 8 N—K1 B—K3 9 B—N5 (or 9 N—Q5) is the consistent follow-up.

After 8 R—N1, Black has a whole range of defensive methods. Since all of these can be used with or without 8 . . . P—QR4 9 P—QR3 thrown in, I have devoted sections A through F to lines without 8 . . . P—QR4 and section G to all variations with that insertion (e.g. 8 . . . P—QR4 9 P—QR3 N—KR4; 9 . . . B—Q2, etc.):

A 8 . . . N—KR4
B 8 . . . B—Q2
C 8 . . . B—B4
D 8 . . . P—KR3
E 8 . . . N—Q5

F 8 . . . R—K1
G 8 . . . P—QR4

A
    8 . . .   **N—KR4**
Closely resembling the Closed Sicilian (e.g. the well-known encounters Spassky—Petrosian (17), 1966 and Spassky—Geller (2), 1968).
   9 P—QN4   P—B4 (37)

37
W

    10 N—Q5
10 B—Q2? P—B5 transposes to Andersson—Tal from the chapter introduction.
   The main alternative to the text is 10 P—N5 N—K2, e.g.
(a) **11 P—K3** (△ 11 . . . P—K5 12 N—Q4) 11 . . . P—KR3 12 N—K1 K—R2 13 B—Q2 (△ P—B4) 13 . . . P—B5! 14 N—B2 P—R3! ∓ Wade—Uhlmann, Hastings 1972/3. The move P—K3 is notoriously dangerous in this kind of position and usually bad. A string of pawns from e2 to c4 and a knight on c3 conspire to make most king-side pawn demonstrations on Black's part futile; but once P—K3 and . . . P—B5 are played, White's f3 becomes weak and moves like . . . P—KN4—N5 or . . . B—N5 force White to capure on f4. Then Black's pieces spring to life. For this reason, P—K3 is usually best if

White can follow up with P—KB4 or effective central action.
   Returning to 10 P—N5 N—K2, White might also contemplate the audacious
(b) **11 P—B5!?** (△ 11 . . . P—K5 12 P×P B×N 13 Q—N3ch) 11 . . . **P×P** 12 Q—N3ch K—R1 13 N—N5 Q—K1 14 N—Q5 etc.; probably no one has played thus because of 11 . . . P—Q4, yet 12 P—Q4 P—K5 13 N—K5 △ 13 . . . P—B5 14 P—B6! is certainly not clear. Less incisive was
(c) **11 Q—N3 K—R1** 12 B—QR3 P—QR3! 13 P—B5 P—Q4 14 P—B6?! P×NP 15 P×P B×P 16 B—B5 P—B3 17 P—K4 P—Q5 ∓ Thorvaldson—Matulović, Helsinki 1972. Finally,
(d) **11 Q—B2!?** P—B3? 12 P×P P×P 13 B—N5! is very awkward for Black: 13 . . . N—B3 (13 . . . **B—B3** 14 B×B and 15 P—B5!; 13 . . . **P—KR3** 14 B×N Q×B 15 N—KR4 Q—K1 16 N—N5!) 14 P—B5 P—KR3 15 P×P Q×P 16 B—K3 N(3)—Q4 17 B—Q2 N×N 18 B×N N—Q4? 19 B×P! ±± Watson—Roy, Phoenix 1976. 11 . . . **P—B5!** is preferable (△ 12 N—K4? P—KR3); White should reply 12 P—QR4 with an interesting fight in store.
    10 . . .   P—KR3(?!)
Never queried, as far as I know, but . . . P—KR3 expends a tempo, both reducing the scope of Black's KB (access to h6 can be handy) and leaving the KNP en prise in some variations (e.g. in the note to 12 . . . P—B5). A more enterprising try is **10 . . . P—B5!**, as played in Watson—Agrachov, Columbus 1977. Then White couldn't decide on **11 N—Q2**

N–Q5!? (△ 12 P–N5 B–N5 or
12 P–K3 N–K3!?) and selected
11 P–N5 N–K2 12 B–Q2 (△ 13
B–R5. Here **12 N–Q2!? N–B4?**
13 N–K4 N–Q5 14 P–K3 P–B6
15 Px N Px B 16 R–K1 Malpert-
Gogol, Columbus 1977, was better
for White, but 12 . . . K–R1! improves.) 12 . . . Nx N 13 Px N
(White has several positional assets,
but he must be careful, as the game
illustrates:) 13 . . . B–N5 15 Q–B2
Q–Q2 15 KR–B1 QR–B1 16
R–N4 B–R3! 17 R–R4!? Qx P
18 R–R5 Q–Q2?! (18 . . . Q–N3!)
19 Rx P N–B3 20 Q–B4 Bx N
21 Px B! P–QN4! 22 Q–N3 P–N4
23 R–N7 P–KN5 24 Qx NP? ∓
½–½ (24 Q–Q1! ±). 10 . . . P–B5!
seems at any rate Black's most
practical choice.
   11 P–N5   N–K2
   12 Q–B2
Universally recommended. Spir-
idinov-Bobekov, Bulgarian Ch 1965
saw the tame **12 Nx Nch?! Qx N**
13 N–Q2 N–B3 14 P–QR4 P–N4
15 P--K3 (see note (a) to 10 N–Q5)
15 . . . K–R1 16 P–R5 R–QN1
17 R–K1 Q–B2 18 B–QR3
R–N1! 19 P–N6 RPx P 20 Px P
P–B4 21 P–Q4 R–R1 ∓.
   12 . . .   P–B5
(a) **12 . . . B–K3?** 13 Nx Nch Qx N
14 N–R4 (Shatskes)
(b) **12 . . . P–N4** 13 B–Q2 N–N3
14 P–B5!; or here 13 . . . P–N5
14 N–R4 K–R2 15 KR–B1
(Shatskes), when the move P–B5
looms over the Black queenside.
(c) **12 . . . Nx N** 13 Px N P–B5
14 R–N4 prepares the assault
on Black's QBP. White will continue with R–QB4, P–QR4,

B–QR3, KR–B1 and perhaps N–
Q2–K4. Black's usual procedure in
such a position begins with . . .
R–B2 and . . . N–K1, when White
has the upper hand but has to do a
lot of shifting to make progress.
   13 N–Q2!
'±' (Taimanov). Indeed, 13 . . .
B–N5 14 Nx Nch and 15 Bx P leads
to the advantage. **13 . . . N–B4!?** is
more troublesome, e.g. 14 P–K3
P–N4! (**14** . . . Px KP 15 Px P
P–B3 16 Px P Px P 17 N–N3!)
15 N–K4 B–K3!? △ 16 P–N4
N–R5 17 Px N P–B6 18 B–R1
B–R6, although White will probably
be able to ward off such an attack.
So '±' seems fair, also as a general
assessment of 8 . . . N–KR4.

B
   8 . . .   **B–Q2**
One of the oldest moves, △ . . .
Q–B1 and . . . B–R6.
   9 P–QN4
A patient player might try **9
P–KR3**, preventing . . . Q–B1 and
. . . B–R6. If Black should advance
his KNP and KRP, then K–R2 and
N–KN1! is a good defensive set-up.
Of course the text is more direct.
   9 . . .   **Q–B1**
   10 P–N5   N–K2
Taimanov and Shatskes criticize
10 . . . N–Q1, since after 11 N–Q5
Nx N 12 Px N, the knight on d8 is
hemmed in and will take some time
to reroute. This is a common 'Closed
English' (2 . . . N–QB3–Chapter 1)
theme.
   11 R–K1
Saving the bishop; but other
moves are not bad, e.g. **11 P–B5!?**
B–R6 12 B–R3 or **11 P–QR4**

B—R6   12 B—R3 Bx B   13 Kx B
Q—K3 (stopping 14 Nx P) 14 Q—N3
P—KR3 (**14 . . . P—N3!**—Taimanov;
White might still play 15 N—N5
and hope for advantage, e.g. **15 . . .
Q—B4 16 B—B1!** or **15 . . . Q—Q2
16 P—B4! ±**)   15 P—B5 P—Q4
('**? . . . 15 . . . N—K1!**'—Keene; then
16 P—R5 ±)   16 P—B6! ± Eising-
Hartoch, Arnhem 1966 (1-0, 47).

    11 . . .   B—R6
    12 B—R1   P—KR3
    Lest 13 N—N5.
    13 Q—B2
A good example of this variation
was A. Hasin-Lanka, USSR 1977:
13 P—QR4 N—R4?! (**13 . . . N—N5**
is better, because after . . . P—KB4,
the thrust . . . P—K5 has more
chance of succeeding, and because
. . . P—KR4—R5 remains an option
after, say, . . . R—B2 and . . . B—B3.)
14 B—R3 P—KB4? (And here 14 . . .
P—N3 keeps the damage down.)
15 P—B5! Q—Q2 16 Px P? (Playing
the White pieces in such a system
can be frustrating; one's advantages,
even large ones, tend to disappear
in one move. Here **16 N—Q2!** and
if **16 . . . P—Q4**, 17 P—B6 wreaks
havoc on the queenside, or **16 . . .
QR—N1** 17 Px P Px P 18 N—B4 ±
—analysis by Tukmakov) 16 . . .
Px P   17 N—Q2 K—R2   18 N—B4
P—K5! 19 R—B1 QR—B1! ≅ (0-1,
35).

    13 . . .   N—N5
Black might consider preserving
his control over d5 a move or two
longer, e.g. 13 . . . Q—K3!?.

    14 N—Q5   Nx N
Shatskes thinks 14 . . . Q—Q2!
better, yet White could play 15
P—R4 ± or 15 N—Q2 ∆ 16 Nx Nch

or 16 P—B5. Taimanov mentions
15 B—Q2 followed by KR—B1 and
B—K1 =/∞. The reason that even
lackadaisical moves such as 15
P—R4 and 15 B—Q2 are feasible is
simply that Black's 'assault' on the
king's wing is at best difficult to
coordinate.

    14 . . . Nx N follows Shatskes-
Muchnik, Moscow 1966: 15 Px N
P—KB4 16 B—Q2 P—B5 17 KR—B1
R—B2 18 R—N4! (Both preparing
to triple on the file and defending
along the fourth rank.) 18 . . . N—B3
19 R—B4 N—K1 20 P—QR4 ±. (38)

    C
    8 . . .   B—B4
Logical, although the sequence
8 . . . P—QR4 9 P—QR3 usually
precedes . . . B—B4 (see G3). Since
Black intends . . . B—R6, he would
rather have his queen on d7 than c8.
But after 8 . . . **B—K3** 9 P—QN4
Q—Q2 10 N—KN5, the bishop
cannot elude exchange for a knight,
and 8 . . . **B—N5** 9 P—KR3 doesn't
help matters. Hence 8 . . . B—B4.

    9 P—QN4
The theoretical problem with
8 . . . B—B4 is
(a) **9 P—K4!?** B—N5 (**9 . . . B—K3**
10 N—Q5 P—KR3 11 P—QN4

K–R2–*11* . . . *Q–Q2? 12 B*×*P!*–12
P–N5 N–K2 13 R–K1 Δ P–Q4–
Shatskes) 10 P–KR3 B×N 11
B×B N–Q5 12 B–N2 P–B3 13
P–QN4 with the bishop pair and
some chances on both wings. Nevertheless, Black's pieces are well-
posted and his position is free of
weaknesses.

(b) **9 B–N5!?** could be considered,
working directly for the control of
e4 and d5, and exploiting the fact
that . . . B–B4 renders . . . P–KB4
more difficult to achieve. The
position after 9 . . . P–KR3 10 B×N
B×B 11 N–Q2 (or 11 P–QN4) can
be considered 'semi-closed,' so that
knights are probably quite as good
as the bishops e.g. 11 . . . Q–Q2 12
N–Q5 B–N2 (12 . . . B–Q1!?) 13
P–QN4 QR–K1?! 14 P–N5 N–Q1
15 Q–R4 P–QB3 (15 . . . P–QR3
16 Q–R5) 16 P×P P×P 17 N–N4
etc. Compare G3, note '(b)': here
Black suffers some discomfiture
from his QRP, there from White's
possession of the QR file.

The text move is in any case
significant, because in any line
where White tries R–QN1 before
P–Q3, Black can play . . . B–B4
(with tempo) and . . . Q–Q2. In
the chapter introduction, the
position before us could be reached
by 7 R–N1 N–B3 8 P–QN4 B–B4
9 P–Q3.

    9 . . .   **Q–Q2**
    10 R–K1

10 N–KN5 is safe: 10 . . . P–KR3
11 N(5)–K4 N×N 12 P×N B–R6
(12 . . . B–K3!?) 13 B×B Q×B
14 N–Q5 N–Q5 ('='–Taimanov)
15 P–N5 K–R2 16 P–K3 N–K3
17 P–B3! **P–QR3** 18 R–B2 P–N3

19 Q–B1 ('±±'–Keene; consider
Black's bishop!) Stein–Vukić,
Sarajevo 1967 (1–0, 42). Shatskes
has the best idea for Black: **17** . . .
P–KB4 18 P×P P×P 19 Q–B2
R–B2 'approximately equal.'
    10 . . .   **B–R6**
11 B–R1 P–KR3 12 P–N5 N–K2
(Again, **12** . . . N–Q1 13 N–Q5
N×N 14 P×N P–KB4 15 R–N4
P–QR4 16 R–QB4 R–B2 17 Q–B2
Udovčić–Damjanović, Yugoslav Ch
1961, restricted Black's elbowroom;
but **12** . . . N–Q5 13 N–Q2 P–B3
is only slightly worse for him.) 13
P–Q4 Q–K3 14 P×P P×P 15
N–Q2 B–B4!? (15 . . . QR–N1!?)
16 P–K4 B–N5 17 B–B3 B×B
18 Q×B P–B3 19 B–R3 ± Dorf-
man–Dvoretsky, USSR Ch 1975.
White is more active.

D
    8 . . .   **P–KR3**
A cautious move, securing the
ideal e6 for Black's QB and preventing B–KN5. . . . P–KR3 is nowa-
days customarily prefaced by 8 . . .
P–QR4 9 P–QR3.
    9 P–QN4   **B–K3**
    10 P–N5
This seems most accurate.
Shatskes and Taimanov criticize
10 P–N5 as 'too straightforward,'
and give instead **10 N–Q2! Q–B1**
11 P–N5 N–K2 12 R–K1 N–R2
13 B–QR3 P–KB4 14 P–B5
P–K5 15 Q–B2 P–Q4 16 P–B6!
Reischenberger–Maricetti, corres
1964, when White was swarming
over the queenside. Against 10
N–Q2, **10** . . . P–Q4 is unwise due
to 11 P–N5 N–K2 12 B–QR3
(impossible had 8 . . . P–QR4

9 P—QR3 been inserted—see G4); and **10 . . . Q—Q2(!)** 11 P—N5 N—Q1 is supposed to be inferior because Black's knight is on the unpromising d8. But, as we shall see often in this chapter, White's knight is itself not very well-placed on d2; it was better off on f3 watching over the centre and helping to prepare P—Q4 or P—B5. After 11 . . . N—Q1, **12 R—K1** can be met by 12 . . . **P—B3** 13 N(2)—K4 N—K1, or by the light-hearted **12 . . . B—R6** 13 B—R1 N—N5 e.g. 14 N—Q5 P—KB4 15 B—R3 N—K3 16 P—K3 R—B2 ∞ Watson–Harari, San Francisco 1976 (30/30 game). And **12 N—Q5** (Δ 12 . . . B—R6 13 N×Nch B×N 14 N—K4 B—N2 15 B×RP ±±) doesn't achieve much against 12 . . . N×N 13 P×N B—R6 e.g. 14 B×B Q×B 15 Q—B2 Q—Q2 16 P—QR4 P—KB4 Δ . . . R—B2, . . . P—N3, . . . N—N2—B4.

10 . . .   N—K2 (39)

39
W

11 P—QR4

Preparing 12 B—QR3. Instead:
(a) **11 B—QR3** runs up against the standard rejoinder 11 . . . P—QR3!.
(b) **11 P—B5!?** is enticing: 11 . . . P×P 12 B—K3 (12 N×P? N(3)—Q4), but Black has 12 . . . P—K5! (not 12 . . . Q—Q3? 13 Q—B1!) 13 P×P

P—N3 =.
(c) **11 Q—B2?!** is not forceful enough. Black's chances in this line are wonderfully demonstrated by Keene–Stein, Hastings 1967/8: 11 . . . Q—Q2 12 R—K1 (12 R—Q1—Keene) 12 . . . B—R6 13 B—R1 N—N5 14 N—Q2 QR—N1 15 N—Q5 N×N 16 P×N (16 B×N ⩲) 16 . . . P—KB4 17 R—N4 QR—K1 18 N—B3 N—N3! 19 P—K4 P—B5 20 B—QN2 N—N5 21 R—B4 R—K2 22 P—R4 R(2)—B2 23 Q—K2 Q—Q1! (Δ . . . P—B3, . . . Q—N3) 24 R—B2 P—KR4 25 B—B1 B—R3 26 B—QN2 P×P 27 RP×P P—R5! 28 B—B1 P×P 29 P×P B×B 30 R(1)×B P—QR3! (Δ . . . Q—N1—R2ch) 31 N—R2 N×N 32 K×N Q—N4! 33 K×B R—R2ch 34 K—N2 Q—R3 0—1. A classic treatment!

11 . . .   Q—B1?!

There is no need to protect the QNP, and Black's intended . . . N—Q2 is too passive. 11 . . . Q—Q2 should be preferred, at least preventing what happens in the text (i.e. the knight on e7 would be protected). The **12 P—B5!?** P×P 13 Q—B2 is obscure (here 13 N×P?! Q—Q5 14 B—N2 Q×N(4) 15 N—K4 fails to 15 . . . Q×B!). The reliable answer to 11 . . . Q—Q2 is **12 R—K1**, e.g. 12 . . . B—R6 13 B—R1 N—N5 14 B—R3 P—N3 15 P—Q4 ±.

12 B—QR3   N—Q2

Defending against the duel threats of 13 N×P! and 13 P—B5.

13 N—Q2   R—N1

14 N—Q5 R—K1 15 N—K4! P—KB4 16 N(4)—B3 K—R2 17 P—R5 B—B2 18 N×N R×N 19 P—N6! (The decisive thrust in a perfectly-

timed assault. White's play could
hardly have been more thematic.)
19 ... RPxP 20 PxP R—R1 (20 ...
NxP 21 RxN! ±) 21 N—N5 NxP
22 NxQP Q—K3 (On 22 ... PxN,
23 BxQP wins material and retains
pressure.) 23 Q—B1 PxN 24 RxN ±
Miles—Belyavsky, Hastings 1974/5
(1-0, 58).

E

8 ...   N—Q5 (40)
40
W

Smyslov's invention. Rather than
watch another competition between
king- and queenside operations.
Black makes his move in the centre,
E1 9 NxN
E2 9 P—QN4
Emma—Smyslov, Mar del Plata
1966 continued 9 N—K1?! P—B3
10 P—QN4 P—Q4! 11 P—N5 PxBP
12 NPxP NxP 13 PxP (13
B—QR3!?) 13 ... QxQ 14 NxQ
N—QR4 15 N—K3 B—K3 16 N—Q3
NxP ∓.

E1
        9 NxN
This capture has a bad reputation,
but at least creates an imbalance.
9 ...   PxN
10 N—N5   N—N5!
10 ... N—K1 11 P—K3 PxP

12 BxKP P—QR3 13 N—B3 (or 13
N—R7!—Gheorghiu) 13 ... N—B3
14 P—KR3 P—B3 15 Q—Q2 B—K3
16 N—K2 P—Q4 17 N—Q4 ± Botvinnik—Gheorghiu, Monaco 1968.
    11 P—QN4
    11 P—KR3 P—QB3! 12 N—R3
(12 PxN PxN 13 PxP Q—N3 ∓—
Smyslov) 12 ... N—R3 13 N—B2
N—B4   14 P—QN4 P—QR3   15
P—QR4 R—K1 16 R—K1 B—K3
17 P—N5 RPxP 18 RPxP Q—Q2
19 PxP PxP 20 N—N4 N—K2
21 K—R2 R—R4! ∓ Benko—Smyslov,
Tel Aviv 1964. The epitome of
efficient Black play.
    11 ...   P—QR3
    11 ... P—QR4!? (Taimanov)
threatens 12 ... P—B3 and 13 ...
PxP. 12 Q—R4!? ∞ looks like the
most interesting answer.
    12 N—R3   R—N1
    12 ... R—K1 13 N—B2
P—QB4!? 14 PxP? (simply 14
P—KR3 N—R3 15 B—B4 ±) 14 ...
PxP 15 BxP R—N1 16 BxB
NxBP! 17 RxR (17 RxN RxR
∆ ... B—R3) 17 ... NxQ 18
RxN Q—B2 19 B—B4 B—K4 20
BxB QxB 21 R—R8 K—B1 22
R—N1 QxKP Vooremaa—N. Popov,
USSR Otborchnii 1974; Black has
too much pressure in the neighbour-
hood of White's king (0-1, 37).
    13 N—B2   P—QB4
White was threatening 14 P—KR3
and 15 NxQP!. Taimanov—Honfi,
Bucharest 1973 continued (after
13 ... P—QB4): 14 P—KR3 N—K4
(14 ... N—R3 15 PxP PxP 16
B—B4) 15 P—B4 N—Q2 16 P—K3!
PxKP 17 BxKP P—QN4?! (17 ...
P—N3—Gheorghiu) 18 P—Q4!?
PxBP (18 ... N—N3 19 PxNP

N–B5 ∞–Taimanov) 19 QP× P P× P
20 P× P ±.

E2

9 P–QN4   N× Nch(?)

Somewhat insipid, not to mention time-consuming. The natural 9 . . . P–B3 (or 9 . . . P–QR3 10 P–QR4 P–B3) would lead to complex positions where Black pits his central prospects against White's plans of queenside intrusion. Compare G5 below. Even 9 . . . R–K1 is preferable.

10 B× N   B–R6

10 . . . P–QR3   11 P–QR4 R–K1   12 P–N5 P× P   13 RP× P R–N1   14 Q–B2 B–R6   15 R–Q1 Q–Q2   16 R–R1! Ignatiev–Yudovich, Moscow 1965, gives an ideal English position: unobstructed diagonals towards the queenside, occupation of the open QR file (with a point of entry at a7), and control of the long white diagonal.

11 R–K1   Q–B1

Bruntrop–Mohring, East Germany 1965. Here Shatskes suggests 12 P–N5 N–N5(?!)   13 N–Q5 Q–Q2   14 Q–B2 P–KB4   15 P–B5! when White holds the reins.

F

8 . . .   R–K1

Though this may not be as effective here as after 8 . . . P–QR4 9 P–QR3, there is one point in its favour: White cannot use the QR file. A game of the author's continued 9 N–Q2 (9 P–QN4 P–K5!) 9 . . . B–K3 10 N–Q5 (10 P–QN4 P–Q4?!   11 P–N5 N–K2   12 B–QR3 ±, but 10 . . . P–QR3! 11 P–QR4 P–Q4 =)   10 . . .

Q–Q2?! (I feared 10 . . . B× N! 11 P× B N–K2 △ . . . P–B3 =) 11 N× Nch B× N   12 N–K4 B–N2 13 N–N5 B–B4   14 P–K4 B–N5 15 P–B3 B–K3   16 N× B ±. Best after 9 N–Q2 is 9 . . . B–N5!, as in the Petrosian–Keres game of G6.

For 9 B–N5!?, compare C, G3, and G6.

CONCLUSION: Without the insertion of 8 . . . P–QR4 9 P–QR3, all of Black's (eighth) moves seem about equally playable; and all of them seem to lead, with precise play, to some advantage for White. 8 . . . N–Q5 or 8 . . . R–K1 (still experimental) probably holds the balance better than, say, 8 . . . P–KR3 or 8 . . . B–Q2.

G

8 . . .   P–QR4

9 P–QR3

The inclusion of . . . P–QR4 makes a big difference in the analysis of:

G1 9 . . . N–KR4
G2 9 . . . B–Q2
G3 9 . . . B–B4
G4 9 . . . P–KR3
G5 9 . . . N–Q5
G6 9 . . . R–K1

Gligorić once played: (a) 9 . . . N–K1 versus Botvinnik (Hastings, 1961–2), but the move has not caught on, for it reduces Black's influence over key central squares (e5,d4) solely for the sake of . . . P–KB4, not always a productive move anyway. On the other hand, the knight on e8 does guard some sensitive spots like c7 and d6: 10 P–QN4 P× P 11 P× P P–B4   12 P–N5 (or 12 N–Q5)

12 ... N−K2 13 N−K1 (13 B−N2
Δ R−R1, or 13 Q−N3 Δ B−QR3, is
more assertive.) 13 ... P−B4!? (13
... P−R3) 14 B−N5 P−R3 15
Bx N Qx B 16 N−Q5 Q−Q1 17
R−R1 Rx R 18 Qx R B−K3 19
Q−R7 R−B2, slightly ± (½−½,
56).
(b) 9 ... R−N1 is a curious idea
which appeared in Schinzel-Krogius,
England 1976: 10 P−QN4 Px P
11 Px P P−N3 (The point: Black
wishes to blockade the queenside.)
12 N−K1 (Here 12 P−N5 N−K2−
12 ... N−QR4 13 B−QR3 Δ B−N4
∞−13 B−N2 and 14 R−R1 could
be tried.) 12 ... N−K2 13 B−N5
('!?'−Schinzel) 13 ... P−R3 14
Bx N Bx B 15 N−B2 P−R4?!
(Black should shift his forces to
the queenside.) 16 P−N5 B−K3
17 N−N4 Q−Q2 18 R−R1 P−R5
19 R−R7 ±.

G1

    9 ...   **N−KR4**
10 P−QN4   Px P
11 Px P   P−B4
12 P−N5

Or 12 N−Q5 P−KR3 13 P−N5
N−K2 14 Q−B2; compare the next
note, (b).

    12 ...   N−K2 (41)

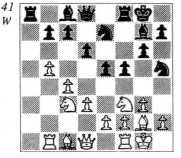

41
W

13 Q−N3!?
(a) **13 Q−B2** P−R3 (**13 ... P−B5!**
14 P−K3?!*−as in A, White should
try to avoid P−K3 unless it breaks
up the centre immediately*−14 ...
B−N5! 15 N−K4 Q−Q2 with a
dangerous attack, Petrosian-Vasi-
ukov, Moscow 1956) 14 B−N2
B−K3 15 R−R1 Q−Q2 16 N−Q2
P−B3 17 R−R4 KR−B1! 18
R(1)−R1 R(R)−N1! = Shatskes-
Seredenko, USSR Master Title
Match 1967.
(b) **13 N−Q5** Nx N 14 Px N P−B5
15 Q−B2 B−N5 16 B−Q2 (**16
B−N2!** Δ R−R1−Shatskes) 16 ...
P−N3 17 KR−B1 R−B2 ∞ Shatskes-
Vasyukov, Moscow 1961.
(c) **13 B−N2** deserves a try, since it
prepares R−R1 and keeps options
open.

    13 ...   K−R1
    14 B−N2   P−KR3
    14 ... P−B5 (Petrosian). Then
15 KR−Q1 Δ P−Q4?
    15 R−R1   R−QN1
16 N−Q5 (or the immediate
16 R−R7, preserving the possibility
of a later N−K4) 16 ... P−B5 17
R−R7 K−R2 (Evidently not liking,
say, **17 ... B−N5** 18 Nx N Qx N
19 N−R4!; nevertheless, **17 ...
P−N4** might have been more
direct in this regard.) 18 Q−R2
B−N5 19 R−K1! N−B4 (White's
19th, among other things, pre-
pared **20 N−Q2**, which is now met
by 20 ... Px P 21 RPx P N(B)x P!.)
20 P−B5 Bx N (Petrosian indicates
a preference for **20 ... QPx P** 21
Nx P Bx N 22 Bx B Px P 23 RPx P
N−Q3 ±.) 21 Px B! (21 Bx B
Q−N4!) 21 ... QPx P 22 Q−B4
N−Q5 (**22 ... Q−Q3** allows

23 P–N4, since the queen does not reach g5.) 23 B×N KP×B 24 B–R3! (24 Q×BP? R–B4) 24 . . . P×P 25 RP×P Q–N4 26 B–N2 R(B)–K1 27 R×R R×R 28 P–B4 R–K8 ch 29 K–R2 Q–N5 30 R–R8 Q–K7! 31 N–B3? (Time pressure must be setting in. **31 R–R2**– Petrosian–maintains a winning position.) 31 . . . Q–K3? (One good turn deserves another. Black overlooked the brilliant **31 . . . N–B3!!**, stopping mate and answering 32 N×Q with 32 . . . N–N5ch and a draw by perpetual check!) 32 B–Q5 Q–K2 33 B–N8ch K–R1 34 B–R7ch 1–0 Andersson–Smejkal, Amsterdam 1973. A superb encounter.

G2

9 . . .   **B–Q2(?)**

Not very suitable here due to the imminent opening of the QR file.

10 P–QN4   P×P
11 P×P   Q–B1
12 B–N5!

To the point; although, as in B above
(a) **12 R–K1 B–R6** 13 B–R1 P–R3 14 P–N5 may be tried, or
(b) **12 P–N5 N–K2** 13 P–B5! P×P 14 N×P B–K3 15 N–R4 B–R7 16 R–R1 B–Q4 17 B–N2 (at least ±) Naranja-Reshevsky, Palma de Mallorca 1970 (1–0, 35).

12 . . .   B–R6
13 B×N
13 B×B?! Q×B 14 B×N B×B 15 P–N5 N–Q5 16 P–K3 R–R6! ∞ was less convincing in Hübner-Uitumen, Palma de Mallorca 1970.

13 . . .   B×B(3)

14 N–Q5

'My plan is to drive Black's KB out of play long enough for me to get control of the QR file.' (Reshevsky)

14 . . .   B–Q1
15 R–R1

Or **15 B×B Q×B** 16 R–R1 R×R 17 Q×R Q–B1? (17 . . . P–KN4) 18 P–N5 N–N1 19 Q–R8 △ R–R1–R7 ±± Andersson-Westerinen, Geneva 1977.

15 . . .   B×B
16 K×B   R–N1
17 P–N5 N–K2 18 N–B3! (Avoiding exchanges. The problem before White now is not the threat of losing, but how to create winning chances—a situation Reshevsky relishes.) 18 . . . N–B4 19 R–R4 N–N2 20 Q–Q2 N–K3 21 Q–R6 ('Forcing black to think about White's possible P–R4–R5'– Reshevsky) 21 . . . B–B3 22 N–Q5 Q–Q1 (22 . . . B–N2!?) 23 N×Bch Q×N 24 R–R7 Reshevsky-Dake, Lone Pine 1977. Endings with this pawn structure and White in control of the QR file are notorious point-winners, and White eventually triumphed.

G3

9 . . .   **B–B4**

A respectable variation.

10 P–QN4
(a) **10 P–K4** differs from 9 P–K4 in C above, to wit: 10 . . . B–N5 11 P–R3 B×N 12 B×B N–Q5 13 B–N2 P–B3 **14 P–QN4** P×P 15 P×P N–Q2 16 N–K2 R–R7 17 N×N P×N 18 Q–N3 Q–R1! = Vereshagin-Dvoretsky, USSR 1967. Black may well be equal after

11 . . . B×N, but White could delay
P−QN4 (he already has secured the
bishop pair) and play to eliminate
the domineering knight on d4, e.g.
by **14 N−K2**, when **14 . . . P−Q4?**
15 N×N P×N 16 BP×P P×P 17
P×P N×P 18 Q−N3 opens up the
board in his favour, and **14 . . .
N−Q2** (14 . . . N×Nch!?) 15 N×N
P×N 16 P−B4 P−KB4 17 P×P
P×P 18 P−QN4 introduces complications. Dynamically equal?
I feel that
(b) **10 B−N5!** would be a promising
strategy here. On 10 . . . P−KR3
11 B×N B×B 12 N−Q2 (or 12
P−QN4) 12 . . . B−N2 13 P−QN4
P×P 14 P×P Q−Q2 comes 15
N−Q5, followed by P−N5 Q−B2,
R−R1, and in some cases P−B5 or
N−K4 and P−N6. Black has two
bishops, but White has definite
chances of winning material on the
queenside, nice outposts for his
knights, and restraint on Black's
centre. Slightly better might be
14 . . . R−N1 15 P−N5 N−K2, yet
after 16 Q−R4 (△ 16 . . . R−R1
17 Q−N4 and 18 R−R1), Black still
faces difficulties.
    10 . . .   P×P
    10 . . . Q−Q2!? 11 R−K1 B−R6
12 B−R1 P−R3 13 P−N5 N−K2
14 N−Q2 ('±'−Raicević) 14 . . .
QR−N1 (14 . . . P−B3!) 15 N−Q5!
N(3)×N 16 P×N P−N3 17 Q−N3
P−KB4 18 B−QN2 B−B3 19 R(N)−
B1 K−R2 20 R−B4 with a com-
manding position, Raicević−Padev-
sky, Vrnjacka Banja 1976 (1-0, 31).
    11 P×P   Q−Q2 (42)
    12 P−N5
    Romanishin−Dvoretsky, USSR
1974, took the course of the Stein-

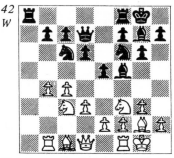

42
W

Vukić game in C above: **12 N−KN5!?**
P−R3 13 N(5)−K4 N−K1 ('?'−
Dvoretsky. He suggests emulating
Vukić by **13 . . .** N×N 14 P×N
B−R6 15 B×B Q×B 16 N−Q5
N−Q5, but as we saw in C, White
may well gain the advantage; in
fact, the open QR file probably
benefits him too, in the long run.)
14 N−Q5 K−R2 15 P−N5 N−K2
16 N×N Q×N 17 N−B3 R−QN1
18 B−QR3! and White dominates
the board (though ½−½, 47, after
errors).
    12 . . .   N−Q5
(a) '12 . . . N−Q1!' (Padevsky),
but Krnić continues '12 . . . N−Q1
13 R−K1 P−B3 14 N−Q2 P−Q4
15 Q−N3 ±'.
(b) **12 . . . N−K2(!)** 13 R−K1
B−R6 14 B−R1 P−KR3 = (Dvoretsky). See C above.
    13 B−K3   P−B4
    14 B−N5!   R−R6
15 R−B1 B−K3 16 B×N B×B 17
P−K3 N−B4 18 N−Q2! B−N2 19
N(2)−N1 R−R4 20 N−Q5 ±
Andersson−Padevsky (3), Sverige
1976 (1-0, 69).

G4
    9 . . .   P−KR3
The most popular variation today.

I doubt that it is objectively best, however.

10 P—QN4	P×P
11 P×P	B—K3
12 P—N5	

12 N—Q2?! (compare D above) has lost its effect, since after 12 . . . P—Q4! 13 P—N5 N—K2, White does not have 14 B—QR3 at his disposal.

12 . . .   N—K2

The first fork in the road. White chooses among:

G41 13 N—Q2
G42 13 Q—N3
G43 13 B—N2

G41
13 N—Q2

Attacking the Black QNP, but releasing pressure on the centre, i.e. moves like P—B5 and P—Q4 are no longer positional threats.

13 . . .   Q—B1!?

(a) **13 . . . P—Q4** 14 P×P N(2)×P (14 . . . N(3)×P 15 N(3)—K4!? ∞) 15 N×N N×N 16 Q—B2 Q—Q2 17 N—K4 P—N3 18 B—Q2 R—R6 19 N—B3 R—R2 20 KR—B1 ± Spiridinov–Westerinen, Orebro 1966 (1–0, 50).

(b) The clearest solution is **13 . . . R—N1!**, when Black simply closes the queenside by . . . P—N3 and builds up slowly on the other wing. Even after White's rook comes to a7 or a8, he will find it difficult to make progress.

14 R—K1	B—R6
15 B—R1	N—Q2
16 B—N2	N—QB4

17 Q—B2 P—B4 18 R—R1 R×R 19 R×R P—B5? (The QR file *and* e4 are to much to concede. Better **19 . . . K—R2** or **19 . . . P—R4**.)

20 N(3)—K4 P×P 21 RP×P Q—B4 22 B—KB3 N×N 23 N×N B—N5 24 B—N2 (or 24 B×B ±) 24 . . . Q—B2 25 R—R7 B—B1 26 P—K3 ± Adamski–Bernard, Poznan 1976 (1–0, 41).

G42
13 Q—N3

White strengthens his grip on d5 and tries to prepare B—QR3. He may also be planning R—Q1, P—Q4, etc. The drawbacks to Q—N3 are that it pins the QBP (no P—B5 break) and may lose a tempo to a knight move like . . . N—Q5 or . . . N—QB4.

13 . . .   N—Q2

The safest, preventing P—Q4, but **13 . . . Q—Q2!?** has its points too: 14 N—Q2 (**14 P—Q4 P—K5** 15 N—Q2 P—Q4 ∞ or 14 . . . P×P △ 15 . . . B—R6) 14 . . . B—R6 15 B—R3 P—N3!? 16 R—R1 QR—B1 17 R—R2 N—R4 18 N—Q5 N×N 19 P×N N—N5 20 B×B N×Bch 21 K—R1 P—KB4 22 P—B3 P—KR4 with a fine attack, Rudofsky–Watson, Providence 1977 (though Black lost . . . sigh).

14 B—QR3

Aimed against . . . N—B4, but **14 B—N2!** is the best chance to justify 13 Q—N3. Then if 14 . . . N—B4, 15 Q—N4!, an idea that hasn't occurred in any games I know of, but ought to be tried. White can continue R—R1 and/or KR—Q1 △ P—Q4.

14 . . .	P—KB4
15 N—Q5	K—R2

Vukić recommends **15 . . . B×N** 16 P×B P—N3 △ . . . N—B4 =.

16 N—Q2   R—R2!?

17 P–N6 N×P 18 N×N P×N 19 Q–N4 N–B1 20 B–N2 R–B2 21 R–R1 R–R3 22 R–R3?! (22 B–Q5! Vukić) 22 . . . P–Q4! ∓ Deze-Vukić, Novi Sad 1976 (0–1, 48)

G43

13 B–N2

The most logical move (Geller's idea in the Closed Sicilian): White intends R–R1 and/or P–QB5, and meanwhile the bishop on b2 helps hold down Black's centre.

13 . . .   N–Q2 (43)

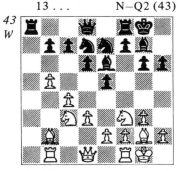

43
W

Black's oldest response. Other ideas:
(a) 13 . . . Q–B1 14 R–R1 N–Q2 (14 . . . R×R 15 Q×R B–R6 16 Q–R7 B×B 17 K×B Q–R1 18 R–QR1 etc. ±–Schinzel) 15 N–Q2 R–K1 16 R×R Q×R 17 Q–B2 P–QB3 18 R–R1 Q–N1 19 Q–N3 Q–B2 20 B–QR3 P–KB4 21 R–N1 ± Schinzel-Novak, Poznan 1976 (1–0, 34). Our first evidence of the strength of B–QN2 and R–QR1.
(b) 13 . . . Q–Q2 14 R–K1 (also 14 P–B5!? B–R6 15 Q–N3 may be ±.) 14 . . . B–R6 15 B–KR1 N–N5 (15 . . . Q–K3!?; 15 . . . QR–K1!? △ 16 R–R1 N–B1) 16

Q–B2 (16 P–Q4 Q–K3! ∞) 16 . . . P–KB4?! (16 . . . QR–K1 ±; 16 . . . Q–B4? 17 N–Q5 N×N 18 P×N QR–B1 19 R–R1 Q–R4 20 R–R7 ±±) 17 R–R1 QR–N1 18 R–R7 ± Valvo-Watson, New York 1977 (1–0, 35).

14 N–Q2?!
This results in little, if anything, for White; but it has been the normal move in grandmaster practice! See the comment on G41 13 N–Q2. Even 14 N–K1, as in a Closed Sicilian is preferable; but the correct moves are:
(a) 14 R–R1!. Also from the Closed Sicilian. This was finally played in the 1977 USSR Championship, and the games are exemplary: 14 . . . P–B3 15 R×R Q×R 16 Q–B2! (I was going to suggest 16 Q–N3! in this position, △ 16 . . . N–B4 17 Q–N4, but 16 Q–B2 also looks effective. Polugaevsky played the less commendable 16 N–Q2? against Rashkovsky in the same event, and after 16 . . . P–Q4 –naturally!–17 NP×P NP×P 18 Q–B2 R–N1! 19 P–K3 Q–R3, Black had equalized.) 16 . . . P–Q4 17 R–R1 Q–B1 (17 . . . Q–N1 ±) 18 BP×P P×QP 19 B–QR3 R–K1 20 B×N! R×B 21 N–K1 Q–B4 (21 . . . N–N3 22 N×P! ±±) 22 N×P winning a pawn, Smyslov-Rashkovsky, USSR Ch 1977.
(b) 14 Q–N3! transposes into G42, note to 14 B–QR3. This move too looks auspicious for White, whose queenside pressure cannot be neutralized.

14 . . .   P–QB3
14 . . . Q–B1, of Flesch-Balashov, Beverwijk 1965, should be answered

by **15 Q—B2** (Keene) or **15 R—R1**.
The game saw **15 N—N3 P—KB4
16 R—R1 P—N4 17 R×R Q×R ∞**
(0—1, 37).

15 R—R1

**15 P—K4 P—KB4   16 KP×P
NP×P   17 P—B4 N—KN3** is hard to
assess, but Black is no worse, e.g.
18 K—R1 (△ P×BP) 18 . . . Q—B1
19 N—N3?! P×P! 20 P×P N—B3
21 Q—Q2 K—R2 ∓ △ . . . N—R5
Polugaevsky—Korchnoi, USSR 1975.

    15 . . .   Q—B2
    16 Q—B2   ½—½
Pachman—Najdorf, Moscow 1956.

G5

    9 . . .   N—Q5
Here Black definitely profits
from the preparatory 8 . . . P—QR4.
To date, 9 . . . N—Q5 has been a
highly reliable line.

    10 P—QN4
As Black can apparently hold his
own against this expansion, White
should investigate the alternatives:
(a) **10 P—K3!?**, as Smejkal gives in
Informant #22, causes few problems
after 10 . . . N×Nch, and if 11 Q×N,
11 . . . P—B3 (△ 12 . . . B—N5,
winning the queen; also 11 . . .
B—B4!?) 12 P—R3 B—K3 =; or 11
B×N P—B3   12 P—QN4 P×P   13
P×P P—Q4   14 P—N5 B—K3 =.
(b) **10 N—Q2?!** P—B3 11 P—QN4
P×P 12 P×P P—Q4 (improving on
12 . . . B—N5?! 13 P—R3 ±—see
Chapter 8, C1!) 13 B—N2 R—K1
14 P—K3 N—B4 15 P×P?! P×P
16 N—N3 P—R4 ∓ Smejkal—Smyslov, Biel 1976 (½—½, 41).
(c) **10 N×N!?** P×N   **11 N—N5?**
N—N5 is obviously better for
Black than E above because White

lacks the retreat square a3. Never-
theless, I would like to recommend
11 N—R4(!) here, when, despite
the apparently clumsy posting of
White's knight, Black has certain
difficulties, e.g. 11 . . . P—B3   12
P—QN4 P×P   13 P×P B—K3   14
P—N5 Q—R4? (14 . . . Q—B2   15
B—B4!)   15 P×P! Q×N   16 P×P
Q×Q   17 P×R(Q) ±±, or 11 . . .
R—K1   12 R—K1 P—Q4   13 P×P
N×P   14 Q—N3 P—QB3? 15 B×N
etc.

Of course Black can do much
better than that, but 10 N×N and
11 N—R4 is worth a try for those
discouraged with White's play in
the text.

    10 . . .   P×P
    11 P×P   P—B3!
This must be the proper plan,
establishing a hold on d5. 11 . . .
N×Nch?! would resemble E above.

    12 P—N5
Natural, yet Black obtains
equality easily. Another productive
move is hard to find: **12 N—Q2?!**
P—Q4 is note (b) above, and the
provocative **12 B—K3!?** (△ 12 . . .
N—N5 13 B—Q2 ±) 12 . . . N—B4!
13 B—Q2 R—K1   14 P—N5 (14
P—R3 P—K5!) 14 . . . P—Q4 doesn't
interfere with Black's comfortable
build-up.

    12 . . .   B—N5! (44)
    12 . . . P—B4?! 13 N—Q2 R—R2
14 P—K3 N—B4 15 B—N2 P—N3
16 R—R1 R×R   17 Q×R B—K3
18 Q—R6 ± Watson—Maxwell, Phila-
delphia 1977.

    13 N×N?!
13 N—Q2 Q—Q2! ∓.
    13 . . .   P×N
    14 N—K4   N×N

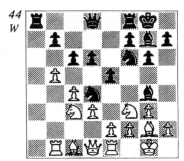

44
W

15 Bx N R–K1   16 R–N2 P–Q4!
17 Px QP Px QP   18 B–N2 R–R8
19 P–R3 B–K3   20 Q–N3 Q–Q2
21 K–R2 R(1)–R1   22 B–B4
R(8)–R6   23 Q–B2 R–B6 ∓
Augustin–Tal, European Team Ch,
1977. Black's mastery of the QB
file led to the win (0–1, 48).

G6
      9 . . .   R–K1
A solid move, and one with
some subtle effects. As in the
Smyslov lines (E and G5), Black
foregoes the opportunity to attack
on the kingside in favour of central
attention. The immediate notion
is . . . P–K5, which White can
ignore or prevent:
G61 10 P–QN4
G62 10 N–Q2
     What about **10 B–-N5** ? For
players of White who are dis-
satisfied with the results of 10
P–QN4 and 10 N–Q2, this continuation contrives to dominate the
light squares in the style of Petrosian
or Andersson. As it did against
9 . . . B–B4, 10 B–N5 stops 10 . . .
P–K5 and prepares to exchange
the dark-squared bishop in a position where . . . P–KB4 will be
cumbersome to organize (with

Black's KR rather misplaced). Nonetheless, White must yield his good
QB and the consequences are unclear, e.g. 10 . . . P–R3 (Otherwise
White plays N–Q5 and/or Q–Q2.)
11 Bx N Bx B   12 N–Q2 N–K2!?
(In G3, the Black QNP would be en
prise now.) 13 P–QN4 Px P 14 Px P
P–B3, and now 15 P–-N5?! P–Q4 16
Q–N3 B–K3 is stereotyped, but
more heedful of White's chances
might be **15 N(2)–K4** B–N2 16
P–B5 P–Q4   17 N–Q6 R–B1
18 N–R4 ±, or perhaps **15 N(3)–K4**
B–N2   16 P–B5 P–Q4   17 N–Q6
△ P–N5, Nx B, etc. Practical examples would be of assistance,
hopefully with Petrosian as White!

G61
      10 P–QN4   Px P
      11 Px P   P–K5
      12 Px P
     On **12 N–K1**, 12 . . . Px P or
12 . . . B–B4, or even 12 . . . N–K4
equalizes.
      12 . . .   Nx P
      13 Nx N   Rx N
      14 N–N5
      14 N–Q2 R–K1   15 P–N5
N–Q5   16 P–K3 N–K3 = Stolyar-
Bannik, 24th USSR Ch 1957.
      14 . . .   R–Q5!
      15 Q–N3   P–R3
16 N–B3 B–B4   17 B–N2 Bx R
18 Nx R B–R7   19 Nx N Px N
20 Q–B2 Bx B   21 Qx B Bx P 22
Bx P = Kivielto–Westerinen, Fin-
land Ch 1970.

G62
      10 N–Q2 (45)
     The 'normal' response, but (as in
D and G4), an early N–Q2 makes it

45
B

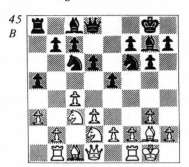

difficult for White to launch a coordinated attack; he has removed a piece from the kingside and from key central squares while still undeveloped.

10 ...   B–K3

Also not bad is

(a) 10 ... N–K2 11 P–QN4 P×P 12 P×P P–Q4 13 P–N5 B–K3 14 P×P N(2)×P 15 B–N2 N×N 16 B×N B–Q4! 17 B×B Q×B 18 Q–N3 and now 18 ... R–R7 would have been equal, but Benkovan Rimsdijk, 1977 saw Black flounder by 18 ... Q×Q?! 19 R×Q R–R7 20 R–N2! R–R6? 21 B×P! R×B 22 N–B4 ±. Black's fundamental equality was also apparent in

(b) 10 ... B–N5! 11 P–R3 B–K3 12 K–R2 P–R3 13 P–QN4 P×P 14 P×P P–Q4 = Petrosian–Keres, USSR Ch 1957.

11 P–QN4

Given '?' by Rukavina and Nemet, who recommend 11 N–Q5, but that allows the typical device 11 ... B×N 12 P×B N–K2 13 Q–N3 P–B3 =.

11 ...   P×P
12 P×P   P–Q4
13 P–N5   N–K2
14 Q–N3?!

14 P×P, transposing to note (a) to Black's 10th, is equal and correct.

14 ...   P–B3
15 B–N2   N–B4
16 KR–B1?!   B–R3! (another advantage of the omission of ... P–KR3) 17 BP×P P×QP 18 Q–Q1 N–N5! (White has organized his pieces aesthetically, but the KR, QB, and KN have all abandoned their kingside defensive functions.) 19 P–K4 (What else? Black threatened both 19 ... N×BP and 19 ... Q–N3.) 19 ... N×BP (or 19 ... N(4)--K6!) 20 K×N Q–N3ch 21 K–K2 Q–K6ch 22 K–B1 Q×Pch (22 ... N–Q5!?) 23 K–K1 N–K6 24 B–B1 N×B 25 N×N P×P! 26 Q×Q P×Q 27 R–Q1 P–K5 Raicević–Matulović, Yugoslavia Ch 1975. Black has three pawns for the piece and an overwhelming game.

CONCLUSION: Not unexpectedly, this Closed Sicilian in reverse often gives White an edge. But his set-up is not particularly telling, and by playing carefully Black can probably emerge from the opening with approximate equality, particularly in the 'centre-oriented' lines such as 8 ... P–QR4 9 P–QR3 N–Q5 and 9 ... R–K1. Older moves such as 8 ... B–Q2 and 8 ... N–KR4 (or 9 ... N–KR4) probably grant the knowledgeable first player some advantage; but they are still critical and can be recommended to the player of Black who enjoys attacking chess.

This entire variation, frequently seen on all levels of play, will repay careful study.

6 KING'S INDIAN II:
5 N–B3 P–Q3 6 0–0 P–K4 7 P–Q3 (7 . . . Others)

1 P–QB4	N–KB3
2 N–QB3	P–KN3
3 P–KN3	B–N2
4 B–N2	0–0
5 N–B3	P–Q3
6 0–0	P–K4
7 P–Q3	

For a discussion of these moves, see Chapter 5. Here we examine the alternatives to 7 . . . N–B3. Noteworthy at the very beginning is that the positions below sometimes come up after 6 . . . P–B3, e.g. 7 P–Q3 P–K4. But that sequence is less convenient for White, since Black can do without . . . P–K4, as in Andersson–Polugayevsky, Hilversum 1973: 6 . . . P–B3 7 **P–Q3** QN–Q2 (or 7 . . . P–Q4 =) 8 R–N1 P–QR4 9 P–QR3 N–N3! 10 B–Q2 (10 P–QN4 P×P 11 P×P P–Q4 12 P–B5 P–Q5! ∓; 11 R×P N(B)–Q4! ∓) 10 . . . P–Q4 (or 10 . . . P–R5!?) 11 P×P P×P 12 P–QR4?! (12 N–QN5! ∞) 12 . . . N–K1! 13 N–QN5 B–Q2 14 Q–N3 N×P!? 15 Q×N N–B2 ∓ (notes by Polugayevsky). A skillful treatment, which indicates that White would do better after 6 . . . P–B3 with **7 P–Q4!**. Then 7 . . . QN–Q2 8 P–K4 P–K4 is a normal King's Indian Defence.

We consider:
A 7 . . . R–K1
B 7 . . . P–B3
C 7 . . . QN–Q2
Even considering Ulf Andersson's recurring use of 7 P–Q3, one encounters these variations in the annals of international chess less frequently than might be expected; hence the lack of theoretical material. Not only does Black sometimes play 7 . . . N–B3; White even more often avoids 7 P–Q3 altogether. I find this neglect a little difficult to understand. True, 7 P–Q3 emphasizes control of the central light squares in a position where N–Q5 can be easily rebuffed (i.e. by . . . P–QB3); but without . . . N–QB3, Black is challenged to find a coherent method of developing. In the long run, White can play R–N1, P–QN4–N5, and P–QB5 or P–QR4–R5, sometimes combined with ideas like N–Q5 and/or N–K1–B2–N4. Another theme is B–KN5, × N, fighting for the central squares. Of course all this uses time, but indicates that Black ought to undertake some counter-action, usually by...P–QB3 and...P–Q4. In that case the relevance of White's formation, especially his idea of P–QN4–N5, becomes apparent.

Naturally the second player has his own ideas about this, and we must turn our attention to specific examples for a realistic view of things. Before tackling the 'main lines' below, however, I should mention the possibility 7...P–KR3, which refrains from commital pawn moves and prepares . . . B–K3 e.g. 8 R–N1 B–K3 9 N–Q2?! N–B3! with a good version of Chapter 5, D. Better 9 P–Q4! (or 9 P–QN4 Q–Q2 10 R–K1 etc.) Also the sequence 7 . . . N–-R4!? 8 R–N1 P–KB4 runs into the annoying 9 B–N5! e.g. 9 . . . B–B3 10 B–R6 or 9...Q–Q2 10 B–Q2!±.

A

    7 . . .   R–K1
    8 B–Q2!? (46)

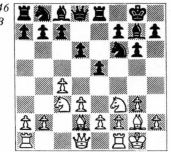

46 B

This remarkable little move we use to illustrate 7 . . . R–K1, even though it is somewhat rare. The customary move has been 8 R–N1, but for one thing 8 . . . P–K5!? (Ljubojević) is unclear, e.g. 9 N–K1 B–B4 10 B–N5 PxP 11 NxP P–B3 =/∞ 8 . . . P–B3 is B below, and 8 . . . P–QR4 9 P–QR3 QN–Q2 is C2, note (a) to 9 . . . P–B3.

Also 'irregular' was 8 Q–B2!? (preventing . . . P–K5) 8 . . .

N–B3 9 R–K1 (anticipating . . . N–Q5) 9 . . . B–N5 10 B–K3 (with the same idea) 10 . . . Q–Q2 11 P–QR3?! (11 N–Q5!?) 11 . . . B–R6 12 B–R1 N–KN5 13 B–Q2 P–KR3 14 QR–B1 N–Q5! ∓ (△ . . . P–QB3, . . . P–KB4) Andersson–Kavalek, Las Palmas 1974 (but 1–0, 89).

    8 . . .   P–B3
    Natural, but
(a) 8 . . . N–B3!? is a possible transpositional trick e.g.
(a1) 9 R–N1 can be answered by 9 . . . B–B4, 9 . . . P–KR3, or 9 . . . P–QR4 10 P–QR3 N–Q5!– all at least equal. Andersson–Najdrof, Wijk an Zee 1978 saw
(a2) 9 R–B1 (compare the text) 9 . . . P–KR3! 10 P–QR3 (10 N–Q5 =) 10 . . . B–K3 11 P–QN4 Q–Q2 12 P–N5 N–Q1 13 P–B5 B–N5 14 PxP PxP 15 Q–R4 N–K3 with an excellent game (0–1, 33). But:
(a3) 9 Q–B1 △ B–N5 seems more consistent with White's eighth move. Then 9 . . . N–Q5 10 B–N5 is a bit awkward for Black (10 . . . N–K3 11 B–R6), so he should consider the direct 9 . . . P–K5!? 10 N–K1 B–B4 11 B–N5 PxP. Then White might try 12 P–K4(!) N–Q5 13 P–B3(±?), since 12 NxP(?) N–Q5 13 Q–Q2 P–KR3! and 12 PxP N–Q5 are clearly satisfactory for the second player.
(b) 8 . . . P–K5!? is already critical. If 9 N–KN5, 9 . . . PxP 10 PxP P–KR3 11 N–R3 P–B3 levels the play; but 9 N–K1! is defter, retreating in order to recentralize after 9 . . . PxP 10 NxP e.g. 10 . . . N–B3 (10 . . . P–B3 11 P–K4

B–K3 12 Q–R4) 11 Q–B1 N–Q5 12 R–K1. Or here 9 . . . B–B4, to maintain e4, fails to do that after 10 P–KR3! and if 10 . . . P–KR4?, 11 B–N5.

9 R–B1!

Petrosian's idea, replacing the mechanical R–QN1 and P–QN4–N5. Despite its passive appearance, sliding the rook to c1 has some marvellously subtle effects. To begin with, it prepares P–QN4 by taking the rook not only off the a1–h8 diagonal, but also off the b1–h7 diagonal (e.g. 9 R–N1), where after . . . P–K5 it would be subject to harrassment from a bishop on f5. Secondly, the move operates against Black's . . . P–Q4. To play that move will give White the QB file and the immediate 9 . . . **P–Q4** 10 Px P Px P 11 P–Q4! works out nicely to White's advantage e.g. 11 . . . P–K5 12 N–K5 or 11 . . . Px P 12 Nx P, an isolated pawn position where R–B1 is useful indeed.

9 . . .   P–QR4!
10 P–QR3   N–R3

Black in turn prevents White's most natural plan, i.e. P–QN4–N5.

11 B–K3(!)   R–N1

11 . . . N–KN5 12 B–N5 would provoke the loosening of Black's kingside, whereas 11 . . . N–B4 12 P–QN4 Px P 13 Px P N–K3, given as equal by Langeweg and Sosonko, remains full of interest after 14 P–N5 P–Q4 15 Px QP (15 NPx P!? P–Q5 16 Nx KP Q–B2!) 15 . . . Px P 16 P–Q4 P–K5 17 N–K5.

12 Q–N3   N–Q2
12 . . . **P–QN4** 13 Px P Px P 14 N–N5 ∞ (Petrosian). After

12 . . . N–Q2, Langeweg and Sosonko suggest 13 **P–Q4** Px P 14 Bx P N(3)–B4 15 Q–Q1 ±. Petrosian handles it more gingerly:

13 Q–B2   N(2)–B4
14 KR–Q1   B–B4
15 R–N1 N–K3 (15 . . . **P–K5** 16 N–Q4 ± –Petrosian) 16 P–QN4 N–Q5 17 Q–R2 Px P 18 Px P R–R1 19 Q–Q2 N–B2 (19 . . . B–N5!?) 20 B–R6 Nx Nch 21 Bx N B–R1? (21 . . . P–Q4 ± – Petrosian) 22 P–N5 Q–Q2 23 R(Q)–QB1 B–K3 24 Q–K3! (△ Q–N6) 24 . . . R–R6 25 B–N2! R–QB1 26 Px P Px P 27 R–N7 B–N2? 28 Bx B Kx B 29 P–B5! (±±) 29 . . . R–R4 30 Px P Qx P 31 N–K4 Q–Q5 32 Qx Q Px Q 33 N–Q6 R–Q1 34 Nx P and White won in a few moves, Petrosian–Planinc, Amsterdam 1973. A surprising game throughout.

B

7 . . .   **P–B3**
8 R–N1

(a) 8 **P–B5?!** Px P! 9 Nx P N–Q4 10 Nx N Px N 11 N–B3 N–B3 (∓) 12 B–K3 N–Q5?! 13 Nx N Px N 14 B–Q2 B–K3 = Miles–Geller, Cleveland, England 1975.

(b) 8 **B–Q2!?** is again worth considering, the more so since 8 . . . N–B3 cannot be played (see A). Skembris–Gheorghiu, Groningen 1977/78 went 8 . . . Q–K2! (8 . . . R–K1 9 R–B1 is A.) 9 Q–B1 (or 9 R–B1) 9 . . . R–Q1 10 B–N5 QN–Q2 11 P–QN4 N–B1! 12 N–K4 N–K3 and Black had equalized.

8 . . .   R–K1
For 8 . . . **P–QR4** 9 P–QR3

QN–Q2 see C2. 8 . . . **P–KR3**
proved rather slow but plausible in
Brasket–Mednis, New York 1977:
9 P–QN4 B–K3 10 P–N5 QN–Q2
11 P×P P×P 12 Q–R4 P–Q4!
(12 . . . Q–B2 13 B–QR3 is not
attractive.) 13 B–QR3 R–K1 14
P×P P×P 15 KR–B1 N–N3 16
Q–R6 ±.

9 B–N5
The most thematic move, in that
White fortifies his influence over
the h1-a8 diagonal. But others have
been successful:
(a) **9 P–K4** N–R3?! (9 . . . P–Q4 ∞;
9 . . . P–KR3 Δ . . . B–K3) 10
P–KR3 N–B2 11 P–Q4 P×P
12 N×P N–K3 13 B–K3 N–B4
14 Q–B2 (the old main line of the
'Classical Fianchetto' King's Indian;
only White is a full tempo up) 14
. . . Q–K2 15 R(N)–K1 (15
R(B)–K1!) 15 . . . P–QR4 16
P–B4 B–Q2 17 B–B2 ± Najdorf–
Bronstein, Mar del Plata 1969
(1–0, 28).
(b) **9 N–Q2** B–K3 (9 . . . P–Q4!?)
10 P–QN4 P–Q4 11 P–N5 P×BP
(11 . . . Q–R4!?) 12 NP×P N×P
13 N×P R–N1 14 B–QR3 B×N
(what else?) 15 P×B Q–R4 16
Q–B1 Seirawan–Winslow, US Open
1977. White threatens to turn his
bishops to good account. He eventually prevailed.
(c) **9 Q–B2** P–Q4?! (9 . . . P–KR3!
Δ . . . P–Q4–Polugayevsky) 10 P×P
P×P 11 B–N5 N–B3 (11 . . .
P–KR3 12 B×N B×B 13 N–Q2
B–K3 14 P–K4 **P–Q5** 15 N–Q5–
Polugayevsky. But **14 . . . P×P!** may
improve e.g. 15 N(3)×P–Δ *N–B5–*
15 . . . N–B3! 16 N×Bch Q×N
17 N–K4 Q–K2) 12 P–K4! P–Q5

13 N–Q5 B–K3 Hug–Polugayevsky,
Palma de Mallorca 1972 and 14
R(N)–K1! ± was the best course.
9 . . .   QN–Q2
The game Spiridinov–Ghizdavu,
Bucharest 1973 saw White quickly
overrun after **9 . . . P–KR3!?** 10
B×N Q×B 11 P–QN4 B–K3
12 N–Q2 P–QR3 ('∓!'–Ghizdavu)
13 P–QR4 Q–Q1 (47) **14 P–N5?**

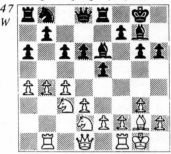

RP×P 15 RP×P P–Q4! 16 Q–N3
P–K5! 17 P×BP NP×P 18 P×QP
BP×P 19 N–N5 N–R3! Δ 20 . . .
Q–R4, 21 . . . QR–N1. Very instructive, but 14 P–N5? was a mis-
calculation. The right move was
14 Q–N3!, stopping . . . P–Q4 and
preparing 15 P–N5. Then even
14 . . . N–Q2 15 P–N5!? N–B4
16 Q–N4! does not make Black's
life easy e.g. 16 . . . **P–QR4** 17
Q–R3 Q–B2 18 N(2)–K4 N×N
19 N×N QR–Q1 20 P–B5; best
therefore is 16 . . . RP×P 17 RP×P
Q–B2 and if 18 P×P P×P 19 Q–N6,
19 . . . R(R)–B1! battens the
hatches.
        10 P–QN4
Ljubojević mentions **10 Q–B1**, a
creditable attempt e.g. 10 . . . Q–B2
11 N–K1! Δ P–QN4–N5, N–B2–
N4. So 10 . . . **N–B1** 11 P–QN4
N–K3 12 B–Q2 N–Q5 ∞ may be

best.

10 . . .	P–KR3
11 B× N	N× B
12 P–N5 P–Q4	13 NP× P NP× P

14 N–Q2 B–B4?! (This doesn't work out well. Is **14** . . . **Q–R4** an improvement? It's hard to believe that White is more than minimally better here . . .) 15 Q–R4 ('±'– Ljubojević) 15 . . . P–K5 16 BP× P KP× P 17 P–K4 B–Q2 and now **18 P–Q6!** (instead of **18 P×P?** B× P! ∓) would have kept a distinct edge, Andersson–Kavalek, Manila 1974 (½–½, 31).

C

7 . . .   QN–Q2

Superficially, one might associate this move with an attempt, by ommitting . . . P–QB3, to deprive White of the simple breaching process P–QN4–N5, × P. In practice, however, 7 . . . QN–Q2 has been most effective conjoined with . . . P–QB3 in an attempt to enforce . . . P–Q4.

8 R–N1	P–QR4

8 . . . N–R4?! (venturesome but decentralizing) 9 P–QN4 P–KR3 10 N–Q2 P–KB4 11 B–N2 N(4)–B3 (Black's pieces are getting in each other's way. Now White slowly breaks ground in the centre:) 12 Q–B2 R–K1 13 P–K3 N–B1 14 QR–K1 K–R2 15 N–Q5 N–K3 16 P–B4 P–B3 17 N× Nch B× N 18 P–B5! ± Keene–Perkins. The foundations are crumbling, and White managed to win in only ten more moves.

9 P–QR3

9 B–Q2 N–B4 10 N–K1 (lest . . . P–K5 gain the initiative) 10 . . .

P–B3 11 N–B2 R–K1 12 P–KR3 (12 Q–B1!?) 12 . . . B–K3 13 K–R2 P–Q4 14 P–N3 P–Q5 15 N–R4 N× N 16 P× N Q–B2 Suttles–Reshevsky, 1970. Drawn shortly thereafter.

9 . . .   P–B3!
(a) 9 . . . N–B4?! 10 P–QN4 P× P 11 P× P N–K3 12 Q–B2 N–R4 13 P–N5 P–KB4 14 B–Q2 (△ R–R1) ± Valvo–Murphy, USA (telephone) 1978.
(b) 9 . . . R–K1 10 N–Q2 P–B3 11 P–QN4 P× P 12 P× P N–B1 (12 . . . N–N3!? 13 P–N5 P–Q4 14 NP× P NP× P 15 Q–N3 ±) 13 N(2)–K4 N× N 14 B× N B–K3 15 Q–N3 Q–Q2 16 P–N5 QR–Q1 17 B–R1! P–Q4 18 B–R3 ± Andersson–van der Sterren, Wijk an Zee 1978 (1–0, 74).

10 N–Q2	N–N3!

Suddenly . . . P–Q4 cannot be prevented, and White is a tempo short of the P–QN4–N5, Q–N3 idea of the preceding note (b). Thus we see the advantage to delaying . . . R–K1.

11 P–QN4	P× P
12 P× P	P–Q4
13 P× P	P× P
14 N–N3	P–Q5

Ree–Polugayevsky, Amsterdam 1970. Black is already slightly better.

CONCLUSION: White has done fairly well with 7 P–Q3, and there is scope for originality (e.g. Petrosian's 8 B–Q2 and 9 R–B1 in A). His traditional English themes of light-square control and queenside infiltration are exemplified by variations such as those in B and in the notes to C. Of course, Black must be faulted for expanding too quickly in the centre in some of these examples; often, too, he has simply defended poorly thereafter. Generally speaking, less committal lines like 7 . . . QN—Q2 seem more effective than creating an early target by, say, 7 . . . P—QB3.

These are objectively equal positions, and players of either colour may feel at home here if they like strategic chess and behind-the-lines manoeuvring.

7 KING'S INDIAN III: 5 P–K4

1 P–QB4	N–KB3
2 N–QB3	P–KN3
3 P–KN3	B–N2
4 B–N2	0–0
5 P–K4 (48)	

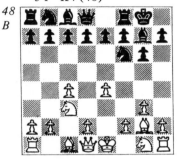

48 B

The Botvinnik set-up (pawns on e4, c4, and g3; bishop on g2; knight on c3) crops up throughout this book. From a King's Indian formation (pawns on d6, g6; knight on f6; bishop on g7), Black has several ways of dealing with it: (1) he can put a pawn on c5 and knight on c6 (often via 1 . . . P–QB4, 2 . . . N–QB3, 3 . . . P–KN3 etc. (*English III*). (2) he can put a pawn on e5 and a knight on c6 (usually via 1 . . . P–K4, 2 . . . N–QB3, 3 . . . P–KN3 etc.), a structure examined in *English I*, Chapter 1. (3) he can avoid both . . . P–QB4 and . . . N–QB3 by a variety of plans, usually involving . . . P–K4 and an early . . . P–QB3 or . . . P–KB4, which form the subject of

this chapter.

Almost nothing has been written on these 'non- . . . N–QB3, . . . P–QB4' ideas, due partly to their relatively infrequent use, and partly to their indefinable character. Nonetheless, both the King's Indian player who does not like alternatives (1) and (2), and the Smyslov system player (see *English I*) who prefers formations with . . . P–KN3 but is already committed to the move . . . P–K4, should find this material useful. As for White, 5 P–K4 constitutes his chief alternative to the main line King's Indian Defence and the systems of Chapter 5 and 6.

By way of introduction, we note that playing for an immediate . . . P–QB3 and . . . P–Q4 against the Botvinnik set-up has not met with great success, but can limit White's choice of move orders. Some illustrations after 1 P–QB4 N–KB3 2 N–QB3 P–KN3 3 P–KN3 B–N2 4 B–N2 0–0:

(a) **5 P–Q3** (allowing the following possibility. 5 P–K4 is simple, if one is already willing to play à la Botvinnik) 5 . . . P–B3 6 P–K4 P–K3!? 7 KN–K2 (**7 P–K5**, which works well after 5 P–K4 P–B3 6 KN–K2 P–K3, is only so-so here after 7 . . . N–K1 8 N–B3 P–Q3

9 P–Q4–*9 P×P N×P △ 10* . . .
N–B4–9 . . . P× P 10 P× P Q× Qch
11 K× Q N–Q2 12 B–B4–*12 R –K1
P–B3!–Gufeld–*12 . . . P–KR3 13
P–KR4 P–B3 Dzhindzhihashvili–
Gufeld, 41st USSR Ch 1st L 1973,
when 14 P× P = was best.) 7 . . .
P–Q4 8 BP× P KP× P 9 P× P N× P
10 N× N P× N 11 0–0 N–B3 12
N–B4 Taimanov–Gufeld, Tbilisi
1967, with a microscopic White advantage (since after . . . P–Q5,
White's KB is stronger than Black's).
Objectively however, a draw should
result from accurate defence.
(b) 5 P–K4 P–B3 6 KN–K2
P–Q4?! 7 BP× P P× P 8 P× P N–R3
9 0–0 N–QN5 10 N–B4 B–B4
11 P–Q3 P–KN4 12 N–R5 N× N
(12 . . . B× P 13 R–K1 B–N3 14
N× B K× N 15 B× P N–B7 16
Q–Q2! ±) 13 Q× N P–KR3 14
P–KR4! (± – Raicević) 14 . . . B–N3
15 Q–N4 N× P(6) 16 P× P P–KR4
17 Q–K2 R–B1 Raicević–Velimir-
ovic, Yugoslavia Ch. 1975. At this
point Raicević suggests 18 N–K4!
(instead of 18 R–Q1 N× NP!) 18
. . . N× B 19 QR× N Q–N3 20
P–N3 ±.

5 . . .   P–Q3
6 KN–K2   P–K4

Black may delay this in favour
of early queenside expansion: 6 . . .
P–B3 7 0–0 P–QR3. If then
8 P–Q3, 8 . . . P–QN4 offsets
White's central superiority, and
8 P–Q4 QN–Q2 9 P–KR3 P–K4
is the kind of King's Indian position
where White's knight would rather
be on f3 (for reasons given in D,
note to 8 P–Q3, below). The game
Hofland–Vliet, Netherlands Ch.

1977, continued 8 P–QR4!?
P–QR4 9 P–Q3 N–R3! (9 . . .
P–KR3, see D, note to 9 P–KR3,
below) 10 P–R3 N–QN5 11 N–R2
(11 B–K3 P–Q4! =) 11 . . . N× N
12 R× N P–K4 (12 . . . P–Q4 =)
13 P–Q4? P× P 14 N× P R–K1
15 R–K1 P–Q4 16 BP× P P× P
17 P× P R× Rch 18 Q× R N× P
19 N–B2 B–K3 20 R–R3 R–QB1 ∓
(0–1, 65).

This plan, delaying . . . P–K4 in
favour of 6 . . . P–B3 and 7 . . .
P–QR3, has much to recommend it.
In practically every example below,
White plays the line-opening device
P–KB4–B5 (△ P–KN4–N5). But
the advance of the KBP comes to
naught with Black's KP still on its
original square (e.g. P–KN4–N5
can be met by a simple knight
retreat).

7 0–0
White sometimes plays 7 P–Q3,
but he will always castle soon
thereafter, since 0–0 is necessary
for any action he might undertake
in the centre, kingside, *or* queenside.
So ignoring transpositions, Black
can deploy in these ways:
A 7 . . . KN–Q2
B 7 . . . B–K3
C 7 . . . QN–Q2
D 7 . . . P–B3
7 . . . N–R4?! is decentralizing.
A game of the author's (White)
continued 8 P–Q4 P–QB3 9
B–K3 N–R3 10 P–B4 P–KB4
11 P× BP NP× P 12 BP× P P× P
13 P–Q5 (creating hanging pawns)
13 . . . B–Q2 14 P× P B× P 15
N–Q5 Q–K1 16 Q–B2 Q–K3
17 R× P! etc.

A

7...	KN-Q2
8 P-Q3	P-KB4
9 P×P	P×P
10 B-K3	N-KB3

Or **10 ... P-B4!?** (Keene). Then 11 Q-Q2 △ QR-K1 and P-B4 is good. White could play N-Q5 and/or B-N5 when appropriate, but his main idea would be to capture on e5 with his KBP, a familiar English motif which forces hanging pawns or, worse, an isolated Black KBP.

11 Q-Q2	P-B3
12 P-KR3	N-R4

13 P-B4! Q-K1 14 K-R2 Q-N3 15 Q-K1 N-Q2 16 R-Q1 K-R1 17 P-Q4 R-KN1 18 Q-B2 B-B3 (As Keene points out, White can prepare the undermining P-KN4 in response to ... P-K5 at its appearance) 19 QP×P P×P 20 R-Q6 ± Pachman-Donner, 1955 (1-0, 32).

B

7...	B-K3

Black opts for quick mobilization, but if he tries to exchange off the enemy KB, he will only expend valuable time and trade a good piece for a mediocre one.

8 P-Q3

8 P-N3! △ P-Q4 is a good idea. Black might counter by 8 ... N-B3, and if 9 P-B4, 9 ... P×P 10 P×P B-N5. Then 11 P-Q4 N-KR4 12 B-K3 P-B4!? 13 P-K5 is complex, and probably slightly in White's favour.

8...	Q-B1

8 ... Q-Q2 9 P-B4 (An unassuming approach was 9 **P-N3** N-B3 10 N-Q5 N-KR4?!-*10 ...*

B×N-11 B-N2 QR-K1 12 P-Q4 ± Filip-Westerinen.) 9 ... P-B3 10 K-R1 B-R6? (**10 ... N-R3** is less obliging. See the note to 7 ... B-K3) 11 P-B5 B×Bch 12 K×B N-R3 13 P-KR3 P-Q4 14 BP×P P×P 15 B-N5! N-B2 16 Q-N3 ± Ivkov-Minić, Yugoslavia 1966.

9 P-B4	P-B3

10 P-N3 B-N5 11 B-K3 N-R3 12 Q-Q2 N-B2 13 P-Q4 ± Dely-F. Portisch. White has a useful advantage in space (1-0, 35).

C

7...	QN-Q2

A flexible move: Black awaits events before deciding upon, say, ... P-KB4 or ... P-QN4.

8 P-Q3

8 P-B4?! (trying to get in P-KB5 before Black can block it by ... P-KB4) was proven premature in Watson-Browne, Vancouver 1975: 8 ... P-B3 9 P-KR3 (△ P-KB5, P-KN4) 9 ... P-QN4! 10 P×NP P×NP 11 P-R3 B-N2 12 K-R2 (**12 P-B5** N-B4 13 P-Q3 P-Q4 ∓) 12 ... P-QR4! 13 P-Q4 P-N5 14 QP×P QP×P 15 BP×P N(2)×P 16 N-Q5 N×N 17 P×N N-B5 18 Q-N3 B-QR3 19 P×P R-N1 20 R-B4!? R×P 21 Q×R P×Q 22 R×B N×P ∓.

8...	P-B3

8 ... N-B4 9 P-B4 (9 P-KR3!?) 9 ... P-B3 10 P-KR3 N-K3? (**10 ... P-QR4** improves considerably, since 11 P-B5 P-Q4! is excellent; so 11 B-K3 ∞) 11 P-B5 N-Q5 12 P-KN4 N-K1 13 B-K3 P-QR3 14 Q-Q2 with a tremendous position, Botvinnik-Shcherbakov, 22nd USSR Ch 1955.

In this example, White's strategy was fully realized.

9 P–KR3 (49)

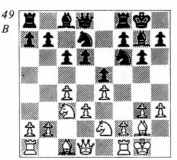

49
B

9 **P–B4** (Schwarz) could be answered by 9 . . . P–QN4! From the diagram, there is a whole row of alternatives. Black must disturb White's threatened incursion on the king's wing or suffer a fate as in the preceding note.

(a) 9 . . . **N–K1** 10 B–K3 P–KB4 11 Q–Q2 N(2)–B3 12 P×P P×P 13 B–N5 ±. Compare the note to A 7 . . . KN–Q2 above.

(b) 9 . . . **N–B4** 10 B–K3 P–QR4 11 P–B4 P×P 12 P×P Q–K2 13 Q–Q2 R–N1 14 QR–K1 N(4)–Q2 15 N–N3 N–K1 16 P–Q4 N–B2 17 P–K5! ± Markland–Hort, Hastings 1970/71 (1–0, 30).

(c) 9 . . . **N–R4(?!)** 10 K–R2?! (10 B–K3!–Kavalek ±) 10 . . . N–B4 11 B–K3 N–K3 12 P–Q4 P–QB4 13 P×BP P×P 14 N–Q5 (±!?) 14 . . . N–Q5 15 P–B4 B–K3 16 P–B5 B×N 17 KP×B? N–KB3 18 P–KN4 P×P! 19 P×P K–R1 20 N–B3 P–K5! (Perfectly timed, since otherwise 21 N–K4 would have been positionally decisive.) 21 K–R1 R–KN1 22 B–N5 B–B1!! 23 N×P N×N 24 B×Q

N–N6ch 25 K–N1 R×B (probably winning!) 26 R–B3!? B–Q3 27 Q–Q3 QR–K1 28 QR–KB1 N(6)×R 29 R×N N–K7ch ∓∓ Bilek–Gligorić, Teesside 1972 (0–1, 36). A dashing game by Gligo, but 9 . . . N–R4 is still dubious.

(d) 9 . . . **R–N1!?** 10 B–K3 P–QR3 11 P–B4 P–QN4 12 P–KB5! P×QBP 13 QP×P N–N3 14 P–N3 ± Kotov–A. Geller, Leningrad ½F, 24th USSR Ch, 1956. Black has no worthwhile break and White can play Q–Q2 △ B–KN5, QR–Q1 etc.

(e) 9 . . . **P–QR3 (!)** 10 B–K3 (10 P–QR4!?) 10 . . . P–QN4 11 P–B4 B–N2 12 P–KB5 P–Q4! ∞. For several examples of this plan, one should turn to:

D

7 . . .   **P–B3**
8 P–Q3

8 P–Q4 is a Classical Fianchetto King's Indian with White's knight on e2 instead of f3. Although his KP is better protected, White exerts less pressure on the enemy centre (e.g. P–QB5 is hardly ever a threat) and in case of P–Q5, Black plays . . . P×P, when White's KN has no effective means of transferring to the queenside e.g. 8 P–Q4 QN–Q2 9 P–KR3 (9 **P–B4** P×QP and 10 . . . Q–N3) 9 . . . Q–N3 (△ . . . P×P), and if 10 R–K1, 10 . . . R–K1 11 P–Q5 P×P 12 BP×P N–B4 13 R–N1 P–QR4 ∓.

8 . . .   **P–QR3**
8 . . . **QN–Q2** transposes to C above. 8 . . . N–R4 9 B–K3 P–KB4 10 Q–Q2 B–K3 11 P×P P×P 12 P–B4 N–Q2 13 QR–K1 (a

typical structure–compare A) 13 . . . Q–B2 14 P–KR3 QR–K1 15 K–R2 K–R1 16 P–N3 N(2)–B3 17 P–Q4 PxBP 18 BxKBP! NxB 19 NxN B–B1 20 P–Q5 ± Bilek-Tisdall, Lone Pine 1975. The exchange on f4 created a position where White's blockading knight counted for more than a bishop, and Black's KBP was sickly (1–0, 37).

9 P–KR3

To be investigated is **9 P–QR4!?**, weakening queenside squares but gaining time to further White's ambitions on the king's wing: 9 . . . P–QR4 (9 . . . **QN–Q2** 10 P–KR3 R–N1 11 B–K3, when 11 . . . P–QN4? 12 RPxP 13 PxP PxP 14 P–QN4! △ R–R5) 10 P–KR3 N–R3 11 B–K3 N–B4 (11 . . . N–QN5 12 P–B4 PxP 13 NxP ±; 11 . . . N(3)–Q2!?–Case) 12 P–B4 B–R3! (12 . . . **Q–N3** 13 P–B5! Q–N6 14 Q–Q2 ±) 13 K–R2 N–R4 ∞.

9 . . .   P–QN4
10 PxP?!

Why give up this important defender of d5? Better 10 P–QR3 or 10 P–N3 (Kavalek), the latter move being the customary one in the corresponding King's Indian Attack (vs. Sicilian) position.

10 . . .   RPxP
11 P–QN4 N–R3 12 R–N1 (Safer was **12 Q–N3** △ 12 . . . B–K3 13 Q–N2 and 14 P–QR4–Kavalek.) 12 . . . B–K3 13 P–QR4 PxP 14 NxP? (14 QxP Q–Q2 15 K–R1 KR–N1 or 15 . . . N–B2 ∓– Kavalek) 14 . . . R–N1 15 B–Q2 Q–Q2 16 K–R2 P–B4 ∓ Popov-Kavalek, Wijk an Zee 1975. Black wins a pawn.

CONCLUSION: Black experiences some difficulty defending against White's kingside attack once he is committed to . . . P–K4; in fact, the irregular idea 6 . . . **P–B3** deserves to be taken seriously. After 6 . . . **P–K4** 7 0–0 has occurred, relatively best seems 7 . . . **QN–Q2** 8 P–Q3 P–B3 9 P–KR3 P–QR3 or 7 . . . **P–B3** 8 P–Q3 P–QR3. Then White must be careful to guard his centre against . . . P–QN4 and . . . P–Q4. These are interesting variations and merit more theoretical attention.

INDEX OF VARIATIONS AND TRANSPOSITIONS

In the English Opening, beginning as it does on the very first move, many variations can be reached by more than one route. The following chart is designed to help the reader find his way through such transpositions to the pages covering a particular sequence.

Alternatives to the main sections of the Index are listed at the beginning of each Part; e.g. 2 N--KB3 is given immediately below 2 N–QB3.

Unless otherwise indicated, parentheses mean that the enclosed moves are analyzed/discussed in notes to the preceding move. Certain obvious transpositions are not listed. For example the move . . . P–QB4 will almost always transpose to a variation of *English III:* . . . *P–QB4*, and in many lines, P–Q4 on White's part will yield a standard Queen Pawn Opening such as the Queen's Gambit or Grünfeld Defence. Moreover, the Index does not always note an elementary transposition from one part of a chapter to another.

The apparent paucity of lines beginning with 2 N–KB3 is due to the convenience of organizing via 2 N–QB3, traditional in works on the English. This stems from the fact that N–KB3 is much more often followed by an early N–QB3 than vice-versa. Page numbers are italicised.

INDEX OF SIGNIFICANT GAMES

This includes complete games (excepting very short ones) and partial games of respectable length (at least 20 moves, with some exceptions) which are important to theory or particularly well-played. An asterisk denotes a complete game.